Shakespeare the Bodger

For Max Altman-Walsh

Shakespeare the Bodger

Ingenuity, Imitation and the Arts of *The Winter's Tale*

Joel B. Altman

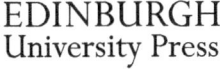
EDINBURGH
University Press

Edinburgh University Press is one of the leading university presses in the UK. We publish academic books and journals in our selected subject areas across the humanities and social sciences, combining cutting-edge scholarship with high editorial and production values to produce academic works of lasting importance. For more information visit our website: edinburghuniversitypress.com

Grateful acknowledgement is made to the sources listed in the List of Illustrations for permission to reproduce material previously published elsewhere. Every effort has been made to trace the copyright holders, but if any have been inadvertently overlooked, the publisher will be pleased to make the necessary arrangements at the first opportunity.

Edinburgh University Press Ltd
13 Infirmary Street
Edinburgh EH1 1LT

First published in hardback by Edinburgh University Press 2023

Typeset in 11/13pt Adobe Sabon by
Cheshire Typesetting Ltd, Cuddington, Cheshire

A CIP record for this book is available from the British Library

ISBN 978 1 3995 0841 4 (hardback)
ISBN 978 1 3995 0842 1 (paperback)
ISBN 978 1 3995 0843 8 (webready PDF)
ISBN 978 1 3995 0844 5 (epub)

Contents

Figures

Acknowledgements

I would like to express my gratitude to several friends and colleagues who read and critiqued different portions of this book as it was being written. I especially benefitted from the suggestions of Louise George Clubb regarding the varied tragicomic forms of sixteenth-century Italian drama, Peter Platt's observations on the growing English interest in *Wunderkammern*, Jeffrey Knapp's healthy skepticism concerning the presence of Giulio Romano's *I modi* in Leontes' imagination during Act 1, Scene 2 of *The Winter's Tale*, and Donald Friedman's characteristic circumspection and supportive enthusiasm. Lorna Hutson, John Baxter, and Stephen Greenblatt posed useful questions concerning conference papers that subsequently became book chapters. And Robert and Rebecca Tracy actually peered into the hollowed shawl of the third caryatid of the Strozzi Monument in Mantua to see whether there was a baby hidden there.

Much of my research on seventeenth-century English art collectors in Chapter 3 was conducted in the British Library with the assistance of an Edward A. Dickson Emeriti Professorship.

Introducing Shakespeare the Bodger

I

In 1589 Robert Greene, a successful if profligate writer of romances and plays, published a tale called *Menaphon: Camilla's Alarum to Slumbering Euphues*, along with a document that contains the first recorded allusion to a tragedy with which Shakespeare was to be associated—though it wasn't his yet. The allusion is made by Thomas Nashe, in his preface addressed to "The Gentlemen Students of both Universities," where Nashe, then twenty-two years old, takes the occasion to broadly criticize the state of English letters.[1] His critique is notable not only for the jaunty self-assertion that characterizes much of his later writing, but also for the vocabulary he uses and the themes he chooses to pursue. He opens with an attack on "inkhorne" men—the common term for writers who abandon their native English fields of russet yeas and honest kersey noes for the exotic shores of Latinate diction and rhetorical amplification. According to Nashe, they've acquired this style not by arduous study but through the "servile imitation of vain-glorious tragoedians"—that is, by picking it up from actors on the stage, especially those who "contend not so seriouslie to excell in action as to embowell the clowdes in a speach of comparison" (308). There's a double critique here: of a newly "lettered" popular theater that is beginning to imitate, in high astounding terms, the high literary—and of a new generation of writers who are going not to the sources for their learning but to popular theatrical imitations.

The social implications of this critique become evident as Nashe pursues his theme, for the languages of market and class now enter the discourse:

> Mongst this kinde of men that repose eternitie in the mouth of a player, I can but ingrosse some deepe-read Grammarians, who, having no more learning in their scull than will serve to take up a commoditie, nor Arte in their brain than was nourished in a serving-mans idlenesse, will take upon them to be the ironicall censors of all, when God and Poetrie doth know they are the simplest of all. (308)

Further charges are thus laid: these writers have only grammar-school educations, their wits are better attuned to surreptitious money-lending practices than to poetry, and they may even have been in service. It's not hard to detect in Nashe's snobbery the clergyman's son from Suffolk come up to London to live by his wits—which are considerable—now further gentrified by a Cambridge degree.

As he proceeds, the issue of imitation expands into a major preoccupation, for he subjects the unguarded borderlands between imitation and theft to a raking search. With a few passing words of praise for Greene, whose romance his preface is intended to introduce, he attacks those (unlike Greene!) who crib continental or classical sources—"the Italianate pen that of a packet of pilfries affoordeth the presse a pamphlet or two in an age, and then in disguised arraie vaunts *Ovids* and *Plutarchs* plumes as their owne" (308–9). Of such writers, he says,

> either they must borrow invention of *Ariosto* and his Countreymen, take up choyce of words by exchange in *Tullies Tusculane* and the Latine Historiographers store-houses, similitudes, nay whole sheetes and tractacts *verbatim* from the plentie of *Plutarch* and *Plinie*, and, to conclude, their whole methode of writing from the libertie of Comical fictions that have succeeded to our Rethoritians by a second imitation: so that well may be the Adage, *Nihil dictum quod non dictum prius* [Nothing is said that has not been said before], bee the most judiciall estimate of our latter Writers. (309)

Under Nashe's critical eye, the scene of writing has become an expedition to a great literary flea market, where an avid rabble of poetasters pores over new and second-hand goods that can be bought, borrowed, or stolen for further recycling on an exchange that trades quotes for futures among the printers of London's Stationers' Company.

In contrast to such trafficking in the commodities of others he celebrates in Greene that quality most evident in himself—what Roger Ascham, nearly two decades before, described in less flattering terms as a "quick wit."[2] "But give me the man," Nashe exclaims, "whose extemporall vaine in anie humor will excell our greatest

Art-masters deliberate thoughts, whose invention, quicker than his eye, will challenge the proudest Rethoritian to the contention of like perfection with like expedition" (309). What is wanting among his contemporaries, he suggests, is the capacity to step out of literary history, as it were—including one's own history of study and deliberate imitation—and to *invent*, to come upon fresh connections that generate new ideas.[3]

Nashe doesn't say much more about the desired "extemporall vaine" but he does deride writers who lack the singularity—read "originality"—that he claims for Greene and himself. These include "unsatiate humorists" who use their "thred bare wits to emptie their invention of their *Apish* devices" and satirists who think they are being "singular" when they produce *ad hominem* detractions. And, most notably, they include translators (309–11).

For Nashe, the word "translation" has a broad, Latinate meaning that comprehends several kinds of carry-over: verbal translation proper, from one language to another; but also poetic imitation, textual interpretation, and a kind of social migration. It's in this context that the Shakespeare connection comes up. In a famous passage, Nashe notes that

> It is a common practice now a daies amongst a sort of shifting companions, that runne through every arte and thrive by none, to leave the trade of *Noverint*, whereto they were borne, and busie themselves with the indevors of Art, that could scarcelie latinize their necke-verse if they should have neede; yet English *Seneca* read by candle light yeeldes manie good sentences, as *Bloud is a begger*, and so foorth; and, if you intreate him faire in a frostie morning, he will affoord you whole *Hamlets*, I should say handfulls of tragical speaches. (312)

This extemporal *lapsus linguae*, familiar in Nashe's despised inkhorn rhetoric as the figure *correctio*, is the earliest known reference to Shakespeare's most famous tragedy, but a pun a few lines later ("the Kidde in Aesop") suggests that it refers to an earlier version attributed to Thomas Kyd. Both play and author are named by Nashe because he is as much concerned with translation as a social phenomenon as he is with translation as a literary practice. What seems especially to vex this university wit is that someone who should have followed in the trade of his father—that of a notary—has translated himself into a poet, taken to writing plays, and is doing it by cribbing not simply from the classics but from *translations* of the classics. And having drained Seneca's bloody English drop by drop, he's now taken "to intermeddle with Italian translations." (Kyd had translated Tasso's *Padre di Famiglia* in 1588, and would try his hand at French tragedy with Robert Garnier's *Cornélie* in the winter of 1593–94, from which he had already pilfered a speech for his own *Spanish Tragedy* [c. 1587][4]—whose plot was climaxed by a play-within-a-play performed in Latin, Greek, Italian, and French![5]) Through all these endeavors, Nashe airily observes, such writers have "poorly plodded" with a "home-born mediocrity" sufficient to "bodge up a blanke verse with ifs and ands" (312)—nothing more.[6]

So, added to the snobbery that informs Nashe's vision of grammarians-turned-poets who learn from and write for the mouths of players, and his belief that poetry is being traded like merchandise on the exchange, is a sense that there are uncontrollable, eclectic translations abroad in the land, translations that have skipped the prerequisites that lead to a university degree, gentlemanly connections, and those dear recognitions—artistic, social, and economic—that one usually expects to enjoy when pursuing such a course of life. These new translations pass in the public eye for their betters. Though Nashe pauses briefly to praise what he calls the "laudable kinde of Translation"—exemplified by Father Erasmus and his followers—he returns as one does to a continuous itch to excoriate the use of compendiums, epitomes, abbreviations, and the "pride of contraction" that infects "our idle age" (312–14). He's referring to the packaged bits and pieces of literary culture that humanist educators had encouraged their students to gather from their own reading and had compiled themselves for classroom use. Alas, they can now be snapped up at a bookstall by almost anyone and passed off as the fruits of genuine erudition.[7]

There is a connection in Nashe's mind between consulting and choosing from a compendium when translating or interpreting, bodging up a blank verse with ifs, ands, and sentences from English Seneca to supply lines for players, and playing itself. The poetaster decking his verse in Ovid's and Plutarch's plumes, the hack dramatist piecing together Senecan phrases with "ifs and ands," and the player who mouths his lines are not only imposters; they share the same livery. That livery is motley. They are all dealers in shreds and patches who "flie, like Swallows in the Winter, from any continuate subject of wit" (316), and in this company the player is king since he's the one who's getting rich. Nashe warns him that his rule is illusory, however, and reminds him of his true place in the social and artistic hierarchy: without the poet, he might have antickt it until this time up and down the countrey with the King of *Fairies*, and dined everie daie at the pease porridge ordinary with *Delphrigus* . . . let subjects for all their insolence dedicate a *De profundis* everie morning to the preservation of their *Caesar*, least their encreasing indignities returne them ere long to their juggling to mediocrity, and they bewaile in weeping blankes the wane of their Monarchie. (319–20)

The king, for all that he is tricked out in taffeta, is only a player king; the true sovereign is the gentleman poet.

I've lingered on Nashe's preface because he sets the terms of the Shakespeare phenomenon that interests me: the bodging-up of a player-poet who works with the materials of others and gets rich in the process. Sometimes, it would appear, he imitates by following "our greatest Art-masters deliberate thoughts," and though he seems to have read "whole sheetes and tractacts *verbatim* from the plentie of *Plutarch* and *Plinie*," to say nothing of the hoards of Hall and Holinshed, he tends not to reproduce them verbatim. Rather, he works by exercising an invention that, if not "quicker than his eye," seems to have been synchronous with it and was enabled by an "extemporall vaine in any humor" that he must have possessed in spades. While this extemporal power did not free him from trafficking in used goods, it did enable him to renovate them, make them over in his own image, and incorporate them in his own work. The practices of imitation, translation, and bodging are deeply pertinent to the self that we call Shakespeare. To see why, we must turn to Robert Greene—but first I want to offer some words about my larger argument.

II

The subject of this book is Shakespeare's ingenuity, particularly as it is exercised in the composition of his late play *The Winter's Tale*. I employ the term "ingenuity" not simply in its common usage today to signify "natural cleverness," "skillfulness," or "inventiveness"— nor, with John Florio, anticipating Iago's description of the noble Moor, to signify "a liberall, free, or honest nature and condition"[8]— though its application to Shakespeare might well take in all these meanings. Rather, I concentrate on ingenuity as a psychological phenomenon related to the matter with which it works, the connections it makes, and the verbal expressions that issue from the convergence of mental attention and perceived, imagined, or recollected texts, events, persons, and material objects.[9] Moreover, what is true of Shakespeare's ingenuity is also true of the ingenuity of the human beings he represents. That is to say, Shakespeare is aware of how minds such as his work and he represents those minds fashioning their discourse in ways we recognize as similar to his—and to ours. This book will therefore emphasize not only Shakespeare's ingenuity but also how Shakespeare *dramatizes* ingenuity.

I begin with some familiar early Shakespeare lore as a way of bringing the subject of ingenuity to prominence in the context of received scholarly discourse. Chapter 1 considers the scene of writing and performing in the late 1580s and early 1590s as it is described by Robert Greene, where the player-author Shakespeare is associated, however allusively, with the practices of translation and imitation, and—in the vulgate—with what was called bodging or botching. The latter variants, native to the clothing trade, signified taking up and stitching together disparate patches of second-hand text to form a fabric of one's own—and they were used disparagingly, even, on occasion, by our playwright.[10] My purpose here is to show how the exercise of ingenuity informs Shakespeare's interpretive practices both intellectually and materially, and to demonstrate his awareness of the way ingenious inference leads to new apprehensions—sometimes approximating closely what has been perceived in writing, speech, and action, but often straying from such "objective" evidence and distorting it in surprising ways. In every case, however, the process is an act of imitation and the result a form of bodging.

Greene's attack on the "upstart Crow, beautified with our feathers," is a conceit that has an ancient lineage in the history of literary imitation. That history concerns the instrument of imitation—what Seneca calls *ingenium*; the formal qualities of the imitation, transshaped in any number of ways from its verbal or visual referents; the imitator's relationship to his *imitatees* or predecessors—son, companion, admirer, rival, thief; the degree of recognition experienced by reader, auditor, or viewer exposed to the transaction; and the kind of self the imitator becomes, publicly and privately, as a consequence of his activity. A range of metaphors invoking genealogy, mellification, and digestion reinforce the organic nature of what seems to be merely a literary practice but which has serious ethical and psychological implications for the practitioner. Greene's feathers metaphor, however true or disingenuous as a description of Shakespeare's practice, suggests more plainly a kind of professional and social lawlessness, ancient in origin but newly resonant in Elizabethan hierarchal society, where sumptuary laws were often violated.[11]

The chapter also explores Shakespeare's posthumous relationship with Robert Greene, who died in 1592. This one-way liaison reaches its climax with his extensive reconfiguration of Greene's *Pandosto* in *The Winter's Tale*, which contains bodges from other works of Greene as well. Equally important for our understanding of Shakespeare's ingenuity in relation to *The Winter's Tale*, the chapter introduces another historical figure who will play a leading role in the ensuing narrative: Giulio Romano, the sixteenth-century Italian designer, painter, and architect whose work, I argue, is patched through verbal allusion into Shakespeare's text from its second scene, though his name is not uttered until the fifth act. Thus the play functions as a kind of fripler's shop, offering an extended display of Shakespearean ingenuity and of the bodging that is its material realization.

Chapter 2 refines the concept of ingenious inference by exploring, through classical and early modern texts—including Shakespeare's—the psychology of phantasia, the organ of faculty psychology through which ingenuity does its job. Because it is an "imaging" instrument, phantasia works by means of internal pictures, which it engenders after having received signals from the various physical organs of sense perception and from the memory. But it also has a cognitive function or, more precisely, a re-cognitive function, and is therefore related to the reason, which helps it to understand that "this" can be connected to "that" in a particular way. Since it takes a subject to cognize something, my analysis then turns to the representation of subjectivity in Shakespeare's plays, making a distinction between two dramaturgic entities, *dramatis persona* and *character*. Only a *character*, I argue, represents a subject, and therefore his or her subjectivity is often expressed in concrete language that assumes a distinctive *colore*—the Latin rhetorical term indicating a particular "slant" or interpretation that an orator may deliberately give to his speech. In drama, however, verbal coloring signifies (unless otherwise indicated) the *character*'s genuine interpretation of what he or she is describing, however inaccurate—from the audience's perspective—it may be. Such vivid theatrical speech is the dramaturgical cousin to the ancient and early modern rhetorical subgenre of ekphrasis (in Latin, *descriptio*), as several twentieth-century scholars have observed—though usually without developing the fact that ekphrasis can be an important instrument for the representation of subjectivity. Hence the subtitle of the chapter: "Portraying the Subject of Ekphrasis."

With this practice in mind, in Chapter 3 I invoke two famous early modern objects of art as intermedial components of *The Winter's Tale*, the better to understand important resonances in the play. The first pertains to Leontes' bizarre interpretation of the courtly exchanges between Hermione and Polixenes in the second scene, which Leontes seems to be reading through lenses provided by Giulio Romano's notorious erotic drawings that were published as engravings accompanied by Pietro Aretino's obscene poems in the mid-1520s, in a little volume known in Italian as *I sonetti lussuriosi* or *I modi*—in English, as the *Postures* or *Positions*. *I modi* was circulated, apparently in the debased form of woodcuts, in the London of Shakespeare's time and was known to Ben Jonson and Thomas Middleton, among others, who refer to the images in their plays. Giulio Romano, identified in Act 5 as the artist who has just completed Hermione's statue, and famously puzzling as the only historical artist Shakespeare ever named, thus makes a silent entrance early in the play. But he is also connected to another, loftier work of art that was even more famous in the sixteenth century. It is *The Transfiguration of Christ*, the last commission of Raphael of Urbino before his death, which was brought to completion by Giulio and his co-heir to Raphael's workshop, Gianfrancesco Penni. Several early copies of this painting are extant, among them those now hanging in the Sistine Chapel, in the Prado, and in the Dulwich College Chapel outside London. This last copy, attributed to Giulio when it was acquired by the College in the late eighteenth century, seems to have been in the possession of English collectors as far back as the early seventeenth century.

The painting makes its ekphrastic appearance in *The Winter's Tale* during the courtiers' awed description of the reunion of the families of the two kings at the court of Sicilia in Act 5, Scene 2. It would seem, then, that even before Giulio Romano's name is spoken at the end of that scene, his work acts as an intermedial subtext anchoring the two most crucial moments in the play—Leontes' apparently inexplicable fit of jealousy in Scene 2 and the coming-to-life of Hermione's statue in the final scene. Tracing the provenance of the painting, from its well-documented existence in England in the eighteenth century to its increasingly less-detailed certification in the seventeenth century, I attempt to demonstrate Shakespeare's familiarity with the alleged Giulio copy and his ingenious appropriation of its gestures and themes to vividly "bodge up" in 5.2 a scene of recognition that is otherwise invisible on the stage.

Perhaps more controversially, Giulio Romano returns in Chapter 4 through his alleged statue of the dead Hermione to raise questions about Shakespeare's awareness of a marble funeral monument still to be seen in Mantua that is commonly believed to have been designed by Giulio. Shakespeare's identification of Giulio Romano as a sculptor has long been regarded as evidence of his ignorance, since Giulio was best known as a painter, architect, and city planner during his long tenure at the Gonzaga court of Mantua, after his departure from Rome in 1524 under the patronage of Baldassare Castiglione. Yet there exists contemporary evidence that modern scholarship has revealed to show that, if Giulio was not a sculptor himself, he was known to have designed sculpture. Following closely the dialogue of Act 5, Scene 3 and its implicit stage directions, I offer an illustrated argument showing how allusions to the women of the Strozzi monument in Mantua inform the "statue scene" of *The Winter's Tale*. They therefore constitute further verbal samples of Shakespearean bodging at work, occasioned most likely by descriptions he had heard from visitors to or players from northern Italy.

In Chapter 5, Robert Greene returns to our attention as we consider in detail Shakespeare's adaptation of *Pandosto: The Triumph of Time* and his indebtedness not only to Greene but also, from the viewpoint of genre, to the recently denizened forms of Italian tragicomedy. Here I further develop a subject introduced in Chapter 3 about which we have been learning more and more in recent years. This is Shakespeare's knowledge of the Italian language and his ability to use Italian sources, such as Giorgio Vasari's *Le vite de' più eccellenti architetti, pittori, et scultori italiani, da Cimabue, insino a' tempi nostri* for his knowledge of Giulio Romano. It also explains his familiarity with fictional narrative and dramatic pieces from whose fabrics he selectively borrowed, and an influential body of Italian dramatic theory. Most notable among these writings are those of Giraldi Cinzio, author of the *Ecatommiti* and *Epizia*, the chief sources of *Othello* and *Measure for Measure*, and his *Discorso intorno al comporre delle commedie e delle tragedie*, as well as those of Battista Guarini, author of *Il pastor fido* and the *Compendio della poesia tragicomica*. To elucidate these imitations, I offer extended analyses of the so-called "problem plays," which clearly indicate Shakespeare's knowledge of Italian tragicomedy, before proceeding to a discussion of *The Winter's Tale* as his distinctive version of Cinzio's *tragedia di fin lieto*.

My epilogue addresses the question of faith, which Paulina implicitly demands of the offstage audience as she addresses those onstage, when the last scene of *The Winter's Tale* draws to an end. The preceding dialogue has evoked both suspicions and denials of

image-making, idolatry, and black magic—practices widely associated with Catholicism in post-Reformation England—and this
sudden insistence on faith alone would seem to indicate a shift to a
more Protestant emphasis, as in the fideist reception of the Eucharist
described by Richard Hooker.[12] Given, however, the theater audience's recent discovery of Paulina's behind-the-scenes plotting—first
that she had kept hidden a hitherto unknown statue of the dead
queen (5.2.93), then that she had "privately twice or thrice a day . . .
visited that removed house" in which it was cloistered (5.2.102–6)—
the valence of her demand at this moment is weighted at least as
much toward theatrical faith as religious faith, though both states
of consciousness require a surrender of rational agency in order
to participate the involuntary pleasures of the proposed miracle.
Why should an attentive audience yield to this temptation? To
explain their anticipated response I offer a blow-by-blow analysis
of the multiple, varied, and often unexpected auditory, visual, intellectual, and emotional pleasures the dramatist has gifted them all
along—and invoke two of Leontes' replies to Paulina in their behalf.
When Paulina threatens to draw the curtain in front of the statue
because "My lord's almost so far transported that / He'll think anon
it lives," Leontes explains, perhaps ventriloquizing an enraptured
theater audience: "No settled senses of the world can match / The
pleasure of that madness" (5.3.69–73). And when Paulina declares,
"It is required / You do awake your faith," he says, "What you can
make her do / I am content to look on; what to speak / I am content
to hear" (5.3.91–3).[13] The larger work of Shakespeare the dramatist
now becomes evident. It is to bodge up theatrical faith by crafting his
audience even as he crafts his play.

Now, let us return to the beginning of the story and meet Robert
Greene.

Notes

1. Quotations that follow are from *Elizabethan Critical Essays*, ed. G.
Gregory Smith, 2 vols. (Oxford: Oxford University Press, 1904), vol.
1, pp. 307–20. Page references will appear in the text.
2. *The Schoolmaster* (1570), ed. Lawrence V. Ryan (Ithaca, NY: Cornell
University Press, 1967), pp. 21–2.
3. "Invention" was one of the five offices of rhetoric—invention, disposition, eloquence, action, and utterance—in which one "invents" material by scanning the topics or "places" of rhetoric and dialectic, such

as who, what, why, how, when, where, by what means, opportunity, nationality, whole, parts, cause, effect, etc., in order to piece out an argument, a lyric, a narrative, or a dramatic speech. By transference, the mental faculty of doing so was also called "invention," as was the product of its activity, which was vulnerable to appropriation, as Nashe, Sidney, and other writers observe. See Lorna Hutson, *Circumstantial Shakespeare* (Oxford: Oxford University Press, 2015) for an excellent review of the topics and their uses in Shakespeare's drama.

4. Smith, *Essays*, p. 426, n. 26.

5. In the extant texts of *The Spanish Tragedy*, the speeches are printed in English "for the easier understanding of every public reader," but in rehearsing the performance, Hieronimo tells his courtly players, "Each one of us must act his part / In unknown languages, / That it may breed the more variety" (4.4, S.D., 4.1.171–3), a gesture likely to have irritated Nashe if he had attended the play. See *Drama of the English Renaissance*, ed. Russell A. Fraser and Norman Rabkin (New York and London: Macmillan, 1976), vol. 1.

6. One who bodges is a "botcher, mender, or patcher of olde garments" according to R. Huloet, *Abcedarium Anglico Latinum* (London, 1552), cit. *Oxford English Dictionary* online. G. Gregory Smith (*Essays*, p. 425) believed Nashe was mocking Lorenzo's line, addressed to Pedringano, in *The Spanish Tragedy*, "What, Villaine, ifs and ands?" (2.1.77).

7. On the use of commonplace books, see R. R. Bolgar, *The Classical Heritage and its Beneficiaries from the Carolingian Age to the End of the Renaissance* (London and New York: Cambridge University Press, 1954); Mary Thomas Crane, *Framing Authority: Sayings, Self, and Society in Sixteenth-Century England* (Princeton: Princeton University Press, 1993); Ann Moss, *Printed Commonplace-Books and the Structuring of Renaissance Thought* (Oxford: Clarendon Press, 1996); and Jeffrey Todd Knight, *Bound to Read: Compilations, Collections, and the Making of Renaissance Literature* (Philadelphia: University of Pennsylvania Press, 2013).

8. This definition is more akin to our "ingenuousness." See John Florio, *A Worlde of Wordes* (1598) (Hildesheim and New York: Georg Olms Verlag, 1972), s.v. ingenuità, p. 181. Cf. *Othello*, 1.3.399. All citations of Shakespeare's plays, unless stated otherwise, are from *The Riverside Shakespeare*, 2nd edn, ed. G. Blakemore Evans et al. (Boston and New York: Houghton Mifflin, 1997).

9. In this broad sense, my argument participates in the recent emphasis on Shakespearean intertextuality. See, for example, Douglas Bruster, *Quoting Shakespeare: Form and Culture in Early Modern Drama* (Lincoln and London: University of Nebraska Press, 2000); Robert S. Miola, "Seven Types of Intertextuality," in *Shakespeare, Italy,*

and Intertextuality, ed. Michele Marrapodi (Manchester: Manchester University Press, 2004), pp. 13–25; Raphael Lyne, *Memory and Intertextuality in Renaissance Literature* (Cambridge: Cambridge University Press, 2016); and John Kerrigan, *Shakespeare's Originality* (Oxford: Oxford University Press, 2018). The widespread practice of intertextuality among Italian Renaissance dramatists and its resonances in Shakespeare is the subject of the seminal work of Louise George Clubb. See especially *Italian Drama in Shakespeare's Time* (New York and London: Yale University Press, 1989).

10. On the relation between the fashioning of plays and the fashioning of clothing in our period, with an emphasis on *Much Ado About Nothing*, see Kerrigan, *Shakespeare's Originality*, pp. 28–40.

11. Ibid. p. 26. The ethical and psychological dimensions of bodging are explored by Montaigne in his essay "We Taste Nothing Purely" (2.20) where he observes, "Man all in all is but a botching and parti-coloured work" (trans. John Florio). See *Shakespeare's Montaigne: The Florio Translation of the Essays: A Selection*, ed. Stephen Greenblatt and Peter G. Platt (New York: NYRB, 2014), p. 192. The editors point out that Feste plays with this materialist idea of self-fashioning in *Twelfth Night*: "bid the dishonest man mend himself: if he mend, he is no longer dishonest; if he cannot, let the botcher mend him. Anything that's mended is but patch'd; virtue that transgresses is but patch'd with sin, and sin that amends is but patch'd with virtue" (1.5.45–9).

12. See Richard Hooker, *Of the Laws of Ecclesiastical Polity*, ed. A. S. McGrade and Brian Vickers (New York: St. Martin's Press, 1975), pp. 291, 294; Joel B. Altman, "Vile Participation: The Amplification of Violence in the Theater of *Henry V*," *Shakespeare Quarterly* 42.1 (1991): 1–32, esp. 4–5, nn. 12, 50.

13. All citations of *The Winter's Tale*, unless otherwise stated, refer to John Pitcher, ed. (London: Arden Shakespeare, 2010).

Shakespeare's Ingenuity: Humanism, Materialism, and One Early Modern Self

I

Confined to his deathbed in the late summer of 1592, Robert Greene seems to have written a pamphlet—part autobiographical fiction, part first-person confession—that was published within weeks after he died at age thirty-four as *Greenes, Groats-worth of witte, bought with a million of Repentance*.[1] Its authenticity has been challenged since the time of its publication, despite its close resemblance to Greene's literary style and its fidelity to his lifestyle. Henry Chettle is the prime suspect—for either forging or liberally adapting Greene's papers, intermeddled with passages of his own invention and those of others—even though in his "To the Gentlemen Readers" of *Kind-Heart's Dream* (published later in 1592) he denies having added anything to Greene's manuscript. "I writ it over [that is, transcribed it], and as neare as I could, followed the copy," he writes; "onely in that letter I put something out, but in the whole booke not a worde in, for I protest it was all Greenes, not mine, nor Maister Nashes, as some unjustly have affirmed."[2] The letter he refers to is that familiar warning to three fellow poets to beware an "upstart Crow, beautified with our feathers," mentioned in my prologue and which we shall examine shortly. Given the uncertainty that hangs over the allegedly mingled authorship of *Greenes Groats-Worth of Wit* to this day, it is a fitting document with which to begin exploring Shakespeare's own ingenuity, imitation, and bodging.[3]

It is the story of two brothers, sons of a new-made gentleman, grown fabulously wealthy as a usurer. Reproved for his trade by his university-educated son Roberto, the usurer confers all his goods upon his foolish younger son Lucanio and bequeaths to Roberto, who clearly doesn't appreciate the value of money, a single groat. In revenge, Roberto tries to make a deal with a courtesan to gull Lucanio out of his inheritance but she betrays him to his brother and he is given Jack Drum's Entertainment and turned out of doors. It's then that his real troubles begin.

Lamenting his destiny, his treachery, and the courtesan's betrayal, he is overheard by a fancy-looking fellow behind a hedge who approaches him with an offer of work. How might you employ me? Roberto inquires. "Why easily," the fellow tells him, "for men of my profession gette by schollers their whole living." To Roberto's astonishment, this would-be benefactor is a player. "A Player, quoth *Roberto*, I tooke you rather for a Gentleman of great living, for if by outward habit men should be censured, I tell you, you would bee taken for a substantiall man" (68). But the player is exactly that. Once, he tells Roberto, "I was faine to carry my playing Fardle a footebacke," but "Tempora mutantur ... its otherwise now; for my very share in playing apparrell will not be sold for two hundred pounds." This raspy-voiced actor ("for that it seems to mee your voice is nothing gratious") is famous for playing "Delphrigus, and the King of Fairies" (plays we know about only from Nashe and Greene). What's more, he's a writer. "I can serve to make a pretie speech, for I was a countrey Author, passing at a Morrall, for it was I that pende the Morall of mans witte, the Dialogue of Dives, and for seven yeers space was absolute Interpreter to the puppets" (69). He's in need of a university wit because his line is now out of date, and Roberto accepts the offer of the player, who obligingly lodges him in a brothel at the town's end.

Falling in with the players is Roberto's undoing. He becomes "famozed for an Arch-plaiemaking-poet" (71), squanders his earnings on dice, drink, and doxies, and becomes companion to "the lewdest persons in the land, apt for pilferie, perjurie, forgerie, or any villany" (72). Learning their tricks but ignoring the consequences of their vicious living, he grows dissipated unto death, and is left with only the single groat his usurer father had bequeathed him, "which looking on, he cryed: O now it is too late, too late to buy witte with thee: and therefore will I see if I can sell to careless youth what I negligently forgot to buy" (75)—evidently planning to write up his experience for sale at the bookstalls. At this point Greene breaks into his narrative, confessing that it is his own tale he tells—"Heereafter suppose me the saide *Roberto*"—and offers (more courteously) to *send* to his gentlemen readers the groatsworth of wit he has gleaned from his folly, thereby attesting his better breeding and change of heart.[4]

After supplying ten general rules to be regarded by gentlemen in pursuing their lives, he writes a more specific address to three particular friends "that spend their wits in making plaies"—a "famous gracer of Tragedians," a "byting Satyrist," and a writer "driven (as myself) to extreme shifts"—apparently Marlowe, Nashe, and Peele. He advises each, respectively, to disavow atheistic "Machivilian pollicy," to prudently "reprove all, and name none," and to realize that "thou art unworthy better hap, sith thou dependest on so mean a stay" (80–3). The implications of this last warning become clear in his next sentence: "Base minded men all three of you, if by my miserie you be not warned: for unto none of you (like me) sought those burres to cleave: those Puppets (I meane) that spake from our mouths, those Anticks garnisht in our colours" (84). Here is the familiar charge that buffoonish players, who appear to be monarchs of their kingdom, are usurping the verbal regalia of gentlemen poets.[5] But it is attached to a second charge—ingratitude—and a warning. "Is it not strange, that I, to whom they all have beene beholding: is it not like that you, to whom they all have beene beholding, shall (were yee in that case as I am now) bee both at once of them forsaken?" (84). To strengthen this argument, he adds a reason for his (and, potentially, his friends') abandonment: he has become redundant. Someone has popped up who has convinced the players that he can supply all their needs. "Yes trust them not," Greene explains, "for there is an upstart Crow, beautified with our feathers, that with his *Tygers hart wrapt in a Players hyde*, supposes he is as well able to bombast out a blanke verse as the best of you: and beeing an absolute *Johannes fac totum*, is in his owne conceit the onely Shake-scene in a country" (84–5). Like the fictional actor who "for seven yeers space was absolute Interpreter to the puppets," this Shake-scene has apparently made the move from base player to play-bodger and now fancies himself master of all theatrical trades. One can only murmur proleptically, with Greene, "Bottom . . . thou art translated."[6]

It is tempting to read the seven years' space in which Greene's fictional player was not only acting but also writing pretty speeches for his fellows as an allusion to Shakespeare's "lost years"—the period between 1585 and 1592 when there is no record of his whereabouts.[7] But I will walk around the temptation because I want to pursue the import of all this talk about imitation, borrowed feathers, social migration, and artistic usurpation that pervades the criticism of Nashe and Greene. The suggestions of plagiarism they use to criticize possible or actual rivals isn't exactly new; one can find allusions to the undercover practices of literary copycats as far back as Horace, Martial, and other classical writers.[8] But their preoccupation with the translation of class—grammarians passing themselves off as erudite scholars, itinerant actors (no better than beggars, according to the 1572 Statute) now fancying themselves gentlemen, tradesmen's sons turning dramatic poets, and all thriving in this new enterprise of the public theater—is a very specific historical response to material changes that are taking place in the society around them. For all their education, talent, and exploitation of the popular press, Nashe and Greene have not made it as they see theater people making it. What I find especially interesting is that they apply to their perception of this contemporary social transgression a language that has an ancient history in the humanist tradition. It is this juncture of current social and material concerns with humanist epithet that offers us a useful insight, I believe, into the formation of the early modern self with whom we're concerned.

The "upstart Crow, beautified with our feathers" is, in 1592, the endpoint of a long line of little crow jokes that began with Horace's Third Epistle (c. 20 BCE), where the poet warns that the writer Celsus should be less ambitious and search for "home treasures" (*privatas . . . opes*)—that is, objects of imitation written to his own meridian—and not attempt to tamper with more august works in the collection of the Palatine library—"lest, if some day perchance the flock of birds come to reclaim their plumage, the poor crow, stripped of his stolen colours, awake laughter."[9] As Scott McGill observes, "The theft consists in the poet's inability to do anything more than inertly echo the superior Palatine poets from whom he borrows."[10] If, as it appears, Greene knew his Horace, he intended to identify Shakespeare with the heedless Celsus, whereby he not only accuses his rival of literally "unadulterated" theft—that is, of insufficiently personalizing his borrowings to make them his own—but in the process of demeaning Shakespeare, he also elevates himself and his friends to the exalted heights of the Palatine poets.[11]

After Horace, according to George W. Pigman, the *cornicula* joke became a commonplace in the discourse of literary imitation.[12] It is repeated during the Renaissance by Petrarch, Pico, Erasmus, Sturm, Nashe, and Harvey, among others, who familiarly describe or allude to the eclectic, unauthorized imitator reduced to his birthday suit by a flock of indignant, avenging models. Greene seems to have super-imposed this family of crows upon another old line, descending from Aesop, Martial, and Macrobius,[13] in which Cicero shames Roscius the actor by comparing him to the cobbler's crow who, having no words of his own, is taught to imitate his master's voice—an anecdote Greene embeds in the anti-theatrical diatribe of *Francesco's Fortunes* (1590). Here the narrator, a Palmer, offers a short history of the theater from the Greeks to the present day for the benefit of the impecunious scholar Francesco, who recently "fell in amongst a companie of Players, who perswaded him to trie his wit in writing of Comedies, Tragedies, or Pastorals, and if he could performe anything worth the stage, then they would largelie reward him for his paines."[14] The theater, the Palmer tells Francesco, once aimed to suppress vice and encourage virtue, but has since declined:

> Thus continued this facultie famous, till covetousnesse crept into the qualitie, and that meane men greedie of gaines did fall to practise the acting of such Playes, and in the Theatre presented their Comedies, but to such onely as rewarded them well for their paines: when thus Comedians grewe to bee mercenaries, then men of accompt left to practise such pastimes, and disdained to have their honors blemisht with the staine of such base and vile gaines."[15]

The actors who remained in the theater, the Palmer remarks, "by continuall use grewe not only excellent but rich and insolent." It's at this point that he cites the example of Roscius, who, having perfected his skills in action, began to believe that he could equal Cicero, "boasting that he could expresse a passion in as many sundrie actions, as *Tully* could discourse it in varietie of phrases: yea, so prowde he grewe by the daylie applause of people, that he looked for honor and reverence to be done him in the streetes." Tully sets him straight:

> Why *Roscius*, what sentence thou utterest on the stage, flowes from the censure of our wittes, and what sentence or conceipt the people applaud for excellent, that comes from the secrets of our knowledge. I graunt your action, though it be a kind of mechanical labour; yet wel done it is worthy of praise: but you worthlesse, if for so small a toy you waxe proud. At this *Roscius* waxt red, and bewraied his imperfection with silence.[16]

The overlay suggests that Greene is exercised not so much by common players who enhance their status by speaking poets' verses as by one particular player who pranks himself up as the poet himself. In this conflation of crows, histrionic imitation shades into professional and social imitation—note the disdainful reference to acting as a "mechanical labour"—and all three are deeply implicated in literary imitation.[17]

To find Shakespeare the dramatist first mentioned within the discourse of literary imitation is not surprising. After all, how did a writer get started in the early modern period if not by imitating? It is suggestive, however, of Greene's own sense of vocation that he uses a humanist epithet to accuse Shakespeare of fraudulent verbal usurpation when the commercial stage normally trafficked, as Janet Clare observes, in "the interplay of imitation, borrowing, and competition."[18] Imitation usually involved some manner of refashioning; borrowing was content with the lifting of words and matter, dishonest if unacknowledged; competition drove the enterprise of playwrights and companies alike. Thus, Shakespeare was doing nothing unusual, though if Greene is referring to collaboration in the early *Henry VI* plays for which Shakespeare was claiming full credit, then he may have had a point.[19] Even so, argues Gary Taylor, this was common stage practice and Shakespeare, for all his genius, was no exception. In fact, Taylor suggests that the word "collaboration" best describes the relationship between a practicing dramatist and his co-writers—whether acknowledged or not—as well as his predecessors, living and dead, since intellectual property was not a legal category at the time. Thus, he observes, "Shakespeare made an honest living stealing other men's work."[20]

A venerable critical tradition has attested to our abiding interest in Greene's Shakespeare by devoting itself to ferreting out Shakespeare's sources, and Shakespeare's early indebtedness to Lyly, Marlowe, Kyd, and other contemporary playwrights—to say nothing of his lifelong researches into Ovid, Virgil, Seneca, Plutarch, and Holinshed—are commonplaces of Shakespeare study.[21] Curiously, though, while the plays have often been compared to the sources—to see how (closely or allusively) Shakespeare worked with them—rarely do we find any exploration of the psychological or existential implications of working with models—a subject that was of great interest to Renaissance theorists of literary imitation. Most source study is closely bound to the notion of intention: to see where and in what manner Shakespeare adhered to or departed from his sources is to become capable of inferring his motive and meaning. This time-honored line of inquiry, as we have become increasingly aware in recent years, is also extremely hazardous, since the play of differences between texts can extend in a variety of directions and assume many configurations in the eye of a reader, which may or may not have been Shakespeare's. Dr. Johnson, well before this poststructuralist insight entered our common parlance, recognized the danger when he was editing Shakespeare's texts.[22] Yet even if we prefer to bracket the deconstructive threat, conventional source study begs a more fundamental question—who *is* this vaunted *meaner*, anyway? That is to say, how do we specify the entity that is doing the meaning, especially if—as it was often thought in the early modern period—making meaning coincides with, even determines, the "who" of the maker. It is here that serious consideration of Renaissance imitation theory can be useful, for it was commonly assumed that as one imitates one creates a self.[23]

The crow beautified with our feathers is but one of many images in the humanist tradition that describes the way one puts oneself together out of the substance of others. As George Pigman, Thomas Greene, Nancy Struever, and others have shown, a writer could imitate in a variety of ways—using one model or many models—and the way one imitated determined one's "kind of self."[24] One could, for example, be a slavish follower, using the model's very words and sentences—"whole sheets and tractacts *verbatim*," in Nashe's sneering terms; one could come onto the field as an open competitor and contend publicly for the laurel with one's predecessor, striving to equal or outdo him; or one might enter the race secretly, dissimulating one's source or alluding to it in only the most covert fashion—thereby allying oneself with the cognoscenti and challenging the envious to find you out. Jonson's got a wonderful moment in *The Poetaster*, where the ignorant Demetrius, a thinly disguised Thomas Dekker, accuses Horace—alias Ben—of plagiarizing through translation: "And (but I would not be thought a prater) / I could tell you, he were a translator. / I know the authors from whence he ha's stole, / And could trace him too, but that I understand 'hem not full and whole."[25] One can also be an emulator, engaged in envious, eristic combat with one's model and unwilling to help him when he is down—the Shakespeare portrayed by Greene.

If these are the "kinds of selves" available to writers who become the people they are by working with models, there is also a language that describes the *process* of becoming and suggests how the imitator is further individuated. Imitating was most commonly expressed in metaphors of genealogy, mellification, and digestion, which derived ultimately from Seneca's eighty-fourth moral epistle, where he speaks of his own reading and writing and speculates on its relationship to the metabolic capacity of the honeybee. Jonson's version is perhaps the most familiar to us. A poet, he asserts in his *Discoveries Made upon Men and Matters*, must "bee able to convert the substance, or Riches of another *Poet*, to his owne use." Like others before him, he recommends that one imitate,

> Not, as a Creature, that swallowes, what it takes in, crude, raw, or indigested; but, that feedes with an Appetite, and hath a Stomacke to concoct, divide, and turne all into nourishment. Not, to imitate servilely, as *Horace* saith, and catch at vices, for vertue: but, to draw forth out of the best, and choisest flowers, with the Bee, and turne all into Honey, worke it into one relish, and savour.[26]

This fanciful description implies that the imitator ingests his model, breaks him down with gastric juices, and converts him into his own substance, which is *then* not what it was prior to the act of imitation. If a king may go a progress through the guts of a beggar, why not Ovid, Virgil, Belleforest—or Robert Greene?

But there was an alternate version of this natural metaphor. The same poetical bee could simply flit from flower to flower and collect, rather than concoct, the assorted fragrances and deposit them raw in his own work, creating a *cento* of flowery essences or, less elegantly, a gallimaufry of undigested literary gobbets. That Shakespeare was alive to this distinction is seen in the fun he has with the pedant Holofernes and Nathaniel the curate in *Love's Labour's Lost*. When these poetasters emerge from a proto-Jonsonian supper of reasons "sharp and sententious; pleasant without scurrility, witty without affection, audacious without impudency, learned without opinion, and strange without heresy," they critique the boastful Armado's diction in so pettifogging a manner that Moth the page is prompted to observe, "They have been to a great feast of languages and stol'n the scraps" (5.1.1–36). Shakespeare knew about eating authors well before Jonson came along and, in this instance at least, was wary of the indigestion that might ensue.

There was also current an imitative notion that had, in its ideal form, a more benign, familial cast. In the same passage of *Discoveries*, Jonson suggests that the poet "make choise of one excellent man above the rest, and so to follow him, till he grow very *Hee*: or, *so like him*, as the Copie may be mistaken for the Principall."[27] This appears to be a condensed version of a more subtle genealogical metaphor also derived from Seneca, but perhaps best known from one of Petrarch's *Familiar Letters*. It goes like this:

> A proper imitator should take care that what he writes resemble the original without reproducing it. The resemblance should not be that of a portrait to the sitter—but it should be the resemblance of a son to his father. Therein is often a great divergence in particular features, but there is a certain suggestion, what our painters call an "air," most noticeable in the face and eyes, which makes the resemblance. As soon as we see the son, he recalls the father to us,

although if we should measure every feature we should find them all different.[28]

Here the imitator is a literary if not a biological son, to be recognized by one who knows his father well. Since it is resemblance that is desired and not identity, differences must be worked into the imitation. In the English sixteenth century, Roger Ascham would formulate this advice for teachers of grammar-school boys in a sentence that defined imitation as either a similar treatment of dissimilar matter or a dissimilar treatment of similar matter, and would insist upon a "deliberate Master-of-Arts" comparison of an author's work with his model if the student were to achieve the same "similarity-in-difference" in his own: "This and that he leaveth out, which he doth wittily to this end and purpose . . . This he addeth here . . . This he diminisheth there."[29] To compare the choices of words and ideas made by your author in relation to *his* model and to make like or unlike choices based upon an understanding of his was to fashion your own "who-ness" within the literary genealogy. But notice, it also implies that you can thereby infer intention.

Several questions arise from all this. First, with such ideas in circulation, would they—or could they—be kept apart? For example, need a son relate to his father in only a benign and respectful fashion? Could he not indulge in an inverse Thyestean banquet and consume his father flesh and bone, with only a few hiccups? One thinks inevitably of *Titus Andronicus*, so long (if unfairly) considered apprentice work, with its gobbets of Ovid, Virgil, and Seneca so confectiously larded into the text. Less obviously, what might be the ethical charge of the allusions to Lyly in *Henry IV, Part 1*, when Falstaff mimics the Euphuism of the 1580s, or of the citation from *Hero and Leander* in *As You Like It*, when foolish Phebe, besotted with passion for a disguised Rosalind, offers passing homage to the departed Marlowe: "Dead shepherd, now I find thy saw of might: / Who ever loved that loved not at first sight?" (3.5.82–3). When Jonson places Kyd's "Eyes, no eyes but fountaines fraught with teares" on the tongue of the dolt Matheo in *Every Man in his Humour* (1.3.135),[30] we think he's indulging in his usual vein of satiric literary criticism. But since we also know Jonson was paid to write "additions" to the very play he is satirizing—Kyd's *The Spanish Tragedy*—a few years after he wrote *Every Man in*, a strain of parasitism may be detected that cannot be separated from the Jonsonian self. What of Shakespeare?

II

However justified Greene's accusation of Shake-scene's usurpation may have been, he continued to endure an uninvited relationship with Shakespeare after his death. It appears that in composing *As You Like It* the upstart crow may have derived Orlando's determination to "carve on every tree / The fair, the chaste, and unexpressive she" (3.2.9–10) from Greene's *The Historie of Orlando Furioso* (itself derived from Ariosto's epic poem), where the evil suitor Sacrepant schemes to madden Orlando by making him believe that his beloved Angelica has been unfaithful. Plots he: "Upon those shrubs that compasse in the spring / And on those trees that border in those walkes / I'll slily have engraven on every barke / The names of Medor and Angelica. / Hard by, Ile have some roundelayes hung up / Wherein shall be some posies of their loves."[31]

When Orlando enters the woods to find those names carved on every tree, and reads the poems attached, he is told by Sacrepant's servant, disguised as a shepherd, that Angelica has betrayed him with Medor and that their love is the shepherds' common song. Maddened, he falls to the ground and begins to babble chiasmatically, "Woods, trees, leaves; leaves, trees, woods: tria sequuntur tria"[32]—a locution resembling that of a later Shakespeare protagonist driven to jealous ecstasy by false report. When Iago tells Othello that Cassio "did—Lie—With her, on her, what you will," the Moor succumbs to the same sort of verbal and logical chiasmus: "Handkerchief—confessions—handkerchief. To confess and be hanged for his labour. First to be hanged and then to confess" (4.1.36–7)—then "falls down in a trance." Othello seems to have picked up another distinctive locution from Greene's Orlando, who claims upon his arrival at the court of Angelica's father that "The savage Moores & Anthropophagi / Whose lands I past might well have kept me backe" (117–20), and explains (as Orlando had not) that the "anthropophagi" are "cannibals that each other eat" (1.2.142–3), before developing further what is only implicit in Greene—that his journey to the city of Desdemona's father has been a "pilgrimage" (1.2.152). Thus within a period of some five years, beginning seven years after Greene's death, Shakespeare seems to have returned to Greene's feast several times and "stol'n the scraps," digesting them along the way and concocting something quite new. He would do so again.[33]

Now if it is legitimate to consider Shakespeare's imitations in the context of social roles, of apiary, digestive, and genealogical metaphors, of simian and aviary analogies, was there a language available in the period that specified the *psychological* dimensions and the *existential* implications of such identity-formation—which might give us an insight into what it was to be an upstart crow simultaneously bodging up one's work and one's self?

The first place to look is in the source of so much imitation discourse—Seneca's eighty-fourth moral epistle. After he passes from apiary to digestive metaphor to explain what happens to him internally as he reads and writes, Seneca turns from the stomach to the mind. "It is the same," he says, "concerning those things with which our *ingenia* are nourished: we should see to it that whatever we have absorbed should not be allowed to remain whole, lest it remain alien to us. We must break it down or else it will merely enter the memory and not the *ingenium*."[34]

What is this *ingenium* he refers to? Although the word appears frequently in discussions of rhetoric and poetry as the *sine qua non* of excellence—a natural gift, talent, mother wit—here it seems to signify the native power with which humans are endowed that enables them to assemble the elements perceived by the senses into new and intelligible configurations. In the Renaissance, *ingenium* was classified as a cognitive instrument—specifically that power of the rational soul that is capable of drawing disparate things together and finding in their relation a *meaning*. According to the humanist Juan Luis Vives, *ingenium* has a foundational role in the life of unaccommodated man. Unlike other creatures, human beings come into the world without the physical means of protecting and preserving themselves, and even though they are in a measure responsible for their present subjection to necessity because of their first disobedience, nevertheless God gave them an instrument by means of which they might free themselves from physical need: "the lively keenness of an *ingenium* full of spontaneous play."[35] From its activities are born all the things invented by man: useful, harmful, worthy, dishonorable. In his treatise on the soul, Vives suggests that we are all natural dialecticians by virtue of our *ingenium*, for we can invent and compose arguments—quickly run through the materials from the outside world that are presented by the exterior to the interior senses, make apt connections among them, and marshal them into effective interpretations of reality. We can even conjecture the future by putting together elements of the present and elements of the past in such a way that what's past becomes prologue and things to come not a copy but a similitude of things that have already happened. In this sense, the future may be considered an existential equivalent of literary imitation.

In more homely language, the English dialectician and rhetorician Thomas Wilson provides an example of the transfer of meaning between apparent dissimilars, and thus of the inventive capacity of *ingenium*. He offers a simple sentence and asks what connection there is between the subject and predicate: "Is a covetous manne poore, or not?" He then replies,

> I maie thus reason with my self, why should a covetous manne be called poore? What affinitie is betwixt theim twoo? Marie in this poincte thei bothe agree, that like as the poore man, ever lacketh and desireth to have so the covetous manne ever lacketh, wanting the use of that whiche he hath, and desireth still to have, being never content though God geve enough. Then seying it is even so, that bothe dooe lacke and bothe doe desire to have, thissame reason is the onely cause, wherebye mine argument is made perfect.

In this way, two apparently dissimilar things—rich miser and pauper—are found to have an affinity and it is *ingenium* that makes the connection.[36]

Sir Philip Sidney offers a more material example. When he urges the importance of poetic imitation in *The Defense of Poesy*, his claim for poetry is rather exalted. A poem is not simply a castle in the air, he says. "So far substantially it worketh not only to make a Cyrus, which had been but a particular excellency as Nature might have done, but to bestow a Cyrus upon the world to make many Cyruses, if they will learn aright why and how that maker made him."[37] He is claiming that a fictional Cyrus outperforms the real Cyrus by providing an intelligible model that living men can imitate if they study the "why and how" of the poet's choices. Clearly they cannot become fifth-century Cyruses—they're sixteenth-century Englishmen—but they can make ingenious adequations between the written Cyrus and themselves to create something new—a contemporary Cyrus that is a behavioral version of the literary imitation advocated by Petrarch.

Of course, there were *ingenia* and *ingenia*. A Renaissance anthropology, derived from Galen's humoral psychology, created a taxonomy of *ingenia*, in which the four humors infiltrated a man's *ingenium* in different proportions to shape his individual talent. Thus, a diversity of capacities was recognized, and a hierarchy of genius established, topped by the melancholic; but each *ingenium* was endowed with a natural faculty for interpreting the world through its own internal eyes, as it were, and thereby to stylize it in what one thought or said, wrote or acted. Common to all *ingenia* was this power of configuring.

But what, we may ask, do complex psychological processes, so lovingly delineated by a humanist elite, have to do with bodging? To bodge up something, whether a blank verse, a pair of old trousers, or a whole suit of feathers—to say nothing of one's self—is to stitch pieces together into a patchwork, an unintegrated whole, an entity that is *only* the sum of its parts. It would seem there is nothing organic in bodging—no need for an ingenuity that digests, mellificates, and engenders a son from a father. Nashe and Greene thought this, and so, on occasion, did Shakespeare, for he used the word and its cognates mockingly at times just as they did.[38] But he also knew that bodging can fashion a kind of coherence that plays into the mind's natural desire for intelligibility. When Henry V confronts his bosom friend Lord Scroop for conspiring against him, he says

> devils that suggest by treasons
> Do botch and bungle up damnation
> With patches, colors, and with forms being fetch'd
> From glistering semblances of piety (2.2.114–17)

in order to deceive their victim—but in Scroop's case they did no such thing and therefore he has no excuse. Here, "botch and bungle" suggests a rough kind of casuistry that disguises the nature of an evil deed with justifying patches and *colores*,[39] and is persuasive notwithstanding its crude handiwork—persuasive enough to enable someone to attempt treason with a good conscience.

The cognitive implications of bodging become even more apparent in *Hamlet* when the Gentleman of Act 4 describes how Ophelia's mad ravings are affecting the Danes who listen to her:

> Her speech is nothing,
> Yet the unshaped use of it doth move
> The hearers to collection. They aim at it,
> And botch the words up fit to their own thoughts,
> Which, as her winks and nods and gestures yield them,
> Indeed would make one think there might be thought,
> Though nothing sure, yet much unhappily. (4.5.7–13)

Ophelia, the Gentleman suggests, is supplying her observers with visual and verbal images that they stitch together as *evidence* that turns their own suspicions into the shape of propositions. Horatio appreciates the potential seriousness of such bodging. "'Twere good she were spoken with," he says, "for she may strew / Dangerous conjectures in ill-breeding minds" (14–16). Bodging can give visible form to a tendentiousness that cannot fully see itself.

What is suggested by these examples is that bodging, for all its bad press, is a practice that does create an interconnected whole through ingenious patching. If not organic in the way digestion, mellification, or engendering is organic, it may be more subtly so, since in its work it reveals that the *ingenium* has a kind of *textual* power that stitches disparate perceptions into reasons, reasons into arguments, arguments into action, and action into existential change. Unfortunately, there is no theory of bodging extant, so far as I know, to which we can attach this practice, but I should like to propose its acceptance as a subset of the theory of ingenious imitation—the materialist verso of a humanist recto. And Shakespeare, from his first literary notice, must be recognized as its most distinguished practitioner in the English Renaissance.

Before tracing him further, as Demetrius might put it, I need to say a few more things about ingenuity in its cognitive and fabricating aspects. The work of the late philosopher of early modern humanism Ernesto Grassi is extremely helpful here. In functioning as a cognitive instrument, he observes, *ingenium* differs from scientific reasoning in several respects. As the word itself suggests, it is a natural capacity for grasping the relations among things rather than an acquired method of logical inference. It fixes upon perceivables—the particulars of its environment—and works with these, instead of proceeding from abstract principles. It therefore fashions, in a very literal sense, only contingent knowledge—bearing the character of probability—rather than a firm system of knowledge based upon necessary implication. And since it is bound to time, place, and person, the work of *ingenium* is historical. It does not so much act upon the concrete materials of its environment as it interacts with them, realizing itself in its materials—its *res*—as it changes these by reconfiguring them. This constitutes its work. Thereafter both *ingenium* and its matter are not what they were, and become the bases of further ingenious activity. It is architectonic metaphor-making, since *ingenium* causes images to signify by transferring to them a signification. Such spontaneous metaphor-making, he remarks, is for the humanist "the original form of cognizance. The metaphor provides the transition to knowledge from the information which is provided by the senses and which is kept present by the memory. It is here that the breakthrough into a new reality occurs: here the metamorphosis of man takes place."[40]

If *ingenium* is the instrument of Shakespearean translation, where do we look for its traces? One might begin with its representations. Shakespeare seems not only to have worked by means of *ingenium* but often dramatized those workings in his plays. His most explicit dramatization is found in the language of Iago, Othello's wily antagonist, a figure whose behavior has puzzled critics from the time of Thomas Rymer, who thought no such person could exist.[41] A century or so later, Coleridge, observing that Iago seems to pick up motives as he goes along, without finding sufficient cause for the evil he inflicts on all the major figures in the play, aptly described his behavior as "the motive-hunting of motiveless malignity."[42] This formulation catches Iago very precisely, but doesn't tell us how Iago *works*. Happily, the villain himself does: "We work by wit, and not by witchcraft," he assures Roderigo (2.3.372). What does this mean?

At the beginning of the play Iago says he holds Othello in his hate and expresses a desire to get back at him—nothing more. He had been passed over for promotion when Cassio was made Othello's lieutenant and he, God save the mark, "his worship's ancient." By the end of the third scene, however, he has begun to realize that he can give formal shape to his feeling. His accretive, disjunctive speech suggests nothing so much as an inventory-taking of circumstances that somehow must be bodged together so he may *realize* his emotion:

> I hate the Moor,
> *And* it is thought abroad, that 'twixt my sheets
> He's done my office; I *know not* if't be *true* . . .
> Yet I, for mere *suspicion* in that kind,
> Will *do as if for surety* (1.3.386–90, italics mine)

First there's hatred, then there's the rumor he's been cuckolded. Even if untrue, it's a piece of evidence that has a useful relation to my hatred, so I'll act on it—and not doubtfully but as if it were a sure thing. Feeling, motive, and action are swiftly bodged together heedless of causality or veracity into a rough cohesive fabric that will allow Iago to proceed.[43] He subjoins to these patches a corroborating element:

> He holds me well,
> The better shall my purpose work on him. (1.3.390–1)

Neatly mended. But *what* purpose? we may ask. We know nothing of purpose, nor does Iago—except insofar as he wants to "serve my turn upon him"—which means, presumably, "revenge my grudge." It is only as Iago encounters new circumstances and sees in them some relation both to his hatred and to his present means that he can acquire a "purpose" in any determinate sense.

Then a new matter passes before his mind's eye:

Cassio's a proper man, let me see now,
To get his place, and to plume up my *will*,
A double knavery . . . how, how? let me see,
After some time to abuse Othello's ear,
That he is too familiar with his wife (1.3.392–6)[44]

Cassio occurs to Iago as an image—a handsome man—and that image is for use. It may be used as a means to a double end, the practical end of winning the lieutenancy and the more obscure one of "pluming up my will." What is Iago's will? Is it the same as his purpose? Or is it something darker, the will of the sonnets that somehow must be *plumed up*, *swelled out*, in the very moment of a consummation whose shape cannot be foreseen?[45] Iago's words reveal the zigzag motions of his mind as he first imagines Cassio's face, then relates it to his double end, then invents the means to that end—abusing Othello's ear that Cassio is familiar with his wife—and finally explains why he thinks this will work:

He has a person and a smooth dispose,
To be *suspected*, *framed* to make women false. (1.3.397–8, italics
    mine)

This is the art of bodging. In a twinkling, the adventitious character of Cassio's good looks—which makes him susceptible to suspicion—is turned into the certainty of a final cause—*framed to make women false*—as Iago works him into the web he has begun to weave. No wonder he exclaims a few moments later, "I ha't, it is engendered; Hell and night / Must bring this monstrous birth to the world's light" (1.3.403–4). Somewhere deep in Iago's *ingenium* he has fathered something new upon the world, something that will bear a family resemblance to the original but will be styled in his own way. This is how he will make himself out of the materials supplied by the daily life he and Othello share.

It is not until the end of the play, however, that we know who he really is, for as he is quick to point out, "'Tis here; but yet confus'd, / Knavery's plain face is never seen till *us'd*" (2.1.311–12). As new perceptibles and old memories pass before Iago's ingenious eye—Roderigo's foolish passion, Cassio's weakness with drink, Desdemona's untimely loyalty, Othello's discarded handkerchief—they are remarked and worked into Iago's unspecified purpose until he has his will, and it is palpable: "Look on the tragic loading of this bed," Lodovico tells him, after Desdemona, then

Emilia, and then Othello have died upon its newly laid-out wedding sheets: "This is thy work" (5.2.363–4). What Iago has become is figured in the violated bodies he finds before him: knavery's plain face is now seen.[46]

It would be overly literal to suggest that when Shakespeare looked over the Deca terza, Novella settima, of Giraldi Cinzio's *Ecatommiti*, his primary source for *Othello*, he said to himself, "Cinzio's a proper novella; Let me see now," and went to work by wit, not witchcraft, on the matter at hand. But that he must have done something like this it is not improper to imagine. For the play *Othello* is a historical translation of Shakespeare in his circumstantiality, circa 1603—the work in which he, like Iago but encompassing Iago, may be seen making himself. To trace him with exactitude in this process is both a theoretical and a practical impossibility, since our conjectures would be made of the same stuff as his—the contingent, ingenious inferences that scholars, editors, and critics, in *their* historicity, bring to their interpretations of texts, guided by the unpredictable criterion of probability.

III

A few years before he wrote *Othello*, however, Shakespeare did represent a play-bodger making himself in precisely the way I am suggesting Shakespeare did. When a company of tragedians arrives at Elsinore during a provincial tour that has taken them from their quarters in the city because "the boys carry it away . . . / Hercules and his load too" (2.2.360–1), Hamlet asks if they can perform a play called *The Murder of Gonzago*, in which he will insert a speech of some dozen or sixteen lines. They agree, and when he's alone he informs us that the players will perform "something like the murder of my father / Before mine uncle" (595–6). He's remembered an old play that can be adapted to *his* circumstances and used for *his* cause—which is, like Iago's, revenge—though even more overdetermined than Iago's, since in his case it seems to be in conflict with his will. Indeed, Hamlet's will is a puzzle, as he himself observes, and it is as arbitrarily defended against as Iago's is plumed up: "The spirit that I have seen / May be a [dev'l]"; "Thus conscience does make cowards [of us all]"; "Why this is [hire and salary], not revenge"; "I do not know / Why yet I live to say 'This thing's to do,' / Sith I have cause, and will, and strength, and means / To do't" (2.2.598–9, 3.1.82, 3.3.79, 4.4.43–6). In this conflict between cause and will,

Hamlet invents ingenious excuses for inaction as rapidly as Iago invents motives for revenge.

But he does bodge up a play and, as is well known, seems to make a botch of it. And that is what makes it interesting. For as the players perform "something like the murder of my father," the dumb show (apparently their invention) is sufficiently vague for Ophelia to ask, "What means this, my lord?"—and then, dissatisfied with Hamlet's cryptic response, to supply her own answer: "Belike this show imports the argument of the play" (3.2.136, 139–40).[47] When, however, the dialogue between Player King and Player Queen begins, Hamlet's "some dozen or sixteen lines" emerge from the generic show of regicide to reveal something more specific—a "seeming-virtuous queen" (1.5.46) who swears eternal fidelity to her sickly husband: "Both here and hence pursue me lasting strife, / If, once a widow, ever I be a wife" (3.2.222–3). Their exchanges rouse Claudius from his silent observation to ask Hamlet if there is any offence in the play, and Hamlet ironically demurs, insisting that it is "the image of a murder done in Vienna; Gonzago is the Duke's name, his wife Baptista"—and twits Claudius for his concern: "Your Majesty and we that have free souls, it touches us not" (3.2.238–9, 241–2). But then some odd bits of information begin to creep in. As the murderer enters, Hamlet identifies him as "Lucianus, nephew to the *King*" (3.2.244) and when the figure starts mugging to the audience, Hamlet hurries him to perform the destined act—"Come, the croaking raven doth bellow for revenge!" (3.2.252–3)—then explains, as the killer "*Pours the poison in the sleeper's ears*" (S.D.), "A poisons him i' th' garden for his estate" (3.2.261). *Nephew* to the *king*? *Revenge*? For his *estate*? These contradictory words confuse the nature of the crime on display, and instead of compelling Claudius to presently proclaim his malefactions they prompt his abrupt walk-out. As a result, his reaction to the play is unclear to the assembled court. Only Hamlet believes his performed similitude has proved the Ghost honest—Horatio is noncommittal, Rosencrantz and Guildenstern interpret the play as a threat against the king's life, and so, apparently, does Gertrude. Claudius, who knows nothing of any ghost, reveals in private that he has received a double message: that his offense is rank and that Hamlet has smelled him out. As public proof of Claudius's guilt, then, the play and its reception are dubious pieces of evidence. As representations of Hamlet's position in time, they are utterly indicative.[48]

It has been customary to regard Hamlet's identification of the murderer as the king's nephew as a *lapsus linguae* suggesting that

as he watched the play it had become the image of his own con-
templated revenge or, more complexly, an Oedipal projection in
which his aggressive feelings toward his father were audibly displaced onto the uncle who had done his job for him (killing his
father and marrying his mother), but who for that very reason had
become an extremely problematic object of revenge who could only
be murdered in play.[49] And there is much in the tragedy to support
these interpretations. In the context of play-bodging, however,
there is something equally interesting going on. For at least part of
this alleged "slip" was already built into the play that Hamlet had
decided to adapt.

The Murder of Gonzago is part of the visiting company's reper-
tory when they arrive, and its victim is someone named Gonzago.
During the performance, Hamlet responds to the growing anxiety
of Claudius and Gertrude by indicating who this Gonzago might be:
a "Viennese" duke named Gonzago with a wife named Baptista. A
few minutes later, the *duke* becomes a *king* with a nephew named
Lucianus. Finally we learn that "The story is extant and written in
very choice Italian" (3.2.262–3). By noting that this is a translation
from the Italian about persons other than Gertrude and Claudius,
Hamlet is, of course, trying to allay the fears of his royal audience
that it is about them, while keeping them in their seats until his dozen
or sixteen lines reveal that it *is* about them. But he also gives us an
insight into the process of bodging up a play. It was common enough
to turn recent history into drama in the sixteenth century, especially
if it was sensational. It is not surprising, therefore, that Hamlet's
remarks have been taken seriously by scholars.[50] For the play is
"something like" the murder of Francesco Maria I della Rovere,
the fourth Duke of Urbino and husband of Eleonora Gonzaga, in
1538—poisoned through the ear by his own barber, who confessed
under torture that the duke's nephew, Luigi Gonzaga, put him up
to it.[51] A few changes have occurred in translation (not including
Hamlet's "dozen or sixteen lines"). Most obviously, there's been a
small spelling change, from Gonza*g*a to Gonza*g*o; more curiously,
the family name of the murdering nephew has become the family
name of the murdered uncle, and the nephew's Christian name,
Luigi, has been Latinized to Lucianus. The faithful Eleonora, who
mourned her husband's death for years, has become the weak-willed
Player Queen, who succumbs to the blandishments of the man who
has murdered her husband. To complete the exchange, as Eleonora's
husband has assumed the name of her kinsman Gonzaga, so she has
taken the name of his kinswoman, Baptista Sforza—and, of course,

the scene has moved to Vienna, though this may be a typographer's slip for "Urbino."[52]

How did this come about? If we consider this question historically, it would seem that Hamlet and, behind him, Shakespeare are only the latest contenders in a long line of play-bodgers. For in Shakespeare's *Hamlet* we have a series of performed similitudes, each "something like" its predecessor. Maximally, in the old play called *Hamlet* to which Nashe alludes in his preface to Greene's *Menaphon* of 1589, hinting that its author was Thomas Kyd; then in the play at Newington Butts listed by Henslowe in 1594; then in the one at the Theatre in Shoreditch where, as Lodge reports in his 1596 *Wit's Misery*, the ghost cried out "like an oyster-wife, 'Hamlet, revenge!'"; then in Shakespeare's play, when the Ghost describes how he was murdered sleeping in his orchard where his brother "in the porches of my ears did pour / The leprous distillment" (1.5.63–4)—and finally as dumb show *and* play in Hamlet's *Mousetrap* where, unlike Shakespeare's version, the murderer is once again a nephew. It is also possible, of course, that *The Murder of Gonzago* did not show up in *Hamlet* until Shakespeare tried his hand at a Hamlet play, in which case the palimpsest would have been less layered but still a set of redactions upon an action previously performed, since if Hamlet knew about *The Murder of Gonzago* so did Shakespeare, who inserted *his* seventeen lines about poisoning through the ears before Hamlet got around to his. And in all three early versions of *The Mousetrap*—Q1, Q2, and F1—the play-within-the-play is initially described by the Prince as the "image" of the murder of a duke.

If we regard *The Murder of Gonzago* in relation to its putative historical model, the various transpositions that we find in it are not at all foreign to the methods of literary imitation that were currently being practiced. "This he ordereth thus, with placing that here, not there. This he altereth and changeth either in property of words, in form of sentence, in substance of the matter, or in one or another convenient circumstance of the author's present purpose." Thus Roger Ascham. And if we acknowledge the *dramatic* fact that the script of *The Murder of Gonzago* lived in the players' memories when they came to Elsinore, then whatever lines Hamlet added to their command performance are not likely to have included a change in the identities of victim and murderer, since the transposition of names had already been made—by someone else. The most—and the worst—Hamlet can be accused of is meddling with a translation, botching his king and queen onto Gonzago's duke and duchess, and cunningly (or was it impulsively?) turning Lucianus into a "nephew to the *King*," from his historical role as nephew to the *Duke*. And, of course, he flagrantly changed the old play to link the murder of the ruler with the seduction of his widow. But that is plenty—enough to make Claudius rise from his seat as soon as he hears, "You shall see anon how the murderer gets the love of Gonzago's wife," and flee the chamber before the performance is over. This is how Hamlet, bodging an old play, turns "something like" the murder of his father into "something like" the murder of his uncle, as he conflates his uncle and himself with one word. Or, to be more precise, how he represents what he has just described to Horatio as "my imaginations . . . foul as Vulcan's stithy" (3.2.83–4).

Which brings us back to *Hamlet*'s author. If *The Murder of Gonzago* came to Elsinore at least partly reshaped from history, who put those changes into the play in the first place? Shakespeare? Kyd? The unknown author of some intermediate *Hamlet*? We don't know. Perhaps more than any other Shakespeare play, *Hamlet* is composed of layers of many wits—Saxo's, Kyd's, Seneca's, François de Belleforest's (whose language filters so oddly through the "To be or not to be" speech), Nashe's, even Thomas Dekker's, whose double portraits of Horace and Ben Jonson in *Satiromastix* reappear when Hamlet confronts Gertrude with the contrasting portraits of her first and second husbands. But all these layerings are precisely what makes the play Shakespeare's—the work of the upstart crow, the imitator, the bodger. If on a thematic level the tragedy of *Hamlet* is preoccupied with fraternal rivalry and filial ambivalence, what is played out as theme is literally written into the act of composition as Shakespeare contends, in a variety of responsive registers, with his predecessors and contemporaries.

Even a current professional controversy gets patched into his script. The so-called War of the Theaters, in which the common players and their writers for the public stage found themselves attacked by the children's acting companies, prodded thereto by poets writing for private theater audiences, seems to be at least partly responsible for Hamlet's players being on the road. "There was for a while," Rosencrantz tells Hamlet, "no money bid for argument unless the poet and the player went to cuffs in the question." This "war" in which Shakespeare's company actually participated—and in which it is participating at this very moment by incorporating (and thus co-opting) its rivals' alleged triumph in its own performance—is a replay at the midpoint of Shakespeare's career of the very issues voiced by Greene and Nashe some ten years previously. But the conflict is now institutional. And given Rosencrantz's news that "the boys carry it away . . . Hercules and his load too"—a line that refers to a Globe Theater emptied of patrons, but which is spoken before a Globe Theater audience—we must infer that it is being managed with considerable confidence.

IV

At the end of his *Groats-Worth of Wit*, Robert Greene offers his version of Aesop's fable of the ant and the grasshopper. The two insects are walking together upon a green, the one carelessly skipping along, the other "carefully prying what winter's provision was scattered in the way," and the grasshopper taunts the little ant with a parable. "The greedy miser thirsteth still for gaine," he says; "His thrift is theft, his weale works others woe," and derides such drudgery, "when mongst faire sweets he may at pleasure go." To which the ant retorts, "The thriftie husband spares what unthrift spends, / His thrift no theft, for dangers to provide" (88). In the winter the grasshopper gets his comeuppance, of course, when he goes to "the Ant his olde acquaintaince," and is told to "Pack hence . . . My house doth harbor no unthriftie mates." "Foodless, helpless, strengthless," he walks to a nearby brook, digs himself a pit in which to die, and composes an epitaph that recapitulates the moral of the *Groats-Worth of Wit*. Greene then identifies the Grasshopper: "Like him my selfe: like me, shall all that trust to friends or times inconstancie" (89).

In a confessional that is a thrice-told tale—with Roberto the first hero, Robert the second, and the Grasshopper the third—it's tempting to see the respective villains as palimpsests as well. If the usurer-father, the upstart crow, and the ant refer to the same person, perhaps, E. A. J. Honigmann has speculated, our poet was improving his fortunes by negotiating loans in 1592.[53] By 1598, the year he was writing *Henry IV, Part 2* and *Much Ado About Nothing*, we do know that Shakespeare's investments were being discussed by his Stratford neighbors and that he was approached for a loan by one of them, Richard Quiney, who was in London on protracted business. When Quiney wrote to his friend Abraham Sturley that "our countryman Mr. Wm. Shak. would procure us money," Sturley drily accepted the report, "which I will like of as I shall hear when, where, and how."[54] However generously or not Shakespeare may have dealt with his friends and business acquaintances, he leaves the paper trail of a provident ant during the later 1590s and the first decade of the seventeenth century. He became a sharer of the Lord Chamberlain's company in 1594; on behalf of his father he applied for and was granted a coat of arms in 1596;[55] in 1597, he purchased a large home, New Place, in Stratford; he struck a deal with the Burbage brothers that made him one of the housekeepers of the newly built Globe Theater in 1599; and he continued to make investments in land, leases, and buildings in the early 1600s, prosecuting debts for as little as thirty-five shillings in Stratford's small claims court. And, of course, he became a liveried servant of King James I in 1604, when the king assumed the patronage of the Lord Chamberlain's company. In August of 1608 he was a partner in the acquisition of the Blackfriars Theater, former home of the boy actors and their poets, now the private theater venue of His Majesty's (uncommon) Players.

The Winter's Tale, which was performed at the Globe some two and a half years later, may as aptly be called *Greene Resurrectus* as, from another point of view, *Greene Hoist with his Own Petard*, for it was adapted from Greene's *Pandosto: The Triumph of Time*, upon which the upstart crow performed operations both salvific and retributive. Shakespeare had written of sexual jealousy several times before. In Greene's romance, however, he found not only a tale of sexual jealousy but one of suspect genealogy originating in the perceived rivalry of two boyhood companions.[56] As he reworked the matter of *Pandosto*, he made the kind of changes we might expect: Aschamlike, he went about transposing places, persons, and actions—reinterpreting their relationships while retaining an unmistakable resemblance to his model. From another Greene romance, *Mamillia*, he took the name of his young prince Mamillius, effecting a sex change along the way, and possibly adapted the name of Mamillia's beloved friend Florion for his Bohemian prince Florizel. But that was not the end of his use of Greene. He bodged a new character, the peddler Autolycus, a "snapper-up of trifles," from Greene's descriptions of the rogue underworld he had frequented—the world of nips, foists, and lifts described in his conny-catching pamphlets of the early 1590s and alluded to in his *Groats-Worth of Wit*. When Autolycus comes across the Shepherd's son going to buy supplies for the sheep-shearing feast in 4.1, he fleeces him even as the young clown is trying to be of service, by pretending to have been beaten and robbed on the road by one Autolycus—a rural transmogrification of an episode that takes place in the middle walk of St. Paul's in *The Second Part of Conny-Catching* of 1592.[57] Robert Greene's feathers flutter all across the landscape of *The Winter's Tale*.

From the perspective I am pursuing here, what emerges most strikingly in Shakespeare's snapping-up of this trifling but still popular romance is his interest in the linked phenomena of ingenuity, imitation, and issue, which are all implicated in the project of remaking Greene in his own image. From the model of the jealous king Pandosto he fashioned in Leontes a portrait of ingenuity diseased that had no precedent in the old romance. "Is whispering nothing?" Leontes asks his faithful counselor Camillo. "Is leaning cheek to cheek? is meeting noses? / Kissing with inside lip? stopping the career / Of laughter with a sigh — A note infallible of breaking honesty . . . Is this nothing? / Why then the world and all that's in't, is nothing, / The covering sky is nothing, Bohemia nothing, / My wife is nothing, nor nothing have these nothings, / If this be nothing" (1.2.282–94).[58] Leontes has been observing his wife and his old friend Polixenes chatting and strolling about the court, where they are behaving affectionately toward one another, but not (as the audience sees them) with the gestures and implications apparent to him. He is amplifying what he sees, then inferring conclusions from his autoerotic vivifications. Iago, making similar inferences from words and images, had recognized the difference between what is "apt and of great credit"—even "probal to thinking"—and what is actually true, though he chose to collapse the distinction as he wove a persuasive verbal net in which to entrap Othello. Leontes makes no such distinction. His ingenious inferences are as coherent, real, and stabilizing to him as the earth he stands on. Which can only mean that he feels his very identity depends on believing that his friend and his wife are cuckolding him. For this is who he has become.

Leontes' investment in being a cuckold is deeply connected to the innocent bonding he and Polixenes had experienced in their boyhood and their subsequent fall into what sounds like a tainted heterosexuality (1.2.67–86). His relationship to his son Mamillius is for these reasons multiplied into a variety of likenesses—infused with love, suspicion, and rivalry—for he sees in him both his own issue and that of Polixenes' ("Art thou my boy?", 1.2.120); himself as a child; even his young friend, with whom "as twinned lambs [he] did frisk i'th'sun"—yet who now (it seems to him) pours fecund tales into his wife's ear (2.1.29–62). Thus the powerful cathexes of an over-metaphorizing ingenuity informs the problem of issue, just as the vexed matter of issue evokes, in turn, the question of imitation.

This question comes up as Leontes anxiously interrogates Mamillius: "What! hast smutch'd thy nose? / They say it is a copy out of mine . . . Thou want'st a rough pash and the shoots that I have / To be full like me: yet they say we are / Almost as like as eggs" (1.2.121–2, 128–30). Then to Polixenes: "Looking on the lines / Of my boy's face, methoughts I did recoil / Twenty-three years, and saw myself unbreech'd / In my green velvet coat; my dagger muzzled, / Lest it should bite its master" (1.2.153–7). Not content with seeing the resemblance of a son to his father, Leontes' mind ranges deep in time to find moments of *identity* with his son, even if he must collapse generational difference to do so.[59] When the court lady Paulina presents Hermione's newborn babe to him—whom he believes is Polixenes' bastard—she caters to this same need of absolute identity through an extended metaphor of natural and mechanical imitation: "Behold, my lords, / Although the print be little, the whole matter / And copy of the father: eye, nose, lip; / The trick of's frown; his forehead; nay, the valley, / The pretty dimples of his chin and cheek; his smiles; / The very mould and frame of hand, nail, finger" (2.3.96–101).

Now I don't mean to reduce a play as rich as *The Winter's Tale* to an allegory of an old relationship between William Shakespeare and Robert Greene, revived and contested on the stage of the Globe Theater nearly twenty years later. It must be remarked, however, that Greene's *Groats-Worth of Wit* was still sufficiently known in 1609 for Jonson to have immense fun with its title in the fourth act of *Epicoene*, where the book is one of two (the other is *The Sick Man's Salve*) that are recommended as a cure for Morose's sudden frenzy upon learning that his new wife talks incessantly. "A very cheap cure," observes Truewit adroitly, for recovering one's wits. When Epicoene inquires where she can procure the books, La Foole replies, "I can help you with one of 'em, Mistress Morose, the *Groat's-worth of Wit*." "But I shall disfurnish you, Sir Amorous," she innocently rejoins. "Can you spare it?" La Foole is quick to oblige: "Oh, yes, for a week or so; I'll read it myself to him" (4.4.110–34).[60] If *Groats-Worth* could provide the matter for an extended joke in 1609, *Pandosto*, too, is likely to have been on many people's minds. It had recently undergone its fifth known printing. First published in 1588, it was reprinted in 1592, 1599, 1607, and 1609—perhaps in the very year that Shakespeare began working on *The Winter's Tale*.[61] Evidently it still commanded a large enough readership to warrant republication, and therefore may have stimulated Shakespeare to revisit Greene. Many in his audiences might have been freshly familiar with the romance—a further incentive to bodge up a play from its story, just as Jonson must have expected that his audience would savor his treatment of the *Groats-Worth of Wit*.

Given the dependence of *The Winter's Tale* on so many parts of Greene and its thematization of fraternal rivalry, the legitimacy of offspring, the imitative crossbreeding of competitive lines, and Leontes' final acceptance of Polixenes' son as a surrogate for his own, it is not improper to ask whether Shakespeare is not bidding Greene a last farewell by rehearsing the questions of ingenuity, imitation, issue, and identity that had informed the original controversy and had continued to shape London theatrical life in the first decade of the seventeenth century—as Rosencrantz attests when he describes the war between the poets, the players, and the "little eyases" who "berattle the common stages" and "exclaim against their own succession" (*Ham.* 2.2.337, 340, 349).

In doing so, he reformulated these issues in *The Winter's Tale* by means of an art that imitates, complicates, and "translates" its model. For he not only emended Greene's work by digesting and transforming the materials of *Pandosto* in many ways, but in a generative stroke of ingenuity he reconfigured the prose narrative, originally printed in 1588, as an Italian *tragedia di fin lieto* in which he effected a *coup de théâtre* unique in his own work. He revised Greene's ending not only by eliminating the suicide of his Leontes figure but by unexpectedly bringing Leontes' dead queen back to life, after having first presented her as a marble statue "newly performed by that rare Italian master Giulio Romano" (5.2.94–5). In thus updating Greene Shakespeare also made him live again, newly embodied in a dramatic hybrid by which the old-fashioned paratactic romance, dominated by the reversals of fortune, is reshaped following the contours of a recently denizened continental genre. Now, although Mamillius and Antigonus remain irredeemably lost, Hermione's statue steps down from her pedestal in the final scene, realizing onstage Giorgio Vasari's quotation from Giulio's epitaph that "Jupiter saw *sculpted and painted* bodies breathe . . . through the skill of Giulio Romano,"[62] embraces her husband, and tells her new-found daughter that she has preserved herself "to see the issue." For Hermione, "the issue" means "the outcome" or, perhaps, "my child," as Pitcher suggests, but in view of Shakespeare's larger endeavor, it also signifies the ingeniously shaped tragical comedy that is the issue of his latest encounter with Robert Greene.

Notes

1. Quotations are from *Greene's Groatsworth of Wit; Bought with a Million of Repentance* (1592). Attributed to Henry Chettle and Robert Greene, ed. D. Allen Carroll (Binghamton: Medieval and Renaissance Texts and Studies, 1994). Carroll conjectures that Greene's death occurred on September 3 (p. 7, n. 21). For a detailed account of the contested authenticity of the pamphlet, see his excellent introduction, pp. 1–31; for the attack on Shakespeare and a judicious account of the scholarly responses it has provoked, see pp. 131–45.
2. *Kind-Hearts / Dream. / Conteining Five Apparitions with their / Invectives agains abuses raigning. / Delivered by severall Ghosts unto him to / be publisht, after Piers Penilesse Post / had refused the carriage. /* Invita Invidia. / by H.C. / Imprinted at London by William Wright [1592], pp. 6–7. It is widely conjectured that the portion Chettle confesses he omitted alluded to Marlowe's alleged homosexuality or his blasphemy (Carroll, p. 2).
3. "Chettle may have been uniquely capable of pulling off such a hoax," observes Carroll, because "his training and life experience as a compositor would have taught him skills of memory that, as a would-be writer, he could exploit in imitating the styles of others" (p. 17 of his edition).
4. It is a matter of some interest that Greene's doppelgänger Roberto became "famozed for an Arch-plaiemaking poet," when none of Greene's plays were printed until after his death, and even then it is unlikely that they bore his name, for the first printings of *Tamburlaine* (1590) and *The Spanish Tragedy* (1592) were without attribution, as were Shakespeare's plays until 1598. His prose works, however, published in the 1580s, did bear his name and did make him "famozed." This suggests the tendentiousness of his narrative fiction, which sets the terms for his attack on the players in the subsequent first-person portion of the pamphlet. See Ronald A. Tumelson II, "Robert Greene, 'Author of Playes,'" in *Writing Robert Greene*, ed. Kirk Melnikoff and Edward Gieskes (Burlington, VT, and Aldershot: Ashgate, 2008), pp. 95–114.
5. The phrase "garnisht in our colours" anticipates the more specific "Crow, beautified with our feathers," which follows. Greene is nothing if not copious.
6. *MND* 3.1.118–19. There is a perhaps unintended irony built into Greene's parody of the Duke of York's description of savage Queen Margaret in *The True Tragedy of Richard Duke of York*. Shakespeare's line "O tiger's heart wrapp'd in a woman's hide!" (1.4.137) is itself an imitation of Petrarch's plaintive sonnet beginning "Questa umil fera, un cor di tigre o d'orsa, / Che 'n vista umana, e 'n forma d'angel vene" ["This humble beast, heart of tiger or bear, / Who comes in human

shape, angelic form"]; *Petrarch: Sonnets and Songs*, CLII, trans. Anna Maria Armi (New York: Grosset & Dunlap, 1968). Thus Greene satirically imitates a Shakespeare who has already parodied Petrarch.

7. The fullest treatment is found in E. A. J. Honigmann, *Shakespeare: The Lost Years* (Manchester and New York: Manchester University Press, 1998).

8. See, e.g., Martial, *Epigrams*, I. 52, 53, 66, 72, and Horace, *Satires*, I.1.120–1; the complex relationship of imitation and plagiarism among classical writers is widely explored by Scott McGill, *Plagiarism in Latin Literature* (Cambridge: Cambridge University Press, 2012).

9. Horace, *Satires, Epistles and Ars Poetica*, trans. H. Rushton Fairclough (London: Heinemann Ltd, 1966), *Epis.* I.iii.15–20.

10. Ibid. p. 27.

11. Kathy Eden has traced the shifting borders between plagiarism, borrowing, and imitation in the early modern period and its roots in the classical tradition. She has shown that the distinction between imitation and borrowing—both furtive and acknowledged—was based on the criterion of the degree to which the imitator made the model his own, not necessarily by changing its matter but by the manner in which he handled it. In this light, Greene's "beautified with our feathers" (*furtivis colores*) indicates wholesale plagiarism, as *colores* signifies interpretation and expression. See "Literary Property and the Question of Style," in *Borrowed Feathers: Plagiarism and the Limits of Imitation in Early Modern Europe*, ed. Hall Bjornstad (Oslo: Unipub, 2008), pp. 21–38.

12. G. W. Pigman, "Versions of Imitation in the Renaissance," *Renaissance Quarterly* 33 (1980): 1–32; for early modern iterations, see p. 8, n. 13. Further references are offered by Kerrigan, *Shakespeare's Originality*, p. 116, n. 24.

13. S. Schoenbaum, *William Shakespeare: A Compact Documentary Life* (New York: Oxford University Press, 1977), p. 152.

14. A. B. Grosart, ed., *The Life and Complete Works in Prose and Verse of Robert Greene, M.A.*, 15 vols. (New York: Russell & Russell, 1964), vol. 8, p. 128.

15. Ibid. p. 131.

16. Ibid. p. 132.

17. Cicero's rebuke to Roscius recalls Philostratus's reply to Shakespeare's Theseus who, puzzled by the description "A tedious brief scene of young Pyramus / and his love Thisbe; very tragical mirth," asks, "What are they that do play it?" "Hard-handed men that work in Athens here, / Which never labor'd in their minds till now" (*MND* 5.1.56–7, 71–3).

18. Janet Clare, *Shakespeare's Stage Traffic: Imitation, Borrowing and Competition in Renaissance Theatre* (Cambridge: Cambridge University Press, 2014), p. 1.

19. On this possibility, see Kerrigan, *Shakespeare's Originality*, pp. 23–4 and n. 18.
20. Gary Taylor, "Collaboration," in *Shakespeare in our Time*, ed. Dympna Callaghan and Suzanne Gossett (London and New York: Bloomsbury Arden, 2016), p. 145. For a stimulating discussion of dramatic intertextuality, here called "quotation," a broad term that can mean the adoption of a single word, a phrase, or a passage—even an allusion—and "position," indicating the quotation's "attitude" toward a source text, see Bruster, *Quoting Shakespeare*, pp. 3–51.
21. See Thomas W. Baldwin, *On the Literary Genetics of Shakespeare's Plays, 1592–1594* (Urbana: University of Illinois Press, 1959); Kenneth Muir, *Shakespeare's Sources* (London: Methuen, 1957); and especially Geoffrey Bullough, *Narrative and Dramatic Sources of Shakespeare*, 8 vols. (New York: Columbia University Press, 1957–75). More recent examples include Jonathan Bate, *Shakespeare and Ovid* (Oxford: Clarendon Press, 1993) and *How the Classics Made Shakespeare* (Princeton and Oxford: Princeton University Press, 2019); Robert S. Miola, *Shakespeare's Reading* (Oxford and New York: Oxford University Press, 2000); and Jason Lawrence, *"Who the devil taught thee so much Italian?" Italian Language Learning and Literary Imitation in Early Modern England* (Manchester: Manchester University Press, 2005).
22. As he was completing his edition of Shakespeare, Johnson wrote, "To dread the shore which he sees spread with wrecks, is natural to the sailor. I had before my eyes, so many critical adventures ended in miscarriage, that caution was forced upon me. I encountered in every page Wit struggling with its own sophistry, and Learning confused by the multiplicity of its views. I was forced to censure those whom I admired, and could not but reflect, while I was dispossessing their emendations, how soon the same fate might happen to my own, and how many of the readings which I have corrected may be by some other editor defended and established" (*Johnson on Shakespeare*, ed. Arthur Sherbo, in *The Yale Edition of the Works of Samuel Johnson*, 9 vols. (New Haven: Yale University Press, 1968), vol. 7, p. 109.
23. This remains valid even as we increasingly tend to emphasize intertextual exchange as a common material practice in the commercial theater of Shakespeare's time, thereby diminishing the ingenious, often agonistic activity of playwrights at work in a competitive market. The humanists' insight into a poet's relationship with his literary predecessors still provides a useful heuristic for understanding how a writer changes himself as he draws upon the material of his contemporaries.
24. Thomas M. Greene, *The Light in Troy: Imitation and Discovery in Renaissance Poetry* (New Haven and London: Yale University Press, 1982); Nancy Struever, *The Language of History in the Renaissance:*

Rhetoric and Historical Consciousness in Florentine Humanism (Princeton: Princeton University Press, 1970).

25. *The Poetaster*, 5.3.310–13, in *Ben Jonson*, ed. C. H. Herford and Percy Simpson, 11 vols. (Oxford: Clarendon Press, 1925–63), vol. 4. (All further Jonson citations are to this edition.) Virgil reminds the jury, as it goes out to deliberate upon the calumnies that Crispinus (John Marston) and Demetrius (Thomas Dekker) have written against Horace: "And, for his true use of translating men, / It still hath been a worke of as much palme, / In cleerest judgments, as t' invent, or make" (5.3.365–7). It is Demetrius's inability to understand Latin "full and whole" that is the true object of satire here, not translation.

26. *Ben Jonson*, vol. 8, pp. 638–9.

27. Ibid. p. 638.

28. Petrarch, *Ad familiares*, 23.19; trans. Thomas M. Greene, *Light*, pp. 95–6.

29. *The Schoolmaster*, pp. 117–18.

30. *Ben Jonson*, vol. 3, Quarto of 1601.

31. Grosart, ed., *The Life and Complete Works*, vol. 13, pp. 140–1, ll. 549–54.

32. Ibid. p. 155, ll. 845–6.

33. For further details of Shakespeare's use of Greene and Greene's sources in Ariosto, see Lawrence, *"Who the devil"*, pp. 154–63. Lawrence points out that though the *Oxford English Dictionary* lists Shakespeare's "anthropophagi" as the first instance of the word in English, Greene had preceded him by many years. A suggestive connection between Rosalind's proposal to cure Orlando's love-madness in *As You Like It* through counsel and Greene's mad Orlando is found in Mary Hale Shackford, "Shakespeare and Greene's *Orlando Furioso*," *MLN* 39 (1924): 54–6.

34. "*Idem in his, quibus aluntur ingenia, praestemus, ut quaecumque hausimus, non patiamur integra esse, ne aliena sint. Concoquamus illa; alioqui in memoriam ibunt, non in ingenium.*" Seneca, *Ad Lucilium Epistulae Morales in Three Volumes*, trans. Richard M. Gummere (Cambridge, MA: Harvard University Press, 1962), vol. 2, Epistle 84, 6–7, slightly modified by me.

35. "*Ingenii acumen vivax, et sua sponte actuosum.*" Juan Luis Vives, *De causis corruptarum artium*, in *Joannis Ludovico Vivis Valentini Opera omnia* . . . (1782–90), 8 vols. (London: Gregg, 1964), vol. 6, p. 8.

36. Thomas Wilson, *The Rule of Reason*, ed. Richard S. Sprague (Northridge, CA: San Fernando State College Renaissance Editions, 1972), p. 55.

37. Sir Philip Sidney, *An Apology for Poetry or The Defence of Poesy*, ed. Geoffrey Shepherd (London: Nelson, 1965), p. 101.

38. *TN* 1.5.45–9, 4.1.54–7; *Tim.* 4.3.285–6; *AWW* 4.3.185–8; *Cor.* 2.1.86–9; *Mac.* 3.1.128–37.

39. The Latin rhetorical term for "slant," attitude," "interpretation" a speaker gives to his argument. See S. F. Bonner, *Roman Declamation in the Late Republic and Early Empire* (Berkeley: University of California Press, 1949), and my *The Tudor Play of Mind: Rhetorical Inquiry and the Development of Elizabethan Drama* (Berkeley: University of California Press, 1978; rpt. 2020), pp. 28–30.

40. Ernesto Grassi, *Renaissance Humanism: Studies in Philosophy and Poetics* (Binghamton: Medieval and Renaissance Text Society, 1988), p. 35.

41. See *The Critical Works of Thomas Rymer*, ed. Curt A. Zimansky (New Haven: Yale University Press, 1956), p. 163.

42. Samuel T. Coleridge, *Shakespearean Criticism*, ed. T. M. Raysor, 2nd edn, 2 vols. (London: Dent, 1960), vol. 1, p. 44.

43. Feeling, motive, and manner of action are, in fact, topics of judicial oratory—the circumstances with which an advocate or prosecutor builds his case, which is what Iago is ingeniously doing. See Hutson, *Circumstantial*, pp. 79–86.

44. The Q text has "make up" instead of F's "plume up," but the latter initiates the sexual trajectory of the passage.

45. Cf. Sonnets 135–6.

46. For a fuller account of Iago's ingenious, willful activity, see my *The Improbability of Othello: Rhetorical Anthropology and Shakespearean Selfhood* (Chicago: University of Chicago Press, 2010), pp. 153–64.

47. Tiffany Stern has pointed out that the lack of an explanatory chorus is unusual for dumb shows in the period. As a result, "the show's significance is never drawn out, so that the fictional and factual audiences' interpretation—indeed the very amalgam of information they draw on—remains undirected. This enables the dumb show to convey one set of symbolic messages to the fictional courtier audience, another to Claudius, another to Hamlet, and a further set to us, the actual audience." See "The Dumb Show in *Hamlet*," in *Shakespeare Up Close: Reading Early Modern Texts*, ed. Russ McDonald, Nicholas D. Nace, and Travis Williams (London: Arden Shakespeare, 2012), p. 276.

48. James Shapiro notes that the line calling for revenge is a parody of one in *The True Tragedy of Richard III*: "The screeking raven sits croaking for revenge." See *1606: William Shakespeare and the Year of Lear* (London: Faber and Faber, 2015), p. 20. It's just one more sign that Hamlet the drama critic is an indefatigable bodger—in this case plucking a line from an old play that lives in his memory to endow another dramatic figure with his own motive.

49. The former interpretation is J. D. Wilson's in *What Happens in Hamlet* (Cambridge: Cambridge University Press, 1967). The latter is the theme of Ernest Jones, *Hamlet and Oedipus* (Garden City, NY: Doubleday, 1955).

50. See Geoffrey Bullough, "'The Murder of Gonzago': A Probable

Source for Hamlet," *MLR* 30.4 (October 1935): 433–44; Rita Severi, *Shakespeare's Mantua: A Cultural Itinerary/La Mantova di Shakespeare: Itinerario Culturale* (Mantua: Sonetti, 2016), pp. 72–81. This would not be the first time Shakespeare had alluded in his own work to an old play with which he assumed his audience was familiar. In the first part of the Induction to *The Taming of the Shrew*, the Lord commends the First Player for playing "a farmer's eldest son. / 'Twas where you woo'd the gentlewoman so well." The Second Player, apparently referring to the character's name, adds, "I think 'twas Soto that your honor means" (Ind. 1.82–3, 86 and note). Brian Morris, editor of *The Taming of the Shrew* (London and New York: Methuen, 1981), suggests that this refers to an early version of Fletcher's *Women Pleased* (pp. 158–9).

51. The fullest account of this event is in Elisa Viani, *L'Avvelenamento di Francesco Maria I della Rovere Duca d'Urbino* (Mantua, 1902).

52. On the substitution of Vienna for Urbino, see *Hamlet*, ed. Harold Jenkins (London and New York: Methuen, 1982), p. 507.

53. *Shakespeare's Impact on his Contemporaries* (London: Macmillan, 1982), pp. 1–14.

54. Schoenbaum, *William Shakespeare*, p. 239; Honigmann, *Shakespeare's Impact*, pp. 8–9.

55. Though it has long been an episode in the Shakespeare biography, recently Heather Wolfe discovered a 1600 copy of the coat of arms specifically made out to "Shakespeare the player" (*New York Times*, June 30, 2016).

56. In Greene's *Groats-Worth*, the narrator refers to the provident ant as the grasshopper's "olde acquaintance."

57. Robert Greene, *A Notable Discovery of Coosnage, 1591; The Second Part of Conny-Catching, 1592*, ed. G. B. Harrison (Edinburgh: Edinburgh University Press, 1966), pp. 40–2. As Katherine Duncan-Jones points out, "Some other details and phrases are drawn from the same work. For instance, Autolycus's stealing of sheets derives from Greene's account of the 'Curber' who removes sheets hung out to dry by means of a long hook; the roguish phrase 'a snapper-up of unconsidered trifles' also comes from Greene." *Ungentle Shakespeare: Scenes from his Life* (London: Arden, 2001), p. 229.

58. As stated above, quotations from *The Winter's Tale* are from Pitcher, ed.; quotations from other Shakespeare plays are from *The Riverside Shakespeare*, 2nd edn, ed. Evans et al.

59. And, perhaps, to express his sense of horned impotence, dagger muzzled.

60. For another example of the intersecting concerns of *Epicoene* and *The Winter's Tale*, see Chapter 4, n. 12.

61. Pitcher, p. 86.

62. *Le vite de' più eccellenti architetti, pittori, et scultori italiani, da*

Cimabue, insino a' tempi nostri, edition by Lorenzo Torrentino, Florence, 1550, ed. Luciano Bellosi and Aldo Rossi, 2 vols. (Turin: Einaudi, 1991), vol. 2, p. 837, translation mine. The quotation appears only in the first edition.

Chapter 2

"Your sorrow was too sore laid on": Portraying the Subject of Ekphrasis

I

I now want to pursue my analysis of Shakespeare's ingenuity beyond exposition of its cognitive, self-fashioning role in literary imitation and, expanding upon Leontes' self-deluding visions, focus on its manifestation as the imaginative activity performed by a dramatized subject who enunciates that activity on the stage. In my study of *Othello* and rhetorical anthropology, I argued that we should make a distinction in Shakespeare's work between *dramatis persona* and *character*, following the usual practice of Elizabethan and Jacobean playwrights as they composed their scripts. A *dramatis persona* is literally a "person of the play," required by the plot as it's sketched out—Hamlet, Prince of Denmark, for example—while *character* emerges from the *dramatis persona* when solicited by the particular circumstances of a scene that has been developed from the plot.[1] Thus one *dramatis persona* can generate as many *characters* as scenic occasion demands, yet subtends them all, just as—outside the drama—the self, which we might think of as the substratum of the subject, holds infinite subject-possibilities which it yields up to varying interpellations—yet is itself a "residual subject," both origin and repository of different "circumstantial subjects."[2]

Through this practice, Shakespeare approximates our modern sense of the self as an entity subject to multiple interpellations, and represents this condition in his plays. We can think of the Prince of Denmark as the originary if not pristine self, born into expectation and subject to his birth, hailed, as it were, *into* that expectation and, in the course of the plot, qualified by further interpellations—student, mourner, friend, lover, revenger, play doctor, drama critic, providentialist, and so on. This is also true of such *dramatis personae* as Shylock the Jew, Othello the Moor, Henry Bolingbroke, "legitimate Edgar," the Thane of Glamis, Cressida, Desdemona, Cleopatra—the list is extensive, as we shall see, only delimited by the degree to which Shakespeare provides scenes in which a given *dramatis persona* is drawn by circumstances into becoming a *character*.

Building on this distinction, I was provoked by a session at the Shakespeare Association of America several years ago, entitled "Depicting the Subject in Early Modern Drama," to reverse the terms and think about "The Subject Depicting in Early Modern Drama"—that is, about the subject as a *dramatis persona* elicited by his or her scene to describe something—and how that might have enabled "Depicting the Subject in Early Modern Drama," notably in the work of Shakespeare.

The depicting subject is a *character* who employs the rhetorical device of ekphrasis (in Latin, *descriptio*), which began its literary-critical, if not its poetic, career in the treatises of Greek and Roman oratory. Ekphrasis is detailed and vivid description, of times, persons, actions, places, natural phenomena, works of art.[3] It was explained metaphorically as "placing things before the eyes" and often referred to as *word-painting*.[4] It was conceptualized and transmitted to the early modern period in the Latin works of Cicero, Quintilian, the author of the *Rhetorica ad Herennium*, and the Latinized Greek of Aphthonius's popular fourth-century CE *Progymnasmata*, which found their way into the Tudor grammar school and were familiar to Shakespeare and his contemporaries.[5]

Ekphrases were originally intended to be used for persuasive purposes in theses, declamations, and full-scale orations, for images transmitted linguistically were thought to be nearly as effective as the things themselves in arousing emotions in the listener—perhaps even more so, if they were presented contextually. But caution must be exercised. As Webb points out, several of the early documents warn the speaker that he had better be careful about what he chooses to describe, for an ekphrasis will reveal where his mind has been dwelling—no furtive glimpses of bridal preparations or lurid scenes of adultery, no details of pederasty, if you don't want to raise doubts about your own morality.[6] Such caution was nurtured by the Aristotelian principle that images in the mind are there because experience put them there, however elaborated by subsequent experience or thought.[7] If we add to this Peripatetic doctrine the Stoic belief that mental images fund language itself, which in its varying enunciations is communicated to others through phonic and lexical signs, we have the outlines of an intersubjective circuit by means of which the speaker's or writer's memory and phantasia (imagination), informed by his or her perceptions—and their analogies—are implicitly conveyed to a listener or reader in whom the transmitter's experience is revealed and, potentially, recycled with further modifications deriving from the recipient.[8]

This occurs for two reasons. In the Aristotelian tradition, the perception received through the senses, registered in the imagination as a phantasma or "image," and preserved in the memory, is tinged with affect. This "image"—whether visual, acoustic, olfactory, gustatory, or tactile—is therefore not innocent, but is imbued with the emotional state of the subject when it was originally impressed on his or her fantasy. The fantasy, an active manipulator, then shapes the affect-saturated image in accordance with the subject's *present* needs or desires, often combining it with associated images, and releases the refashioned phantasma in speech.[9]

Ekphrases, then, can be indices of the mind, registering actual experiences and the fictions we weave from them and to which we are subject.[10] This makes ekphrasis an especially rich expository instrument that enables a dramatist to depict a *character's* subject even as he or she is depicting something else. That Shakespeare was familiar with the persuasive function of ekphrasis is evident: just recall Edgar's dizzying description of the cliff at Dover to which he claims he's led the blinded Gloucester, or Enobarbus's erotic survey of Cleopatra sailing upon the river Cydnus to meet Mark Antony, with which he beguiles the erected ears of Agrippa and Maecenas. Note that in each case the object of ekphrasis is not present; it is through language alone that the object is, as it were, "placed before the eyes" of the listener—turning him from auditor to spectator.[11] This "placing before the eyes" occurs, the rhetorics tell us, because the ekphrastic speaker amplifies details and illuminates them with *enargeia*, a glowing vivacity created by concrete diction and metaphor—which is infused with *energeia* when the elements described are in motion, so that the transaction seems to be happening *now*. In the course of its deployment a sonic phenomenon *heard* becomes a visual one *seen*.[12]

The *locus classicus* that explains how this common psychological phenomenon can be deliberately exploited for professional use is Quintilian's exhortation to budding orators in his *Institutio oratoria*:

> There are certain experiences which the Greeks call φαντασίαι [phantasiai] and the Romans *visiones*, whereby things absent are present to

our imagination with such extreme vividness that they seem actually to be before our very eyes ... When the mind is unoccupied or is absorbed by fantastic hopes or daydreams, we are haunted by these visions of which I am speaking to such an extent that we imagine that we are travelling abroad, crossing the sea, fighting, addressing the people, or enjoying the use of wealth that we do not actually possess, and seem to ourselves not to be dreaming but acting [*non cogitare sed facere*]. Surely then, it may be possible to turn this form of hallucination to some profit. I am complaining that a man has been murdered. Shall I not bring before my eyes all the circumstances which it is reasonable to imagine must have occurred in such a connexion? Shall I not see the assassin burst suddenly from his hiding-place, the victim tremble, cry for help, beg for mercy, or turn to run? Shall I not see the fatal blow delivered and the stricken body fall? Will not the blood, the deathly pallor, the groan of agony, the death–rattle, be indelibly impressed upon my mind?[13]

He then recalls that he has often seen actors leave the theater "still drowned in tears" after performing a moving role, and asks:

But if the mere delivery of words written by another has the power to set our souls on fire with fictitious emotions, what will the orator do whose duty is to picture to himself the facts and who has it in his power to feel the same emotions as his client whose interests are at stake?[14]

Readers will recognize this as the source of Hamlet's astonished response to the First Player who, "But in a fiction, in a dream of passion, / Could force his soul so to his own conceit / That from her working all his visage wann'd, / Tears in his eyes, distraction in his aspect, / A broken voice, an' his whole function suiting / With forms to his conceit. And all for nothing, / For Hecuba!" (2.2.552–8).[15] The Player's impassioned ekphrasis of "the mobled queen" acting out her despair before audiences human and divine so affects Hamlet that he roars—paraphrasing Quintilian—"What would he do / Had he the motive and the cue for passion / That I have?" (559–63). Here, in a Shakespearean *imitatio*, is a dramatized gloss on the psychosomatic process by which a perception, entering the mind via immediate or secondary experience (seeing and hearing Hecuba in person or reading, memorizing, and reciting lines about her), enters the phantasia and memory and informs the phantasma or "conceit," which in turn produces the physical symptoms expressive of that mental image. Clearly Shakespeare has mastered the concept and through a double tour de force is professionally exploiting it to his profit, by exhibiting its workings not only in the Player but also in Hamlet's anguished self-questioning, as one who actually *has* "the motive and the cue for passion"—that is, the inciting phantasma supplied by the Ghost—yet cannot even match the Player's passion, which is based on fiction. As students of the play have long recognized, the problem may lie in the conflicting emotions attached to Hamlet's *visio*, which, Shakespeare has already shown, repeatedly bleed through his speech, as he distinguishes his uncle from his father, and conflates himself with his uncle, and his father with himself.[16]

But what of Enobarbus? Where does his phantasma of Cleopatra's sumptuous pageant upon the river of Cydnus come from? The answer is more complicated than it may initially appear. His description is of course meant to register the report of an eyewitness and give credence to Antony's infatuation. But that leaves unexplained why Shakespeare makes this particular eyewitness break *charac-ter*—or, more precisely, *dramatis persona*—to deliver this particular speech. Before and after the speech Enobarbus is the tried soldier and boon companion, wise, practical, loyal, wry, convivial, and cynical (in a barracks sort of way) about women, a deeply moral man who is so rational that he is capable of deserting Antony when he finds his captain's reason hopelessly compromised by his passion, and who then dies of shame on discovering Antony's continuing generosity towards him—declaring himself a master-leaver and a fugitive: "I am alone the villain of the earth" (4.6.29). Yet for some fifty-odd lines this tough soldier envisions a voluptuously sexual-ized world of nature besting art. As Robert Miola has pointed out, all the physical data—"gold poop, purple sails, silver oars, music, pavilion (cloth of gold of tissue)"—are found in North's Plutarch.[17] But Shakespeare has given to Enobarbus sails "so perfumed that / The winds were love-sick with them," oars that "made / The water which they beat to follow faster, / As amorous of their strokes," and silken tackle that "Swell with the touches of those flower-soft hands" (2.2.219–20, 201–3, 216). His language becomes not only erotic but also synaesthetic. We see, hear, smell, and touch the elements of the scene. Moreover, though the description is couched mainly in the past tense, at times the verbs shift to the present and through their *energeia* invite the hearer to enjoy an immediate experience of the object: "At the helm / A seeming mermaid *steers*. The silken tackle / *Swell*"; "A strange invisible perfume *hits* the sense / Of the adjacent wharfs" (214–16, 218–19, italics mine).

Enobarbus, too, has the motive and the cue for passion—and it is his phantasma of Cleopatra. This is what his words tell us as he emerges from his *dramatis persona* to become a *character* revealing how his visit to Egypt has affected him. The audience must be meant to infer that—perhaps to his own surprise—this weathered soldier, this counselor who accompanied Antony to Cydnus, was so sensually aroused by the spectacle of the queen and her attendants on the barge that he has preserved the entire scene in his memory as a voluptuous medley of sights, sounds, smells, touches that come flooding forth at his comrades' questioning. Shakespeare is using ekphrasis to depict not only an object world but also the subject of the speaker, whose very probity attests to the enchantments cast by Cleopatra's Egypt.[18]

Returning to Edgar's description of Dover cliff, however, we find his speech virtually a textbook example of the sort of amplification prescribed by Erasmus in his widely read schoolbook, *De copia verborum ac rerum*.[19] Quoting Quintilian, Erasmus notes:

> If someone should say that a city was captured, he doubtless comprehends in that general statement everything that attends such fortune, but if you develop what is implicit in the one word, flames will appear pouring through homes and temples; the crash of falling buildings will be heard, and one indefinable sound of diverse outcries; some will be seen in bewildered flight, others clinging in the last embrace of their relatives; there will be the wailing of infants and women, old people cruelly preserved by their fate till that day, the pillaging of profane and sacred objects.[20]

For Quintilian (and Erasmus) it is a matter of analyzing and then giving voice to what would otherwise lie implicit and silent when one says a city was sacked. Shakespeare does something similar with Edgar's exquisitely detailed ekphrasis of the place called Dover cliff, but he also provides Edgar with a psychological etiology by engaging him in a dialogic prompt earlier in the play. In Act 4, Scene 2, Gloucester gives Edgar (and the audience) a cue for the passion that will be uttered three scenes later, when he poses a question to Poor Tom:

> *Gloucester*: Dost know Dover?
> *Edgar*: Ay, master.
> *Gloucester*: There is a cliff whose high and bending head
> Looks *fearfully* in the confined deep.
> Bring me but to the very brim of it,
> And I'll repair the misery thou dost bear
> With something rich about me. From that place
> I shall no leading need. (4.1.71–8, italics mine)

The lines are terse, but they supply the fearful image-seeds with which Edgar's fantasy shapes and amplifies the verbal scene when they arrive at the non-existent cliff:

> Come on, sir: here's the place. Stand still. How *fearful*
> And dizzy 'tis, to cast one's eyes so low!
> The crows and choughs that wing the midway air
> Show scarce so gross as beetles. Halfway down
> Hangs one that gathers samphire, dreadful trade!
> Methinks he seems no bigger than his head.
> The fishermen, that walk upon the beach,
> Appear like mice . . .
> . . .
> I'll look no more,
> Lest my brain turn, and the deficient sight
> Topple down headlong. (4.6.11–18, 22–4, italics mine)

Audiences at *King Lear* are often hard put to reconcile what they see—a flat stage—with what they hear. So vivid and *fearful* is Edgar's description that it can unmoor a sensitive listener. Notice that instead of the "high and bending head" of a cliff that "looks fearfully in the confined deep," it is Edgar himself who pretends to do the looking—assuming the cliff's anthropomorphic persona—and perhaps even sways at the vertiginous sight. No wonder the blinded Gloucester is persuaded, even though he has remarked, "Me thinks the ground is even" (4.6.3) and claims he cannot hear the sea. This occurs because Edgar's fantasy, nourished by the mnemic traces of Gloucester's own words and moved by the pitiful hoax he is about to enact for the benefit of his beloved father, is, for this moment at least, nearly overpowering his sense of actuality. Nearly—for he does come out of it: "Why I do trifle thus with his despair / Is done to cure it" (4.6.33–4). He is like the advocate envisioned by Quintilian—using the actor's skills for his own cause and forcing his soul so to his own conceit that for a time he believes and physically responds to his own fantasy. He must, in order to redeem his client.

II

So far I've discussed the psychology of ekphrasis and offered a few examples of its practice in Shakespeare's hands. Before I develop further the different ways Shakespeare uses ekphrasis to depict the subject, it would be useful to reflect upon the oddity of such a practice in the theater. To return to Erasmus for a moment, he instructs students writing letters and declamations that "We shall enrich speech by description of a thing when we do not relate what is done, or has been done, summarily or sketchily, but place it before the eyes painted with all the colors of rhetoric, so that at length *it draws the hearer or reader outside himself as in the theater.*"[21] This suggests that a certain irony—if not a threat of supererogation—adheres to the use of ekphrasis in staged drama. Although, as Murray Krieger has argued at length, the phonic and the lexical sign have been striving to achieve visuality since Homer described Achilles' shield in Book 18 of the *Iliad*, that struggle has taken place largely within a lyric and narrative tradition, not drama.[22] In the earliest literary criticism, it is *tragedy* that claims to realize this ambition—to its philosophical shame, according to Plato, for imitating mere phenomena, not reality;[23] to its greater respectability, according to Aristotle, since it is an imitation of the actions of men according to the philosophical principles of probability and necessity.[24] For both critics, albeit with contrary valences, it accomplishes what non-dramatic literature cannot: it exhibits *in real time*, without the disruptions of a non-mimetic narrator, *real people* impersonating others speaking and acting before the ears and eyes of auditors and spectators. Drama offers presence.

This might seem to render ekphrasis either superfluous or, as suggested above, supererogatory in drama, but there are actions and words that poets have felt they cannot or should not directly imitate in action onstage, for practical, moral, or aesthetic reasons. It may also be recalled that Aristotle thought tragedy did not have to be performed to remain tragedy,[25] and that Seneca wrote tragedies that were probably declaimed without any physical action or spectacle. The use of ekphrasis in both kinds of drama, however—the fully staged or the merely spoken—has a similar psychological function for an audience. It effects what we might think of as a change in depth-of-focus from the foregrounded plane of present action to a time and place (initially in the imagination of only the speaker) that expands the play's focal length, whether the original plane of action is actually observed by an audience or is only inferred from ongoing speech. And it is not just a change of scene that is brought about, but a change in what we might call psychosomatic condition, as we move from the status of witness to the status of imaginer.[26]

Thus ekphrasis, that device intended to "turn the listener into a spectator," has a place even when the listener is already a spectator.[27] Moreover, it is capable not only of placing a new scene "before the eyes," but also of inducing the listener to share the speaker's response to what he or she is called upon to describe, as in the case of Edgar and of Enobarbus. It has an ancient history in the messenger speech. Recall the horrified self-referential detail of the Second Messenger in Sophocles' *Oedipus Tyrannos* as he brings to Creon news of Jocasta's suicide and Oedipus's self-blinding, which, as Aristotle argues, effects the turn to pity and fear that is critical for tragic response, or the gloating language in which Seneca's Atreus reports Thyestes reclining, drinking, and belching with content after consuming the filial supper he's prepared for him—which, if it doesn't bring about pity, certainly induces disgust and confirms Atreus as villain.[28] To leap ahead fifteen centuries, consider two latter-day messenger speeches: Ophelia's frightened account of Hamlet's intrusion into her chamber, "his stockins fouled, / Ungart'red, and down-gyved to his ankle" (*Ham.* 2.1.76–7), and Gertrude's poignant description of Ophelia drowning "in the glassy stream," with its sympathetic images of "envious sliver" and "weeping brook" and its moralized gloss on "long purples" (*Ham.* 4.7.167–75).

For such early modern descriptions, the late Francis Berry once coined the term "Shakespearean Inset," which he aptly characterized as providing a "hinterland" behind the present of the dramatic action, drawing a distinction between foreground and background by analogy with Italian and Northern Renaissance religious paintings. He showed—through close readings of verbal tense, tone, diction, and theme—how such Insets brought the "hinterland" into the foreground, temporarily halting the progress of the plot, and thereby provided important background information, added new points of view, and enriched the material concerns of the play and its vocal sonorities in a variety of ways.[29]

Berry was primarily interested in the function of the Inset as an expository plot device, which accounts for his emphasis on narrative and his tendency to dismiss other kinds of description, however vividly rendered. Though he is concerned with the effect of the Inset on both stage and theater audiences, he is not inclined to explore its function as a means of depicting the psychology of its *speaker*. Neither is Richard Meek, who more recently has written extensively about the use of ekphrasis in Shakespeare's plays and major poems. Meek is primarily interested in the continuing *paragone*, often thematized, of the verbal and the visual in these works, and he argues persuasively that Shakespeare reveals the interdependence of the two modes in rendering his fictions lifelike and believable—even in situations defying credibility. He repeatedly emphasizes, however, the illusoriness of any interiority in Shakespeare's characters—a metatheatrical argument with which I have no quarrel, though my interest is in the way Shakespeare uses ekphrasis as a dramaturgic tool to create that illusion of interiority.[30] Reading the work of Meek and other contemporary writers on ekphrasis raises even more urgently, it seems to me, the question of the uses Shakespeare makes of ekphrasis to reveal where his speakers' minds have been dwelling.

We have seen how Edgar and Enobarbus respond to external stimuli to reveal upon emergent occasions the firmly rooted phantasmata that suddenly branch into elaborated expressions of their experiential origins. These are occasions when the speaker not only seems to be persuading his listening interlocutor, but is also listening—in effect, persuading himself even as he persuades another.[31] One is therefore tempted to ask, is self-persuasion a common function of ekphrasis in Shakespeare?

The answer must be a qualified "yes," for even here fine distinctions must be recognized. First, it is evident that the two Shakespeare examples I have mentioned earlier in this discussion—Ophelia and Gertrude—are spoken by *dramatis personae* interpellated by their scenes to become *characters*, that is, circumstanced subjects; yet their ekphrases are quite different from one another in the manner in which they are delivered and in our impression of their respective origins. Ophelia's agitated account of Hamlet's intrusion into her chamber while she was sewing evokes a setting in which we can picture her, but also presents an unfamiliar speaker. The wry but obedient girl of 1.3 is seized by fear, pity, and confusion as she describes the scene in which she has just participated:

> Lord Hamlet, with his doublet all unbraced,
> No hat upon his head, his stockins fouled,
> Ungart'red, and down-gyved to the ankle,
> Pale as his shirt, his knees knocking each other,
> And with a look so piteous in purport
> As if he had been loosed out of hell
> To speak of horrors—he *comes* before me. (2.1.75–81, italics mine)

Though the moment has passed, she is re-experiencing it, describing the details of Hamlet's dress and demeanor in the passive preterite and active present as though she were seeing him now. So vivid is the event in her mind's eye that she even enacts what she yet sees:

> He *took* me by the wrist and held me hard,
> Then *goes* he to the length of all his arm,

And with his other hand *thus* o'er his brow
He *falls* to such perusal of my face
As a would draw it. Long *stayed* he so.
At last, a little shaking of mine arm,
And thrice his head *thus* waving up and down,
He *raised* a sigh so piteous and profound
That it *did seem* to shatter all his bulk
And end his being. (2.1.84–93, italics mine)

By mimicking Hamlet's actions she seems to be persuading not only Polonius but herself of their reality. Continuing her narrative in the active past tense, she quickly turns it into an ongoing action, as the reiterated "thus," accompanied by present-tense verbs, indicates. Then her account gradually recedes into an action completed—"he lets me go," "seem'd to find his way without his eyes," "out a' doors he went," "bended their light on me" (2.1.93, 95, 96, 97)—as the tense turns back to the past and she is released by the image. An audience hearing this description will have little doubt that a real event has taken place and that Ophelia's display of details like "stockins fouled" and "knees knocking each other" are based in actual recollections of Hamlet's fear and perplexity, which have precipitated her own. Polonius's initial response to her cry "Alas, my lord, I have been so affrighted"—"With what, i'th'name of God?"—and his immediate conclusion—"Come, go with me, I will go seek the King" (2.1.76–7, 102)—frame her speech with alarm and reinforce our impression that Hamlet *has* intruded in her chamber and filled her fantasy with his unexpected, wild behavior.

Gertrude's ekphrasis functions quite differently, as befits the interpellations she has undergone since she first appeared in 1.2. The once-opaque queen who has evolved, scene by scene, into a worried, then frightened, then angry, then guilty mother-widow-wife now speaks an elegy that honors the tormented girl and reveals her own growing despair. She does this by evoking a landscape that seems alien to the Elsinore of platform, cellarage, presence chamber, closet, stairs, and lobby, which have hitherto been the scenes of action. She also recalls the brief, tender moment one scene earlier when Ophelia, in her madness, distributed imaginary flowers to the standers-by. It is not clear, however, how Gertrude learned of Ophelia's death. Did she witness it? Her words reveal no hint of how she came upon the scene. Did she hear about it from another? There is no clue that she is passing on someone else's report. She is simply offering a finely detailed narrative, setting the scene—a pastoral *locus amoenus*—and recounting what Ophelia did there and how she died as a consequence of her actions: fashioning "fantastic garlands," "clamb'ring" to hang them on the "pendant boughs," and falling into "the weeping brook," which eventually "Pulled the poor wretch from her melodious lay / To muddy death" (4.7.143–6, 153–4). Gertrude's ekphrasis makes something beautiful of Ophelia's death and, in doing so, also tells us something about herself—her affection for the girl, her sadness, her fatalism—but it is so palpably a pastoral elegy that it cannot be claimed that it is rooted in personal witness. Rather, it creates a "subjectivity effect" through mood and mode.

Now let us consider Cesario's melancholy recollection of "his" fictitious sister, who sat "like Patience on a monument, / Smiling at grief" (*TN* 2.4.114–15), and Othello's proud description of his "[travel's] history" (*Oth.* 1.3.139). It is immediately apparent that they are different from Ophelia's frightened report to Polonius and Gertrude's sympathetic elegy before Claudius and Laertes, insofar as they are so ostentatiously *self-persuasive*. Neither of these ekphrases is properly a messenger speech, since they don't report news. But they do suggest that self-persuasion is proceeding perhaps even more strongly than persuasion of another. For both Cesario's projection of Viola's love-longing onto "his" supposed sister, as "he" proclaims the power of a woman's love to Orsino, and Othello's narrative recasting of himself from *exotic foreigner among Europeans* to *European explorer among exotic foreigners* as he speaks before the Duke's council, express the speaker's attitude toward the speech object and the emotions that object arouses, but are marked by fantasies of self-transformation.

That is because they are representations of a subject hard pressed to defend itself in the face of new exigencies. Viola/Cesario tries to prove to her beloved Orsino how deeply a woman can love by obliquely making the Count see *her* in the *him* she has adopted as her persona or—even more inwardly—to make *herself* see *herself* in *herself* as a monument, so as to control her own passion. Othello aims to "whiten" himself, against a racially colored charge of witchcraft, before an audience of Venetian aristocrats. His ekphrasis enfolds two earlier reported ekphrases—when he ran through the story of his life for Desdemona's father and when he did it once more for Desdemona, who had heard the first only "by parcels . . . but not intentively" (1.3.154–5). By means of his second ekphrastic performance, he tells his audience, his wife "lov'd me for the dangers I had pass'd, / And I lov'd her that she did pity them" (1.3.167–8). His self-revelation is attested by Desdemona a few moments later: "I saw Othello's visage in his mind, / And to his honors and his valiant parts /

Did I my soul and fortunes consecrate" (1.3.252–4). Ekphrasis has done multiple duty here: it has been literally *self-reflexive*—mirroring in language the speaker's introjection of European cultural values, attesting this transformation in Desdemona's response, and, in so doing, rendering him that much more outwardly persuasive to his audience. Even the Duke is convinced: "If *virtue* no delighted beauty lack, / Your son-in-law is far more fair than black" (1.3.289–90).[32]

Yet both speeches are clearly the ekphrases of a *character*. This needs to be emphasized because Shakespeare also writes ekphrases that are spoken by *dramatis personae* that do not depict the subject. Strictly speaking, a *dramatis persona* has no subjectivity to express, because he or she is generic—a Moor, a Jew, a Prince, a Lover, or a Tyrant. We might imagine what goes on in the minds of such stereotypes, but stereotypes are not subjects—unlike a *character* hailed forth by a scene to address circumstances that elicit resources that he or she may not have previously exhibited to him- or herself, or to others.[33] I can offer a very simple example.

In *Love's Labour's Lost*, Armado writes a letter to the King of Navarre, who reads it to an assembly of mockers (1.1.219–78). It describes in detail how he discovered Costard courting Jaquenetta. All the circumstances are on display: "The time when? About the sixth hour, when beasts most graze, birds best peck, and men sit down to that nourishment which is called supper. So much for the time when. Now for the ground which—which, I mean, I walked upon. It is yclept thy park. Then for the place where . . ." (235–40). We can stop here. Long ago, T. W. Baldwin demonstrated that Armado's method comes straight out of Aphthonius's *Progymnasmata*, which supplies the topics for such a narrative and advises copious amplification.[34] It is that author's voice that Armado is ventriloquizing as he reveals the mind of a point-devise Braggart, not even a particularly Spanish Braggart, just a Renaissance Braggart given to rules and inkhorn terms. Now one might argue that in ventriloquizing Aphthonius, Armado reveals that he has been inducted into the Symbolic Order with a vengeance, and is therefore a subject. That is, his *dramatis persona* represents a self already interpellated by the Tudor educational system. Fair enough: there are no pristine selves. But—at this moment at least—he is no more than that, uninflected by the "time when," "place where," and "ground which" of the variable life enjoyed by a *character*.[35] In dramatic terms, he remains a *dramatis persona*, and his language shows it.[36]

More problematic regarding its expression of the speaker's psyche is the language of the Chorus in *Henry V*, which is imaginative, vivid, and seductive. It would be a mistake, however, to try plumbing the subjectivity of the Chorus, ekphrastic though his speeches may be, for he is just doing his job—which is to persuade the audience to imagine what they cannot directly experience: "*Suppose* within the girdle of these walls / Are now confined two mighty monarchies"; "O do but *think* / You stand upon the rivage and *behold* / A city on th'inconstant billows dancing"; "Now *entertain conjecture* of a time / When creeping murmur and the poring dark / Fills the wide vessel of the universe" (Prol. 1.19–20, Chor. 3.13–15, Chor. 4.1–3, italics mine). Urging the audience to play with their fancies and "eke out our performance with your mind" (Chor. 3.35), he attempts to produce the same effect that Quintilian reported he experienced when reading Cicero's oration against Verres:

> Is there anybody so incapable of forming a mental picture of a scene that, when he reads the following passage from the Verrines, he does not seem not merely to see the actors in the scene, the place itself and their very dress, but even to imagine to himself *other details* that the orator does not describe? "There on the shore stood the praetor, the representative of the Roman people, with slippered feet, robed in a purple cloak, a tunic streaming to his heels, and leaning on the arm of this worthless woman." For my own part, I seem to see before my eyes his face, his eyes, the unseemly blandishments of himself and his paramour, the silent loathing and shame of those who viewed the scene.[37]

Like Quintilian reading Cicero, Shakespeare's audience must "Piece out our imperfections with your thoughts" (Prol. 1.23), and see more than is shown or spoken. Still, one would be hard put to make a case that, in urging the audience to visualize the English fleet upon the sea or a little touch of Harry in the night, the Chorus is projecting his own vision as a *character* would, for he, too, is a *dramatis persona*. His speeches would have to be traced to the visions of "our bending author" who, "with rough and all-unable pen . . . hath pursued the story" (Epil. 1–2)—that is, to the subject for whom he speaks, who is attempting to fashion an *epic* in the confines of a wooden O. For all the writers in the tradition insist that in order to transmit a vision one has to experience it first.[38]

But that is not part of *my* story. What I'd like to do is compare the Chorus's urgings to Harry's threats. When he stands before the gates of Harfleur and demands that the governor surrender the city, Henry V is embellishing one of the most famous examples of ekphrasis available to Tudor grammarians—that very description of the sacking of a city quoted earlier, which originated in Quintilian and was picked up by Erasmus in his *De copia*. Harry's speech, you'll recall, describes "the flesh'd soldier . . . / In liberty of bloody hand . . . / With conscience wide as hell, mowing like grass / Your fresh fair virgins and your flow'ring infants" (3.3.11–14) and includes such disclaimers as "What is't to *me*, when you *yourselves* are cause?" (96, italics mine)—which is lifted from Erasmus's adjoining theme, "We will charge the war to your account."[39] Unlike the words of the Chorus, these are words of a *character*. Why? The Archbishop of Canterbury tells us: "Hear him but reason in divinity, / And, all-admiring, with an inward wish / You would desire the King were made a prelate; / Hear him debate of commonwealth affairs, / You would say it hath been all-in-all his study" (*H5* 1.1.38–42). Harry is drawn to become what the circumstances demand. Hence his *dramatis persona* may be said to harbor the imaginative possibilities required by this scene, and since *character* represents a *subject*, we may infer that Shakespeare wants us to recognize that a Tamburlainian lust for blood lies within the capacities of this mirror of all Christian kings.[40]

III

I now want to suggest a more revealing means of depicting the subject of ekphrasis. It is to allow the speaker to put his own gloss on an object the audience also views—thus enabling auditors to compare what the speaker describes with what they see or know. This technique lays bare what happens in *all* ekphrases: a sense perception or thought actualizes the subject's organ of fantasy, and the resulting phantasma or *visio* mingles with previous phantasmata or *visiones* released by the memory to gloss the present image, telling the subject, "That is such-and-such." This composite fantasy is then described as if it were actually being perceived.[41]

The process by which an object perceived feeds a passion-infused phantasia and issues as an eroticized description—then becomes the source of a description with a far different coloration when that passion has passed—may be seen in the second act of *Titus Andronicus*. Here Tamora, who has been shown up till now as a sullen captive, outraged mother, and scheming revenger, welcomes her lover Aaron the Moor to a secluded place in the woods, coaxing him to linger with her, sequestered from the imperial hunting party:

The birds chant melody on every bush,
The [snake] lies rolled in the cheerful sun,
The green leaves quiver with the cooling wind,
And make a checker'd shadow on the ground.
Under their sweet shade, Aaron, let us sit,
And whilst the babbling echo mocks the hounds,
Replying shrilly to the well-tun'd horns,
As if a double hunt were heard at once,
Let us sit down and mark their yellowing noise;
And after conflict such as was suppos'd
The wand'ring prince and Dido once enjoyed,
When with a happy storm they were surpris'd,
And curtain'd with a counsel-keeping cave,
We may, each wreathed in the other's arms,
(Our pastimes done), possess a golden slumber,
While hounds and horns and sweet melodious birds
Be unto us as is a nurse's song
Of lullaby, to bring her babe asleep. (2.3.12–29)

Tamora's ekphrasis not only renders the present landscape—however it may actually appear onstage—an irresistible *locus amoenus* for the consummation of a powerful sexual desire; it further links that space and act to its heroic precedent in an epic past, even "supposing" that the amorous "conflict" once enjoyed by Aeneas and Dido followed the same rhythm of excitement, fulfillment, and repose as the two of them may enjoy now. One would think it should persuade. Aaron, however, is less preoccupied at the moment with venery than with vengeance, and his would-be Dido is left alone to be confronted only moments later by a suspicious Bassianus and Lavinia who come upon her in this place so conducive to lovemaking, quickly followed by her sons Chiron and Demetrius. When the latter asks why she looks so pale, she replies:

These two have 'ticed me hither to this place:
A barren detested vale you see it is,
The trees, though summer, yet forlorn and lean,
Overcome with moss and baleful mistletoe;
Here never shines the sun, here nothing breeds,
Unless the nightly owl or fatal raven (2.3.92–7)

In a trice, the cheerful, secluded space of amorous overture has become a place wholly inimical to life because Tamora's lust has been frustrated and her mind is new-set on entrapment, murder, and rape. Even in a tragedy often thought to be short on characterological subtlety, Shakespeare uses ekphrasis to trace the shifting passions of his speaker.[42]

As we have discovered, the taxonomies into which ekphrases fall are made of fine distinctions. Although we know that the *dramatis persona* Romeo is a lover, not a tyrant (Tybalt is cast in that role), and is thus given by fiat to high Petrarchan conceits, when he gazes on the cold, still body of Juliet in the Capulets' tomb in 5.3, he says something remarkable even for him:

> O my love, my wife,
> Death, that hath suck'd the honey of thy breath,
> Hath had no power *yet* upon thy beauty:
> Thou art not *yet* conquer'd, beauty's ensign *yet*
> Is crimson in thy lips and in thy cheeks,
> And death's pale flag is not advanced there. (5.3.91–6, italics mine)

Romeo is solicited by what he sees to express a triumphalist grief not hinted at earlier when he purchased poison from the Apothecary in Mantua. It is activated only now as he looks on her. He describes what the audience cannot see but will understand by comparing his words, with their reiterated, death-defying "yet," to those of Friar Laurence just a few scenes back—that signs of life are returning to Juliet's cheeks and lips as the sleeping potion wears off (4.1.91–106). But Romeo glosses what he sees in the language of heroic transcendence, creating a tragically ironic gap between what the audience knows and what he does not know. He goes further:

> Ah, dear Juliet,
> Why art thou *yet* so fair? Shall I believe
> That unsubstantial Death is amorous,
> And that the lean abhorred monster keeps
> Thee here in dark to be his paramour?
> For fear of that, I will still stay with thee,
> And never from this [palace] of dim night
> Depart again. (5.3.101–8, italics mine)

He does not simply predict his own suicide here, or even its erotic, metaphoric equivalent—"Well, Juliet, I will lie with thee to-night" (5.1.34)—but imagines an *afterlife* as Death's *rival*, to which end he turns Petrarch's worn conceit of Amor as "conduct" of his "seasick weary bark" into an epithet for the poison he drinks in order to enter a post-mortem competition for Juliet's love (5.3.116–18). Clearly Shakespeare is depicting a subject whose immersion in Petrarchan erotics leads him to accurately describe but fatally misinterpret the living Juliet he perceives before him. Yet this is but prologue to what Leontes does in *The Winter's Tale*.

IV

The Winter's Tale is unique in the canon for several reasons, though I shall discuss only two of them in this chapter: the apparently spontaneous jealousy of Leontes in Scene 2 and the sudden aural introduction of Giulio Romano later in the play. The two figures are linked by the remarkably lifelike representations each can create, which deceive the eye and confound the mind. Indeed, Giulio was reputed to have fooled even the gods. The epitaph on his tomb, according to the first edition of Vasari's *Vite*, read: "Jupiter saw sculpted and painted bodies breathe, and the dwellings of mortals made equal to those in heaven, through the skill of Giulio Romano. Angered, therefore, he called a council of all the gods, and swept him from the earth, because he would not suffer to be conquered or equaled by an earth-born man."[43] Shakespeare paraphrases this tribute in Act 5, Scene 2, when the Third Gentleman, with slightly more reserve, proclaims that a statue of Hermione has been "newly performed by that rare Italian master Giulio Romano, who, had he himself eternity and could put breath into his work, would beguile Nature of her custom, so perfectly is he her ape" (5.2.94–7).

Since Hermione's statue turns out to be no statue at all, but the queen herself posing as a statue, alive after sixteen years during which she was presumed dead, neither is it the work of Giulio Romano. Why, then, is his name invoked? There are several answers to this question that reveal the range of Shakespeare's ingenuity, and I will address them in due course. For now, it will be sufficient to consider the fact that Giulio's belated entrance into the dialogue enables Shakespeare to comment indirectly on the issue that has vexed the action from the second scene of the play: for what Giulio has done to the gods, according to Vasari, or to Nature, according to the Third Gentleman, Leontes has done to himself. That is, both have created threatening works of mimetic art, but the historical Giulio's are out there in actual space for all to see, while Leontes' are images seen only in his mind and, issuing from his lips, can only be realized as subjective ekphrases that persuade no one but the speaker. Among its other functions, then, the name and reputation of Giulio Romano is used as a benchmark (ironically, as it turns out) to distinguish a physical work of art from a wholly imaginary work of art that is realized only in words. Yet because the speaker is a king, these words have the power to substantially change the world in which he, his family, his friends, his courtiers, and his subjects dwell.

Unlike the earlier examples of ekphrastic subjectivity we have examined, in the case of *The Winter's Tale* Shakespeare takes us step by step through the process by which the subject forms his vision from the words he hears and the images he sees. Shakespeare even provides background information to the audience before we are aware of its significance in the creation of that vision. I will begin by addressing the process of image formation.

Leontes crafts his ekphrasis while observing the behavior of his wife and closest friend in Act 1, Scene 2, as they chat with one another—Polixenes reserved and courtly, Hermione teasing and affectionate. Their conversation unfolds in three stages. First, at Leontes' prompting—"Tongue-tied, our queen? Speak you" (1.2.27)—Hermione breaks the serious, formal tone of the scene's opening dialogue between Leontes and Polixenes with a playful rebuke: "I had thought, sir, to have held my peace until / You had drawn oaths from him not to stay" (28–9). Whereupon she offers Leontes some stronger arguments to use on Polixenes before she turns to Polixenes himself and assails him with more of her own. To his refusal to delay his departure—"I may not, verily" (45)—she replies, "Verily? . . . A lady's 'verily' is / As potent as a lord's . . . Will you go yet? / Force me to keep you as a prisoner, / Not like a guest . . . How say you? / My prisoner? Or my guest? By your dread 'verily' / One of them you shall be" (50–6). When Polixenes finally relents and chooses to be "Your guest, then, madam. / To be your prisoner should import offending / Which is for me less easy to commit / Than you to punish" (56–9), Hermione's assigned task is successfully completed. Yet Leontes, who has remained silent during this exchange while apparently listening, soon reveals that his mind has been elsewhere, for thirty lines after Polixenes has—in his presence—agreed to stay, he asks, "Is he won yet?" (86), as though he had not been listening at all. What had he been attending to during this first conversation—and what was he thinking during the subsequent one?

It would seem that Leontes *had* been listening, but his imagination had become fixed on the words Hermione had used to offer Polixenes his choice—"guest" or "prisoner"; the reciprocal power the pair would exercise on each other should he choose the latter—"*force me to keep you* prisoner"; the dominant role Hermione would assume in either case—"your gaoler," "your kind hostess." Polixenes' diction, too, had suggested disturbing possibilities—"offending," "commit," "punish." Whatever the intention of the sentences in which these words were embedded, there is a tendentiousness in the listener's imagination that has led them in another direction. Particularly so because it is *Leontes'* friend to whom Hermione has been speaking, and Leontes himself has disappeared from the "my" and "your" that define the proposed relationships.

What had happened next is that the couple actually moved away from him: "Come, I'll question you / Of my lord's tricks and yours when you were boys" (60–1). The word "Come" indicates that Hermione had taken Polixenes' hand or arm—and thus commenced the second stage of their increasingly personal colloquy. They can't have been too far away. Polixenes' response is apparently sufficiently audible to Leontes for him to think of himself and his old acquaintance as "twinned lambs that did frisk i'th'sun" changing "innocence for innocence," but who "have tripped since," for "Temptations have since then been born to's" (77). Following which he must also have heard at least part of Hermione's ironic riposte—"Your queen and I are devils"; "Th'offences we have made you do we'll answer"; "first sinned with us"; "You did continue fault"—for that is the troubling direction in which his imagination has been drifting, as we discover shortly (82, 83, 84, 85).

This second stage of his wife's conversation with Polixenes ends when she answers Leontes' question "Is he won yet?" with the words "He'll stay my lord," which prompts the jealous reflection "At my request he would not" (86–7). His words are not unmotivated. Shakespeare has fashioned the preceding exchange to show that Hermione has exceeded her commission, and is pursuing her own line of inquiry, eagerly assisted by Polixenes' own courtly mischievousness. Left by himself, Leontes gradually did become detached from their dialogue, picking up verbal cues only—"higher reared / With stronger blood," "guilty," "tripped," "devils," "sinned," "fault," "slipped"—and, watching the fun the two are having together, had bodged up a scenario of unwonted familiarity between wife and friend. No wonder he is moved to say "At my request he would not"!

But he tries to put a good face on it: "Hermione, my dearest, thou never spok'st / To better purpose" (88–9). Yet even here, Hermione's own high spirits play into the invisibly spreading phantasma of which she is unaware. "What? Have I twice said well? When was't before? / I prithee tell me; cram's with praise, and make's / As fat as tame things ... You may ride's / With one soft kiss a thousand furlongs ere / With spur we heat an acre" (90–6). "Cram's," "fat,"

"ride's," "kiss," "spur," "heat"—innocent words that bear a darker
signification to the increasingly jealous husband of a pregnant
woman. His reply, evidently sincere, is tinged with bitterness and
ends with a cautionary note:

> Why, that was when
> Three crabbed months had soured themselves to death
> Ere I could make thee open thy white hand
> And clap thyself my love. Then didst thou utter,
> '*I am yours for ever.*' (101–5, italics mine)

Heedless of this warning, Hermione leads Polixenes off once more,
presumably by the hand,[44] in keeping with the symmetry of her
words: "Why, lo you now, I have spoke to th'purpose twice. / The
one for ever earned a royal husband; / Th'other for somewhile a
friend" (106–8).

The third stage of Leontes' creation of the ekphrastic relationship of Hermione and Polixenes becomes audible immediately after
these lines, as the couple stroll off to pursue their conversation. At
this point, Leontes seems to have become completely detached from
what they are saying (we don't hear them either), but is attentive
only to the succession of *images* they present, which he describes
as he watches them. What is extraordinary about his description is that it must be quite different from what is viewed by the
audience—exponentially outdoing Romeo's misinterpretation of
Juliet's recumbent body. Leontes glosses what he sees as a moving
image of "paddling palms and pinching fingers," "making practiced
smiles," "to sigh, as 'twere / The mort o'th'deer—O," increasingly
heated acts that compose an "entertainment / My bosom likes not,
nor my brows" (1.2.118–19), for they are ongoing intimacies that
denote a foregone conclusion: his wife's visible pregnancy. Just as
Quintilian, reading Cicero's description of Verres and his courtesan,
imagined to himself other details that the orator does not describe,
so Leontes easily inserts the missing scene of sexual intercourse as he
witnesses the spectacle of wife and friend behaving in what the text
heretofore has suggested is a familiar but certainly decorous manner.
Why should he do this?[45]

To begin answering this question we need to examine the opening
lines of this scene, and then go back one more scene to listen atten-
tively to the exchange between Archidamus and Camillo. In a sensitive reading of the opening lines of 1.2, B. J. Sokol has pointed out
that Polixenes' words express ideas more appropriate to Leontes'
concerns than to his own:

Nine changes of the watery star hath been
The shepherd's note since we have left our throne
Without a burden. Time as long again
Would be filled up, my brother, with our thanks,
And yet we should for perpetuity
Go hence in debt. And therefore, like a cipher,
Yet standing in rich place, I multiply
With one 'we thank you' many thousands moe
That go before it. (1.2.1–9)

Nine months, a royal seat lacking the weight of its rightful occupant, filling the time with thanks for debt insufficiently paid, standing in rich place, there multiplying. It is not surprising that when Polixenes replies to Leontes' further urging to linger—"I have stayed / To tire your royalty"—Leontes responds almost pugnaciously, "We are tougher, brother / Than you can put us to't" (1.2.14–16).

Sokol notes that "In his very first speech, begging permission for an immediate departure from Leontes' court, hints are conveyed of several topics and motifs centrally important to the play, but not concerning Polixenes himself." Of his reply to Leontes' urging him to stay—"I am questioned by my fears of what may chance / Or breed upon our absence" (11–12)—Sokol observes that "Here again his imagery breaks his characterological outline by suggesting suspicions of cuckoldry and conspiracy which are native to Sicilia, not Bohemia."[46] Sokol is concerned to show that the thematic, structural, and characterological interpenetrate in Shakespeare, especially in the late plays. His thesis supports my specific argument concerning the depicting subject and the attentive auditor. For Polixenes' opening lines serve two important dramaturgic functions. First, they are verbal "seeds" sown in Leontes' fantasy and memory, much as Gloucester's are in Edgar's, thence to issue forth at Dover. Once they have been bodged together with other thoughts that have been collecting in his mind over an unspecified period of time—probably augmented by the unwelcome discovery that he has become part of a foursome since Polixenes' arrival[47]—he hears a challenge even in his friend's expression of concern that "I have stayed / To tire your royalty." Second, they help an attentive audience to comprehend Leontes' bizarre ekphrases of Polixenes' and Hermione's behavior later in the scene after she has (implicitly, if not textually) taken his friend's hand, visually imitating in Leontes' mind her acceptance of him after she had agreed to "clap thyself my love" (1.2.103). In this way, auditors are themselves enabled, through their aural participation, to bodge up the motive and the cue for passion that drive Leontes as his jealousy suddenly emerges into audibility.[48]

Here is where an understanding of ekphrastic psychology helps. To more fully unpack the phenomenon of what we may call the "intersubjective thematic" of Polixenes and Leontes that Sokol points out, and explore its back-story, we need to consult Scene 1, where the play's preoccupation with significant representation is first sounded. Camillo and Archidamus are commenting on the enduring friendship of the two kings. "Sicilia cannot show himself over-kind to Bohemia," says Camillo:

> They were *trained* together in their childhoods, and there *rooted* betwixt them such an affection which cannot choose but *branch* now. Since their more mature dignities and royal necessities made separation of their society, their encounters, though not *personal*, hath been royally *attorneyed* with the interchange of gifts, letters, loving embassies, that they have seemed to be together, though absent, shook hands as over a vast, and embraced as it were from the ends of opposed winds. The heavens continue their loves. (1.1.20–30, italics mine)

The topiary metaphor used to describe the boyhood friendship of Leontes and Polixenes implies a shared origin and nurture, and in the very next scene Polixenes confirms their common identity using the natural simile cited above: "We were as twinned lambs that did frisk i'th'sun, / And bleat the one at th'other" (1.2.66–7). This felt twin-ship has been sustained during their separation by representations of mutual love, following a practice that, as Lisa Jardine has shown, was often used "to bridge the geographical and emotional distance between friends separated by circumstances, to cement and register shared interests and pursuits."[49]

In this case, however, the seemingly benign practice of love "royally attorneyed" has had an adverse effect: self and twin seem to have become conflated as present perceptions enter Leontes' *phantasia* and memory, where his boyhood identification with Polixenes functions as a palimpsest showing through their "more mature dignities." Hence the vision that discerns in the courtesies of Polixenes and the swollen-bellied Hermione a hidden scene of adultery that exhibits to Leontes' shaping fantasy the signs of lust he describes. If I am Polixenes and he is me, and I have had sex with my wife, then *he* has had sex with my wife: thus runs the literally "fantastic" logic of Leontes' reasoning, freshly activated by the suggestive diction of Polixenes' opening speech and his subsequent dialogue with Hermione. Love by *representation*, which fosters the art of symbolical interpretation—indeed, of *indexical* interpretation—has reinforced the innate art of reading one's world *phantasmatically* and, as a result, present perceptions mingle with earlier phantasmata to fashion a multi-layered vision propelling Leontes into an adult homosocial rivalry with his childhood twin for his own wife.

This would help to explain not only Leontes' fantasy concerning Hermione's current pregnancy, but also its bizarre proliferation as he gazes alternately at the strolling couple and at Mamillius, irrationally questioning the paternity of his seven-year-old son—"Mamillius, / Art thou my boy?" (1.2.118–19)! Looking on the boy's face, his mind recoils twenty-three years as he sees himself in Mamillius ("methoughts I . . . saw myself unbreeched" [154–5]) and, by implication, Polixenes too—for in the next scene, as he synaesthetically *listens* to the report of Polixenes' escape and *watches* Mamillius whispering in Hermione's ear, he violently pulls the boy from her. Mamillius has become the nodal attraction for Leontes' fantasy of geminal adultery.[50]

At this point one may ask if ekphrasis is not enabling a deeper depiction of the subject. Is there something in engendering itself that Leontes finds repugnant, and which requires a surrogate for self-purification? Heterosexual disgust is familiar in Shakespeare. We need only recall "Th' expense of spirit in a waste of shame" of Sonnet 129 or Lear's "Down from the waist they are Centaurs, / Though women all above; / But to the girdle do the gods inherit. / Beneath is all the fiends'; there's hell, there's darkness, / There's the sulphurous pit, burning, scalding, / Stench, consumption" (4.6.124–9). The expression closest to Leontes' fantasy in form and function is Iago's ekphrasis of the fight between Cassio and Montano in *Othello*: "Friends all, but now, even now; / In quarter, and in terms like bride and groom / Devesting them for bed; and then, but now— / (As if some planet had unwitted men), / Swords out, and tilting one at other's [breast], / In opposition bloody" (2.3.179–84). Here ekphrasis issues from one man's fantasy and solicits another's, as Iago so powerfully recalls Othello to his nuptial bed that the Moor displaces the image of aroused bridegroom onto Montano: "Worthy Montano, you were wont to be civil . . . What's the matter, / That you *unlace* your reputation thus, / And *spend* your rich opinion for the name / Of a *night brawler?*"—then vows that whoever "is approv'd in this offence, / Though he had *twinn'd* with me, both at a birth, / Shall lose me" (*Oth.* 2.3.190–7, 211–13, italics mine).

And sure enough, confidant Cassio, Othello's point man in wooing Desdemona, becomes thenceforth his sexual surrogate.[51]

V

Some seven years after Iago's voyeurist take on the night brawl in Cyprus, Shakespeare still locates sexual tragedy in the subject's ekphrastic imagination. But in *The Winter's Tale*, the text is also thickly "colored" with allusions to the visual arts.[52] Giulio seems to have intensified Shakespeare's lifelong meditation on the relationship of the naturally given and the artfully imitated. The strangest of these allusions is the one quoted in the title of this chapter, which might pass unnoticed if not for the litany of more explicit references that precedes it. In Act 5, Scene 3, Camillo is trying to comfort Leontes after Paulina warns Perdita not to kiss the effigy's hand, for, she says, "The Statue is but newly fixed; the colour's / Not dry" (47–8):

> *Camillo*: My lord, your sorrow was too sore *laid on*,
> Which sixteen winters cannot blow away,
> So many summers *dry*. (5.3.49–51, italics mine)

Camillo's words are infected by Paulina's. Real paint on a supposedly polychromed statue becomes a metaphor for immaterial sorrow, which—like the statue's coloring—seems recently applied. Leontes' grief, that is to say, remains fresh and alive, and he himself is described as though he were the portrait of a man whose internal life can be discerned through its external rendering by an artist's hand. This makes him virtually a duplicate of Hermione's statue, which is also a living human being, though no one but Paulina yet realizes it. Reading the subjectivity of a portrait's model through its medium is a familiar topos in the early modern period. In a letter to Veronica Gambara in 1537, Pietro Aretino writes that in Titian's portrait of Francesco Maria della Rovere "the colors with which he is painted do not simply make manifest the boldness of his flesh, but also reveal the manliness of his mind," and in an accompanying sonnet he specifies the qualities of soul that may be seen in the subject's painted eyes, brows, forehead, and chest.[53] Ironically, it is *internal* "painting" that has brought Leontes to this state.

The idea that artificial imitation and biological nature are contiguous modes of existence recurs several times in the play—famously in the formal debate of Act 4, where it is argued that art is an extension of nature. "Over that art," says Polixenes to Perdita, "Which you say adds to Nature, is an art / That Nature makes ... This is an art / Which does mend Nature—change it rather—but / The art itself is Nature" (4.4.90–7). Such scripted moments acquire a dynamic trajectory when the theater audience hears that a statue of the dead queen—so like Hermione that "they say one would speak to her and stand in hope of answer" (5.2.98–9)—has been created by a rare Italian master. The words stimulate in the listener that "greediness of affection," voiced by the Third Gentleman, finally to "sup" at a visual feast that incarnates the paradox that has only been talked about so far: that copy and original exist interchangeably along a single continuum where art arises from and has the power to alter nature. The paradox is actualized by the posed and painted Hermione when her *artificial* performance induces *genuine* self-abnegation in Leontes, which then releases her to descend from her pedestal and resume sentient life.[54]

Giulio Romano, the alleged sculptor of a simulated statue, is the medium of that actualization, but it is Shakespeare who has pressed its psychological significance. Just as the received *stone* image of Hermione prompts a collective ekphrasis from its viewers—"Her natural posture"; "not so much wrinkled, nothing / So aged as this seems"; "our carver's excellence, / . . . lets go by some sixteen years, and makes her / As she lived now"; "The very life seems warm upon her lip"; "The fixture of her eye has motion in't"—just as apparent *stone* now receives such glosses, so the *living* image of Hermione and Polixenes had been refashioned into an icon of lust by the naturally artificial glossing of Leontes' fantasy. Ekphrasis is an art that does not always "mend nature"; sometimes it does "change it rather." But "the art itself is nature" and often reveals where its subject has been dwelling.

Notes

1. I am not implying that these terms were actually used by practicing dramatists, merely that they are useful to designate the products of their work. In the 1623 Folio, examples of *dramatis personae* may be seen at the end of seven plays—*The Tempest, The Two Gentlemen of Verona, Measure for Measure, The Winter's Tale, The Second Part of King Henry the Fourth, Timon of Athens,* and *Othello*—under variants of the heading "Names of the Actors." These briefly identify the major dramatic figures by the roles they play.

2. For full discussion of *dramatis persona* and *character* in relation to contemporary play composition, see Altman, *Improbability,* esp.

chapters 8 and 9. The distinction between the two designations is supported by the work of Simon Palfrey and Tiffany Stern on cue scripts in *Shakespeare in Parts* (Oxford: Oxford University Press, 2007), esp. pp. 91–110, 118–23.

3. It was only in the twentieth century that ekphrasis came to be thought of more narrowly as a verbal description of a work of art. See Ruth Webb, *Ekphrasis: Imagination and Persuasion in Ancient Rhetorical Theory and Practice* (Burlington, VT: Ashgate, 2009), esp. pp. 28–38; Jean Hagstrum, *The Sister Arts: The Tradition of Literary Pictorialism and English Poetry from Dryden to Gray* (Chicago: University of Chicago Press, 1958); James A. W. Heffernan, *Museum of Words: The Poetics of Ekphrasis from Homer to Ashbury* (Chicago: University of Chicago Press, 1993); and John Hollander, *The Gazer's Spirit: Poems Speaking to Silent Works of Art* (Chicago and London: University of Chicago Press, 1995). Murray Krieger offers the most theoretically based historical account of the fluctuating relationship between the mimetic natural sign—associated with the visual arts—and the arbitrary-conventional sign, through which objects are represented by words needing imaginative transformation. See *Ekphrasis: The Illusion of the Natural Sign* (Baltimore: Johns Hopkins University Press, 1992).

4. The marginal scholia of Reinhard Lorichius, for example, included in Aphthonius's fourth-century *Progymnasmata*, translated and edited by Rudolph Agricola and Giovanni Maria Cataneus, which, T. W. Baldwin has shown, was "the form of Aphthonius current in England at least from 1572," quotes Quintilian (*Institutio oratoria*, first century CE) thus: "*Descriptio* is speech in which the whole matter that concerns us is, in a manner, an image painted by words." See Baldwin, *William Shakspere's Small Latine and Lesse Greeke*, 2 vols. (Urbana: University of Illinois Press, 1944), vol. 2, p. 288. Quoting Erasmus's *De copia*, Baldwin adds that we use *descriptio* "when, for the sake of amplifying, ornamenting, or delighting we expound a matter not simply, but expressed, as it were, in colors, and we set it forth on a canvas to be seen so that it seems to have been painted, not narrated and the reader has viewed, not read it. This will happen if first we illuminate the very nature of the whole matter and every circumstance, so as to make evident its full shape to the mind. Next we so fashion the matter in words and suitable figures that it is rendered as visible and transparent to the reader as possible" (ibid. pp. 281–2, translation mine).

5. See Baldwin, *William Shakspere's Small Latine and Lesse Greeke*; Peter Mack, *Elizabethan Rhetoric: Theory and Practice* (Cambridge: Cambridge University Press, 2002); and Lynn Enterline, *Shakespeare's Schoolroom: Rhetoric, Discipline, Emotion* (Philadelphia: University of Pennsylvania Press, 2012), esp. pp. 109–12. The device is also prescribed in such vernacular guides as Henry Peacham, *The Garden of*

Eloquence (1577), and George Puttenham, *The Arte of English Poesie* (1589), where it is called *hypotiposis* (ed. Baxter Hathaway [Kent: Kent State University Press, 1970], p. 245).

6. Webb, *Ekphrasis*, pp. 113, 120–1, 157–8.

7. This is stated repeatedly in *De anima, De memoria et reminiscentia*, and elsewhere in the Aristotelian corpus. For helpful discussions, see Jonathan Lear, *Aristotle: The Desire to Understand* (Cambridge: Cambridge University Press, 1988), pp. 96–151; Malcolm Schofield, "Aristotle on the Imagination," in *Essays on Aristotle's De Anima*, ed. Martha C. Nussbaum and Amelie Oksenberg Rorty (Oxford: Clarendon Press, 1992), pp. 249–77; and Dorothea Frede, "The Cognitive Role of *Phantasia*," ibid. pp. 279–95.

8. On the Stoic concept of the *lekton* linking the "presentation" perceived by the senses, deposited in the fantasy, then tested against the subject's "common ideas" by the *hegemonikon* or ruling principle, and its expression in speech, see Gerard Watson, *The Stoic Theory of Knowledge* (Belfast: Queen's University Press, 1966), pp. 41–6. For the Stoics, "Language is man's special way of paralleling or modeling external events, constructing another world of physical sounds which yet (because of an 'incorporeal' process) coheres and permits of testing, and therefore will allow, to the Sage at least, the construction of the perfect theory which will be the complete expression of the universe" (p. 44). Regarding the Stoics' view of perception, cognition, and speech, Diogenes Laertius writes, "For presentation comes first; then thought, which is capable of expressing itself, puts into the form of a proposition that which the subject receives from a presentation" ("Zeno," II.vii.49, in *Lives of Eminent Philosophers*, trans. R. D. Hicks [London: Harvard University Press, 1970], vol. 2, pp. 111–262). Though not all sense presentations are reliable, attentive comparison of each particular with resident "common ideas" can result in "rational presentations" which become the signifieds of speech. As a result, observes Webb, "*Phantasia* is the basis of language and, as in the rhetorical theory of *enargeia* [vividness], language serves as the medium by which *phantasiai* are communicated from the speaker's mind to that of the listener" (*Ekphrasis*, p. 114).

9. On the way emotion distorts perception, see Aristotle, *De somniis*, 460b3ff. Shakespeare's familiarity with these ideas is revealed by Theseus's reflection upon the lovers' stories of their night in the woods: "Such tricks hath strong imagination / That if it would but apprehend some joy / It comprehends the bringer of that joy; / Or in the night, imagining some fear, / How easy is a bush supposed a bear!" (*MND* 5.1.18–22).

10. By "actual experiences," I mean not only direct perception of real-world objects but also the experiences of reading and of viewing works of representational art.

11. This phrase is used frequently by Webb, drawing upon Aristotle and other classical rhetoricians (*Ekphrasis*, pp. 52–6).

12. On the linking of *enargeia* and *energeia* in Aristotle, Cicero, the author of the *Rhetorica ad Herennium*, and Quintilian, see Lucia Calboli Montefusco, "Ἐνάργεια et ἐνέργεια: l'évidence d'une demonstration qui signifie les choses en acte (*Rhet. Her.* 4, 68)," in *Demonstrare: Voir et faire-voir: forme de la demonstration à Rome*, Proceedings of the International Colloquium in Toulouse, 18–20 November 2004, compiled by Mireille Armisen-Marchelli (Toulouse: Presses universitaires du Mirail//Centre national du livre, 2005), pp. 43–58.

13. Quintilian, *Institutio oratoria*, trans H. E. Butler, 4 vols. (Cambridge, MA: Harvard University Press, 1961), vol. 2, pp. 433–5, Book VI, II. 29–31.

14. Ibid. II. 35.

15. Peter Platt has recently pointed out that Hamlet's description of the Player's pallid complexion and distracted aspect derives from Montaigne's addition to Quintilian's recollection of tearful actors in the essay "Of Diverting or Diversion," where the actor exhibits "the paleness of countenance and behavior of a man truly dejected with grief" (Florio's translation). See *Shakespeare's Essays: Sampling Montaigne from Hamlet to The Tempest* (Edinburgh: Edinburgh University Press, 2020). A small but significant bit of Shakespearean bodging.

16. "So excellent a king, that was to this, / Hyperion to a satyr"; "My father's brother—but no more like my father / Than I to Hercules"; "A little month, or ere those shoes were old / With which she follow'd my poor father's body, / Like Niobe, all tears" (1.2.139–40, 152–3, 147–9), etc.

17. *Shakespeare's Reading*, p. 13.

18. Here it will be useful to make a finer distinction in the concept of *dramatis persona*. I have defined the term literally as "person of the play"—Hamlet, Prince of Denmark, for example, or Polonius, a foolish counselor—in essence, a type. But often, a *dramatis persona* is given an opportunity to exhibit what the rhetoricians called an *ethos*, his or her moral qualities, as does Enobarbus when he discovers that, despite his desertion, Antony has sent his treasure after him: "This blows my heart. / If swift thought break it not, a swifter mean / Shall outstrike thought, but thought will do't, I feel . . . I will go seek / Some ditch wherein to die" (4.6.33–7). There is no hint here of the voluptuary that Enobarbus momentarily becomes as the circumstances of his recounting to Agrippa and Maecenas his memories of Cleopatra's barge on the river Cydnus transform him into a character, in the sense I am using here.

19. After its initial appearance in 1512, some 150 editions were published in the sixteenth century. See *Desiderius Erasmus of Rotterdam, On Copia of Words and Ideas*, ed. and trans. Donald B. King and H. David Rix (Milwaukee: Marquette University Press, 1963), p. 2.

20. Ibid. pp. 47–8.
21. Ibid. p. 47, italics mine.
22. Krieger, *Ekphrasis*, ch. 2.
23. *Republic*, Book X, 595a–599e.
24. *Poetics*, 1451a–b.
25. "Spectacle is something enthralling, but is very artless and least particular to the art of poetic composition. The potential of tragedy exists even without a performance." *Poetics*, trans. Richard Janko (Indianapolis and Cambridge: Hackett, 1987), 1450b15–18.
26. I speak here of performed drama, however attenuated. This would not be so, of course, in the case of closet drama, where we are always imaginers.
27. For detailed discussion of the various functions of ekphrasis in early seventeenth-century English theater, see my "Ekphrasis," in *Early Modern Theatricality*, ed. Henry S. Turner (Oxford: Oxford University Press, 2013), pp. 270–90.
28. In *De utraque verborem ac rerum copia*, Erasmus's fifth method of amplifying thought is *enargeia*, which he translates as *evidentia*. "We use this," he writes, "whenever, for the sake of amplifying, adorning, or pleasing, we do not state a thing simply, but set it forth to be viewed as though portrayed in color on a tablet, so that it may seem that we have painted, not narrated, and that the reader has seen, not read." Among his examples of descriptions of "things" are the messenger speeches of Euripides, Seneca, and Sophocles (King and Rix, pp. 47–9).
29. Francis Berry, *The Shakespearean Inset: Word and Picture* (London: Routledge, 1965).
30. Richard Meek, *Narrating the Visual in Shakespeare* (Burlington, VT: Ashgate, 2009). See also Judith Dundas, *Pencils Rhetorique: Renaissance Poets and the Art of Painting* (Newark and London: University of Delaware Press, 1993); Rawdon Wilson, *Shakespearean Narrative* (Newark: University of Delaware Press, 1995); Barbara Hardy, *Shakespeare's Storytellers: Dramatic Narration* (London: Peter Owen, 1997); Alison Thorne, *Vision and Rhetoric in Shakespeare: Looking through Language* (New York: St. Martin's Press, 2000); Alastair Fowler, *Renaissance Realism: Narrative Images in Literature and Art* (Oxford: Oxford University Press, 2003); and Patrick Cheney, *Shakespeare, National Poet-Playwright* (Cambridge: Cambridge University Press, 2004). More recently, Lorna Hutson in *Circumstantial Shakespeare* has shown how Shakespeare exploited the dialectical and rhetorical topics of place, time, and person from judicial oratory to evoke extra-mimetic scenes and to enable audiences to infer the interiorities of characters onstage.
31. By the time Edgar gets to the line "I'll look no more," having traced Gloucester's imminent fall from "here's the place" to "the midway air" to "Halfway down" to "The fishermen . . . upon the beach / Appear

like mice," one senses that he is making himself dizzy even as he speaks falsehoods. As to Enobarbus, although he eroticizes Cleopatra's approach to Antony upon the river to impress Agrippa and Maecenas, the very cadence of his speech suggests he is lingering the description to savor anew the sensory influences felt on the occasion.

32. Othello's speech to the Venetian Council is thus a well-burnished arti-fact: it is an ekphrasis that includes the circumstances in which he first fashioned his life as an ekphrasis, *plus* the circumstances surrounding his second ekphrasis. Its status as a set-piece is suggested by the Duke's response to his offer to "present / How I did thrive in this fair lady's love": not "Tell us, Othello," but "*Say* it, Othello" (italics mine).

33. We have just seen how an exotic Moor can transcend his *dramatis persona* through ekphrasis when elicited by his scene to become a *character*. What of a Jew? Shylock is cast almost unequivocally as the villain of *The Merchant of Venice*, yet there are moments during which his *dramatis persona* of avaricious Jewish moneylender suffers fissures that reveal a *character* who harbors unsuspected sentiments. One instance is his treatment of an Old Testament story as a cherished family anecdote: "When Jacob graz'd his uncle Laban's sheep ..." Antonio rejects his attempt to moralize the tale of cunning Jacob as "thrift is blessing, if men steal it not," asking, "Was this inserted to make interest good? / Or is your gold and silver ewes and rams?" Thus rebuffed, Shylock instantly wriggles back into his *dramatis persona* of cynical Jew: "I cannot tell, I make it breed as fast" (1.3.71–96). Again, when he learns that Jessica has sold his ring for a monkey in Genoa, he cries, "Thou torturest me, Tubal. It was my turkis, I had it of Leah when I was a bachelor. I would not have given it for a wilder-ness of monkeys!" (3.1.120–3). If his conclusion is rather grotesque, his tender burst of feeling for his dead wife comes as a surprise, even though it is embedded among savage responses to his daughter's theft of his jewels ("I would my daughter were dead at my foot and the jewels in her ear!") as well as predatory expressions of joy at news of Antonio's losses ("I thank God, I thank God"). Yet his passionate defense of revenge to Salerio a few minutes earlier—"Hath not a Jew eyes" (3.1.51–73)—reveals to his audience what it feels like to be made a *dramatis persona*, through the logical voice of a *character*. In this instance, the experience of living as a *dramatis persona* is the object of ekphrasis.

34. *William Shakspere's Small Latine and Lesse Greeke*, vol. 2, pp. 310–15.

35. Rhetorically he is a *notatio*, which Erasmus defines as a "character sketch of a voluptuous lover, a miser, a glutton, a drunkard, a slug-gard, a garrulous person, a braggart, a show off, an envious person, a sycophant, a parasite or a pimp," referring his reader to Book IV of the *Rhetorica ad Herennium* (King and Rix, p. 51). Indeed, Navarre's description of him (1.1.162–76) suggests in the form of a fifteen-line

sonnet that he is "a garrulous person." Symptomatic of his dramatic ontology is the frequency with which Folio stage directions and speech prefixes refer to him as "Braggart," though G. R. Hibbard notes that Shakespeare recasts him as more punctilious stylist than *miles gloriosus* after Navarre's speech. See *Love's Labour's Lost* (Oxford and New York: Oxford University Press, 1990), pp. 29–30.

36. Armado acquires "character" only when he defends dead Hector against the mocking gallants (5.2.647–9) and when he repents getting Jaquenetta with child (5.2.705–7), as does Holofernes when he admonishes his audience: "This is not generous, not gentle, not humble" (5.2.617). As Hibbard remarks, "Depths we had not expected are being sounded" (*Love's Labour's Lost*, p. 21).

37. *Institutio oratoria*, 8.3.64–5, quoting Cicero, *Verrine Orations*, 5.33.86. Bernard F. Scholz points out that Quintilian has added not only facial features to the persons described but also an audience of witnesses with whom he can participate in communal disgust at the praetor's behavior, revealing how his own mind amplifies the ekphrasis Cicero provides. See "*Ekphrasis* and *Enargeia* in Quintilian's *Institutionis Oratoriae Libri XII*," in *Rhetorica Movet: Studies in Historical and Modern Rhetoric in Honour of Heinrich F. Plett*, ed. Peter L. Oesterreich and Thomas O. Sloane (Leiden: Brill, 1999), pp. 3–24, esp. 10–11.

38. The Chorus thus functions precisely like the actor described by Quintilian and observed by Hamlet, as he performs the playwright's lines. As for the playwright, we must ascribe his *visiones* to his reading, his listening, or his (unknown) travels.

39. King and Rix, p. 47. This suggests that Erasmus, not Quintilian alone, may have been Shakespeare's primary source.

40. In the epilogue to *Henry V*, the Chorus reminds the audience of the foreign loss and civil strife that followed Henry's triumph in France, "Which oft our stage hath shown" (Epil. 13). It may be of interest in this regard that, according to *Henry VI, Part 1*, ekphrasis was an efficient cause of the War of the Roses. In the last act of that play, Suffolk, in love with Margaret's "natural graces that extinguish art," vows to "Repeat their semblance often on the seas, / That when thou com'st to kneel at Henry's feet / Thou mayst bereave him of his wits with wonder" (*1 Henry VI*, 5.3.192–5). Two scenes later he has achieved his wish, for Henry says, "Your wondrous rare description, noble Earl, / Of beauteous Margaret hath astonished me" (5.5.1–2), then declares his passion and intent to marry her. In the ensuing debate among the angry peers, who have arranged a marriage far more profitable to England, Henry is adamant about crowning the woman who will increasingly antagonize the York faction—unaware that Suffolk has verbally transmitted his own phantasmata of Margaret into the royal phantasia via ekphrasis in order to achieve his sexual and political ambitions through this royal marriage. See my "Virtual Presence and

Vicarious Identity in the First Tetralogy," in *Shakespeare Up Close*, ed. Russ McDonald, Nicholas D. Nace, and Travis D. Williams (London: Arden Shakespeare, 2012), pp. 234–44.

41. In Aristotelian psychology, perception and fantasy are separate functions utilizing different organs. Aristotle's distinction between potentiality (*dynamis*) and actuality (*energeia*) underlies the relationship of perception, fantasy, thought, and what we might call "subject position." The movement of an external object through its medium (e.g. color through light) actualizes the potentiality of a sense organ, which sends the sense perception to the fantasy, actualizing it from its condition of potentiality, and the resulting phantasma or "image" is "seen" as a "presentation." (It can be visual, auditory, olfactory, gustatory, or tactile.) "Presentation" is always subsequent to perception—in effect, a mnemic trace of the perception, which then enters the memory and can be re-actualized when the fantasy is stimulated by a new perception or a thought. Phantasmata (images) thus inform and contextualize perceptions and thoughts, thoughts being dependent on fantasy to do their work (*De anima*, 427b27–8, 431b2; Frede, "The Cognitive Role of *Phantasia*," p. 290; Schofield, "Aristotle on the Imagination," p. 273). Though Aristotle believes that "proper" objects of perception (color, sound, odor, texture, flavor) are perceived truthfully by their respective sense organs in healthy and temperate animals, there are "accidental" objects of perception (e.g. the "what" or "who" of the object) and "general" objects of perception (e.g. the size and shape of the object) that are often falsely perceived. Moreover, since phantasmata are always belated, they are alien by nature to the objects perceived and to that extent detached from the object world. Observes Ronald Polansky on *De anima*, 427b27–428b9: "Because animals [including humans] can have inaccurate perceptions and have perceived things in the past and retain remnants of their sense perception, they are capable of having things appear to them otherwise than they are, especially when they are in a passionate state. The current perception somehow links with *phantasia*, that arising from past perceptions and perhaps a current perception, to make a misleading presentation or appearance ... In these cases we might say that the *phantasma* is not merely an image but the appearance resulting from the combination of *phantasmata* with the current perception to offer an illusory appearance." See Polansky, *Aristotle's "De anima"* (Cambridge: Cambridge University Press, 2007), p. 415. *Mutatis mutandis*, this concept informs the Stoic, Neoplatonic, and Christian traditions as well. It illuminates what I describe below as Leontes' "multi-layered phantasia," which distorts his perception of Hermione and Polixenes in *WT* 1.2. Aristotle's interrelated concepts of potentiality and actuality can be usefully read against Lacan's account of the subject, though a notion of the unconscious is only adumbrated in Aristotle. Like Aristotle's

psyche, the Lacanian subject is *potentially* equipped to be inducted by stages into the Symbolic Order, growing progressively alienated from the Real of the object world and also from the drives of its own body as it is *actualized as a subject*, dependent on the fantasies and desires of an unconscious that is produced from within the world of the Other.

42. With this in mind, we need to reassess the words of Marcus, brother of Titus, who comes upon the ravished Lavinia one scene later, her tongue cut out and her hands cut off: "Why dost not speak to me? / Alas, a crimson river of warm blood, / Like to a bubbling fountain stirred with wind, / Doth rise and fall between thy rosed lips, / Coming and going with thy honey breath" (2.4.21–5). Rather than regard his words as incongruously "pretty," we might consider that he is responding to his own horror by aestheticizing the loathsome sight of his mutilated niece.

43. VIDEBAT IUPPITER CORPORA SCVLPTA PICTAQVE / SPIRARE, ET AEDES MORTALIVM AEQVARIER COELO / IVLII VIRTVTE ROMANI. TVNC IRATVS, / CONCILIO DIVORVM OMNIVM VOCATO, / ILLVM E TERRIS SVSTVLIT, QVOD PATI NEQVIRET / VINCI AVT AEQVARI AB HOMINI TERRIGENA. Vasari, *Le vite*, vol. 2, p. 837, translation mine.

44. F supplies no stage direction, but neither does it for "Come" (60). We must infer the blocking from the text.

45. Here, Scholz's explication of Quintilian is useful. He persuasively argues that for Quintilian, ekphrasis is a dispositive concept. That is, a passage of description can be disposed to elicit powerful emotions from a listener or reader through its fullness of vivid detail, but in order for it to work, its intended audience must also be disposed to respond. If we extrapolate from this to Leontes' situation, the not merely lifelike but live actions of Hermione and Polixenes play into his predisposition to read the scene as he does. The audience, not thus disposed, sees differently ("*Ekphrasis* and *Enargeia*," pp. 21–3).

46. *Art and Illusion in The Winter's Tale* (Manchester: Manchester University Press, 1994), pp. 24–5. He notes that later in the scene "Polixenes identifies original sin with sexual maturing," citing the lines about his youth spent with Leontes (1.2.69–75). This speech, he suggests, "reveals an even stranger breach of Polixenes' identity, which so ignores his characterization as to imply the total fusion of his psychology with Leontes'" (p. 25).

47. I include in this number the fetus swelling Hermione's belly, not Mamillius.

48. Cf. the way in which Ophelia's mad ravings affect the Danes who listen to her and "move / The hearers to collection" (*Ham.* 4.5.8–9), discussed in Chapter 1.

49. The exchange of courtesies and material objects described here—means of sustaining the intimacy of friendship across time and distance—was common practice in the period, when travel was more difficult and

less frequent. Jardine describes the letters, verses, and artifacts circu-
lated self-consciously for this purpose among Erasmus and his friends
in "Towards Reading Albion's Classicism: An Exchange of Gifts
between Northern Classical Scholars," in *Albion's Classicism: The
Visual Arts in Britain, 1550–1660*, ed. Lucy Gent (New Haven and
London: Yale University Press, 1995), pp. 19–28. See also Raymond B.
Waddington, *Aretino's Satyr: Sexuality, Satire, and Self-Projection in
Sixteenth-Century Literature and Art* (Toronto: University of Toronto
Press, 2004), pp. 45–55, for Aretino's adaptation of Erasmus's *De
conscribendis epistolis* in fashioning vivid imagistic bonds with his
addressees.

50. Which may be why his death is announced at the climax of Leontes'
fantasy, when—unlike Greene's Pandosto—Leontes declares "There
is no truth at all i' th' oracle." Instantly the king confesses, "I have
too much believed mine own suspicion" (3.2.149). Notice that when
Leontes looks upon Florizel in Act 5 and is again drawn to youthful
reminiscence, he does not use the locution "methoughts," which in
1.2 signalled his phantasmatic delusion; instead he uses a conditional
phrase, "Were I but twenty-one" (5.1.125), followed by conditional
verbs, indicating the temptation but also a resistance to falling into
phantasmatic identification a second time.

51. I realize that this "thicker" description pushes my argument beyond the
depiction of Leontes' subject into that of his maker, as it did in the case
of the Chorus in *Henry V*, but again it does not obviate my primary
point about Shakespeare's expressive use of ekphrasis. Indeed, in this
context ekphrasis would seem to be a parapraxis ready to hand for a
seventeenth-century dramatist. See Webb's classical cautions regarding
ekphrases above, in n. 6.

52. This has already been touched on in Chapter 1 in the context of imitation (1.2.121–2, 2.3.96–101, to which should be added 5.1.123–5),
and will be developed further in Chapter 3. As we shall see, much of
Act 5, Scene 2 is an extensive ekphrasis of the reunion of the two families, viewed as a kinetic painting.

53. For further examples, see Norman E. Land, *The Viewer as Poet*
(University Park: Pennsylvania State University Press, 1994).
Shakespeare offers an abbreviated version in *Timon*, 1.1.30–8.

54. I use the term "sentient" advisedly and take my cue from Paulina:
"Be stone no more . . . Bequeath to death your numbness." Although
Hermione has been alive these sixteen years, that life has been cloistered, set apart from the fullness of feeling that is promised by the
reunion of family and good friends at the end of the play—despite the
irreparable losses sustained.

Chapter 3

Julio at the Crossroads: Sex and Transfiguration in the Court of Sicilia

I

In the previous chapter, I argued that Shakespeare deployed the powers of ekphrasis to reveal the subjectivity of characters in his plays. And I proposed that in *The Winter's Tale* he silently referenced the reputation of Giulio Romano for creating lifelike representational objects to counterpoint Leontes' purely *mental* representations of the *visible* actions of his wife and childhood friend. Some two hours, therefore, before his name was even mentioned, Giulio was already present in the imagined world of the play, though he did not come to audibility until the gossipy penultimate scene. Then, after the Third Gentleman has described the reunion of King Leontes and his daughter Perdita—who is accompanied by Florizel, her betrothed, pursued by *his* father, King Polixenes of Bohemia and the courtier Camillo, along with the two shepherds and Autolycus—he is asked by a fellow Gentleman what the royal families did next. I now quote his reply in full:

> The Princesse hearing of her Mothers Statue (which is in the keeping of *Paulina*) a Peece many yeeres in doing, and now newly perform'd, by that rare Italian Master, *Julio Romano*, who (had he himselfe Eternitie, and could put Breath into his Worke) would beguile Nature of her Custom, so perfectly he is her Ape: He so neere *Hermione*, hath done *Hermione*, that they say one would speake to her, and stand in hope of answer. Thither (with all *greediness* of affection) are they gone, and there they intend to *Sup.* (5.2.92–101, italics mine)[1]

So eager is the Third Gentleman to express his admiration of Giulio Romano's skill that he turns a simple one-sentence answer into three distinct grammatical periods, leaving the first one, with its heaped-up modifying clauses, dangling without its complement until he catches his breath. But his amplification provides a staged advertisement for the artist, a man of nearly supernatural powers, it would seem, and cues the theater audience that they are about to see something marvelous.

As we know, what they see is something even more marvelous than was advertised: someone *has* "put Breath into his Worke" and those who "would speake to her, and stand in hope of answer" *are* answered. In a dramatic demonstration of the rhetorical figure *litotes* (disguised understatement) Shakespeare is doing Giulio one better. A good enough reason—with some sly obfuscation thrown in—for all the ballyhoo. But it raises some specific new questions that need to be addressed: what did Shakespeare know about Giulio Romano and what did he expect his audience to know? One does not normally engage in hyperbolical name-dropping of this order without expecting to impress.

Scholars have pondered these questions for generations, though they may seem self-explicating. An audience is prepared, by means of a staged script, to see a lifelike statue, and their expectations are more than fulfilled: the statue comes to life. Shakespeare knew this much about Giulio Romano and so, perhaps, did many in his audience: that he was an artist whose works exhibited extraordinary *vivacità*. Big joke, case closed.

But the issues become more complicated when we consider that Giulio is the only historical artist named in the Shakespeare canon. Shakespeare had shown interest in the theory and practice of visual art before—playfully in the workings of perspective in Sonnet 24; cunningly in Bushy's explanation of the Queen's grief in *Richard II*; in the viewer's response to what she beholds in a real painting in *The Rape of Lucrece*; in the painter's engagement with his subject in the casket portrait of Portia in *The Merchant of Venice*; in the *paragone* of painter and poet in *Timon of Athens*; in the interpretation of *imprese* in *Pericles*, to name a few instances. But in none of these is a given artist mentioned by name.[2] This suggests that the words "Giulio Romano" had unusual rhetorical force for the dramatist and that he was counting on Giulio's name recognition to stir at least part of his audience to fresh surmise. In the person of the Third Gentleman he may have been touting their shared knowledge and also bringing his own preoccupations into focus.

But what was that knowledge? And what preoccupations did those two puffs of air signify? In the first edition of Giorgio Vasari's

Le vite de' più eccellenti architetti, pittori, et scultori italiani, da Cimabue, insino a' tempi nostri, as we saw in Chapter 2, he might have read that the following Latin epitaph was placed on Giulio's tomb on his death in 1546. Here is the full text:

> Jupiter saw *sculpted and painted* bodies breathe, and the dwellings of mortals made equal to those in heaven, through the skill of Giulio Romano. Angered, therefore, he called a council of all the gods, and swept him from the earth, because he would not suffer to be conquered or equaled by an earth-born man. Dying, Giulio Romano carried off three of the arts with him—no wonder: he alone was four. (Italics mine)[3]

In comparison to this inscription—which implies that Giulio was a sculptor, painter, and architect—the Third Gentleman's praise of "that rare Italian master," quoted above, seems modest, with "nature" standing in for "Jupiter" and the epitaph's hyperbolical claim translated from the indicative to the conditional mood ("had he . . . could put . . . would beguile"). Nonetheless it is a paraphrase. This suggests that Shakespeare must have been familiar with Vasari's 1550 *Vita*. Eye contact or someone else's quotation would seem to have been requisite for the reference.[4]

The first part of the Third Gentleman's speech, however, which describes "a piece many years in doing and now newly performed by that rare Italian master," is a different matter. It alludes to, yet contradicts, a passage in the longer and definitive edition of the *Vita*, published in 1568, in which Vasari characterizes Giulio Romano's practice in this way:

> It may be affirmed, indeed, that Giulio always expressed his conceptions better in drawings than in finished work or in paintings, for in the former may be seen more vivacity, boldness, and feeling; and this may have happened because he made a drawing in an hour, in all the heat and glow of creation, whereas on paintings he spent months, and even years, so that growing weary of them, and losing that keen and ardent love that one has at the beginning of a work, it is no marvel that he did not give them that absolute perfection that is to be seen in his drawings.[5]

Here, Vasari stresses that Giulio's strength lay in his drawings, and that pieces "many years in doing" lacked the liveliness of work he turned out in an hour.[6] The logical inference is that Shakespeare, a playwright and not an art historian, did not refer to the 1568 life of Giulio, using only the volume he had at hand or paraphrasing it from another printed or personal source. Yet it is in the later version that Vasari repeatedly emphasizes (without recurring to his initial qualification) the astonishingly lifelike imitation of nature seen in Giulio's finished work. A lion in an altarpiece in the Fugger Chapel of S. Maria dell' Anima at Rome has short wings "with feathers so soft and plumy, that it seems almost incredible that the hand of a craftsman could have been able to imitate nature so closely." In the marriage of Cupid and Psyche, painted on the vault of the Stanza di Psiche in the Palazzo Te at Mantua, the figures are foreshortened so skillfully that "besides seeming to be alive (so strong is his relief), they deceive the human eye with a most pleasing illusion." Vasari reserves his most extravagant praise for the Sala dei Giganti at the Te, where the Titans' assault on Olympus is portrayed in a room "all of rustic stones rough-hewn as if by chance, and, as it were, dis-jointed and awry, in so much that they appeared to be really hanging over to one side and falling down." After describing the painted fury of Jupiter hurling thunderbolts, the fearful departure of other gods, and the terror of the giants, lying among "falling temples, columns, and other pieces of buildings," he concludes: "let no one ever think to see any work of the brush more horrible and terrifying, or more natural than this one; and whoever enters that room and sees the windows, doors, and other suchlike things all awry and, as it were, on the point of falling, and the mountains and buildings hurtling down, cannot but fear that everything will fall upon him." *Vivacità, fierezza, affetto*—all are present here.[7]

It would not be unlike Shakespeare to alter his textual sources—even to play oppositional games with them. That is at the heart of the art of bodging. He does precisely this in adapting Greene's *Pandosto*, where he exchanges the Bohemia of Greene's Leontes figure for the Sicilia of Greene's Polixenes figure and makes Leontes' queen the daughter of the emperor of Russia, whereas in Greene it's the Polixenes figure who has the Russian wife.[8] So while Occam's law recommends the simpler alternative—consulting one version only—we should not rule out the possibility that he was familiar with the 1568 edition of Vasari too. After all, Inigo Jones owned a copy, and *The Winter's Tale* notably alludes to the dance of satyrs in Jones's and Jonson's contemporary *Masque of Oberon*—an instance of intermedial exchange that may also have been an exchange of courtesies.[9]

But this leaves two related, yet still more crucial, questions unad-dressed. Could Shakespeare read Italian? And if he could, why choose Giulio Romano, when other Italian painters were praised for their lifelike illusionism? Scholarly opinion was long undecided on the first question, since many of the known Italian sources of the plays were available in French or English translation, and on the evidence of the language lesson in *Henry V* he could certainly handle himself in French. Yet more than sixty years ago Mario Praz argued that he did indeed know Italian and even read Italian drama. "In *Measure for Measure*, for example," observed Praz,

> he must have taken the idea of the substitution of the bodies [of Ragozine for Claudio] from Cinthio's drama *Epitia*, since that substitution does not occur in the story of the *Hecatommithi* (Deca VIII, Novella 5), of which *Epitia* is a dramatic version. Neither does it occur in Whetstone's rehandling of Cinthio's story. Since Italian books were widely read in the society in whose midst Shakespeare lived, there is nothing extraordinary in his acquaintance with Italian literature; rather the contrary would have been surprising.[10]

More recently, Keir Elam has emphasized Shakespeare's familiarity with the works of John Florio: his *First Fruites* (1578), *Second Frutes* (1591), *A Worlde of Wordes* (1598), and *Queen Anna's New World of Words* (1611). "Florio," he writes, "provides not only the venues but some of the actual dialogic material that Shakespeare employs in his representations of Italy . . . thereby rendering superfluous any mere physical journey to the peninsula. Shakespeare's explorations of Italy, its language and culture begin and end within—although they are certainly not limited to—the confines of Florio's texts."[11]

This view of Shakespeare's use of Florio is further developed by Jason Lawrence, who has shown convincingly that Shakespeare could read Italian, and read it quite well by the time he was writing *The Winter's Tale*.[12] Lawrence's account of foreign language study in early modern England and the habits of reading it fostered also turns the possibility that Shakespeare consulted both editions of Vasari into a strong probability. He shows how the method of instruction by means of parallel texts, like those found in Florio's *First Fruites* and *Second Frutes*, inculcated the habit of comparative and selective reading in such writers as William Drummond of Hawthornden, Samuel Daniel, John Marston, and Shakespeare himself. Moreover, knowledge of Italian did not preclude consulting translations. Even an accomplished Italianist like Marston, son of an English father and a first-generation English-Italian mother, who made self-conscious use of Italian in *Antonio and Mellida* in 1599, consulted the new English translation of Guarini's *Il pastor fido* when writing *The Malcontent* three years later.[13] Shakespeare used Florio's *First Fruites* in many plays, notably for the exchange between Petruccio and Hortensio in the second scene of *The Taming of the Shrew* (c. 1592). As we saw in Chapter 1, he was parodied by Greene in *Groats-Worth of Wit* during the same year for having imitated Petrarch's line "Questa umil fera, un cor di tigre o d'orsa / Che 'n vista umana, e 'n forma d'angel vene" as "O tiger's heart wrapp'd in a woman's hide!" (*3 Henry VI*, 1.4.137), perhaps prompted by Florio's own reference in his first manual.[14]

Shakespeare's connection to Florio was proposed as far back as the eighteenth century, when William Warburton suggested that Holofernes the Pedant in *Love's Labour's Lost* was modeled on the Italian Englishman, and in the twentieth century Charlotte Stopes, Frances Yates, and G. P. V. Akrigg argued that Florio's presence as tutor in the household of Shakespeare's patron Henry Wriothesley, 3rd Earl of Southampton, and as instructor of William Herbert, 3rd Earl of Pembroke (a candidate for the "young man" of the sonnets), brought him into Shakespeare's ambiance.[15] But it is Lawrence who has offered the strongest argument for Shakespeare's dependence on Florio by demonstrating that borrowings from Florio's language books can be traced from the early 1590s—not only in *Shrew*, but also in *Love's Labour's Lost* and *Richard III*—and that by 1596 Shakespeare was capable of reading Italian without an English text beside him, for he wholly depended on Ser Giovanni Fiorentino's *Il pecorone* while writing *The Merchant of Venice*, the only source known to contain all the major elements of the play.[16] By the time he wrote *Measure for Measure* and *Othello* (1603–4), he was sufficiently proficient in Italian to draw on Giraldi Cinzio's *Ecatommiti* for both plays, though there is evidence that he also consulted Chapuys's French translation. And, as noted by Praz, he had begun to use Italian drama as well as *novelle* for source material. Even earlier, John Manningham's comparison of *Twelfth Night* to the comedy *Gl'inganni* when recording a performance of Shakespeare's play at the Middle Temple in February 1602 points to one of two plays with the same name, one of which, that of Curzio Gonzaga, features a cross-dressed heroine who disguises herself as the young man Cesare, anticipating Viola's disguise as Cesario. And there is a larger "*Ingannati* family" that must be considered as well.[17] So once more we encounter a Shakespeare exercising his ingenuity by poring selectively over narrative and dramatic sources—but this time in a foreign language—to bodge up a new play.

II

The second question, why did Shakespeare fix on Giulio Romano, when other artists—Titian, for example, or Raphael himself—were also praised for their lifelike imitations of nature, is more intriguing.[18] Giulio, I suggest, can be detected straddling the crossroads of the sacred and the profane in *The Winter's Tale*. Let us enter upon the latter road first. Although it is not reported in Vasari's life of Giulio—nor in Shakespeare's play—"that rare Italian master" was involved in a notorious sex scandal that is described in Vasari's 1568 life of the engraver Marcantonio Raimondi, which was included in the same volume owned by Inigo Jones. Giulio had served as Raphael's assistant from his early teens and rapidly became his favorite, finishing many works designed by his master, in Rome and elsewhere. At Raphael's death in 1520 he was, in effect, his professional heir, completing Raphael's unfinished commissions and undertaking new ones, partnered with his workshop fellow Gianfrancesco Penni.[19] Sometime in 1524 he proposed a novel project to Marcantonio, who had engraved many of Raphael's drawings and paintings. This is Vasari's account of their enterprise:

> Giulio Romano caused Marc' Antonio to engrave twenty plates showing all the various ways, attitudes, and positions in which licentious men have intercourse with women; and, what was worse, for each plate Messer Pietro Aretino wrote a most indecent sonnet, insomuch that I know not which was the greater, the offence to the eye from the drawings of Giulio, or the outrage to the ear from the words of Aretino. This work was much censured by Pope Clement; and if, when it was published, Giulio had not already left for Mantua, he would have been sharply punished for it by the anger of the Pope. And since some of these sheets were found in places where they were least expected, not only were they prohibited, but Marc' Antonio was taken and thrown into prison; and he would have fared very badly if Cardinal de' Medici and Baccio Bandinelli, who was then at Rome in the service of the Pope, had not obtained his release. Of a truth, the gifts of God should not be employed, as they very often are, in things wholly abominable, which are an outrage to the world.[20]

Modern scholars have found Vasari inaccurate in several details. The drawings were not twenty in number, but sixteen; Giulio continued to enjoy the favor of Gian Matteo Giberti, the Vatican Datary, in spite of their initial publication;[21] Aretino did not write his *sonetti lussuriosi* until Marcantonio had been released (according to

Aretino, through *his* influence); and the sonnets, inspired by Giulio's drawings (as Aretino later wrote to his friend Battista Zatti), caused a new furor when they appeared with Marcantonio's engravings sometime between 1525 and 1527, in a book known as *I modi*, i.e. "ways and means," or, as Englished in the seventeenth century, "postures" or "positions." Just as Marcantonio's original engravings had been confiscated by papal authorities anxious not to add fuel to Reformers' accusations of Church immorality, these books were seized where they could be found, destroyed, and banned.[22] But they had a long afterlife in pirated editions using engravings and wood-cuts based on the originals, and they circulated widely in northern Europe.[23] About eighty years later Ben Jonson, critic, rival, and self-declared bosom friend of Shakespeare—"I lov'd the man, and doe honour his memory (on this side idolatry)"[24]—evoked recollections of *I modi* in *Volpone* and *The Alchemist* through two of his most fashionable voluptuaries, Lady Politic Would-be and Sir Epicure Mammon respectively—plus one wittold, *Volpone*'s Corvino—and the book was cited by other English writers, such as Thomas Nashe, John Donne, Thomas Middleton, and even Robert Greene.[25]

There is also an allusion to *I modi* in the Induction to *The Taming of the Shrew*, when the Lord instructs his servants to carry Christopher Sly "to my fairest chamber / And hang it round with all my wanton pictures" (*TS*, Ind. 1.45–6). As Elam argues, this can be traced to the Italian versions behind George Gascoigne's *Supposes*, from which Shakespeare derived his Bianca plot. In the Prologue Gascoigne tells his audience, "some I see smyling as though they sup-posed we would trouble you with the vaine suppose of some wanton Suppose," a line that refers to Ariosto's original prose version of *I suppositi* (1507), where the prologue says, "Benign auditors, do not interpret this supposing in the wrong way: not in the quite different manner which it is supposed Elephantis left illustrated in her lascivi-ous books"—a reference to the notorious Greek poetess Elephantis, whose pictures are also evoked by Jonson's Mammon (*Alchemist*, 2.2.41–5).[26] In his verse adaptation of the play (written in 1532, after the *I modi* scandal), Ariosto adds a new reference: "My sup-poses, however, are not like those antique ones, that Elefantis, in diverse actions, forms, and various positions, allowed to be painted; and which now, in our own times have been renewed and printed on sheets of paper, more beautiful than honest, so that the whole world might have a copy of them."[27] It is thus highly likely that Shakespeare was familiar with *I modi*, and may have even picked up a copy at the booksellers' stalls in London.[28]

A piquant connection, perhaps, but what does it have to do with
The Winter's Tale? As we observed in the previous chapter, in Act
1, Scene 2, Leontes suddenly breaks into a violent expression of jealousy as his wife and best friend chat together, refashioning the easy
familiarity of their stroll about the stage into an ekphrastic sequence
of lurid images. These are prompted, the play's language suggests, by
Polixenes' words announcing his departure after a nine-month stay
(1.2.1–16); Hermione's words of persuasion to prolong his visit—as
requested by Leontes—and Polixenes' response; Leontes' own lifelong
bonding with Polixenes (1.1.21–31, 1.2.67–71), which seems to have
had the psychological effect of conflating their identities; his wife's
visible pregnancy; and his own carnal knowledge. Given Giulio's
audible presence later in the play, however, there may also be a more
publicly recognizable source of his fantasies. Like the female voyeur
in the eleventh position of *I modi*, peering unobserved through a
window at a man and a woman whose vigorous sexual activity has
caused the mattress on which they have been sporting to fall to the
floor (Fig. 3.1), Leontes seems to have looked through the glasses of
Giulio's eyes and witnessed a scene of copulation. Aretino's intruder
exclaims: "Oh lewd lady, oh ribald rogue, on floor and bed. / I see

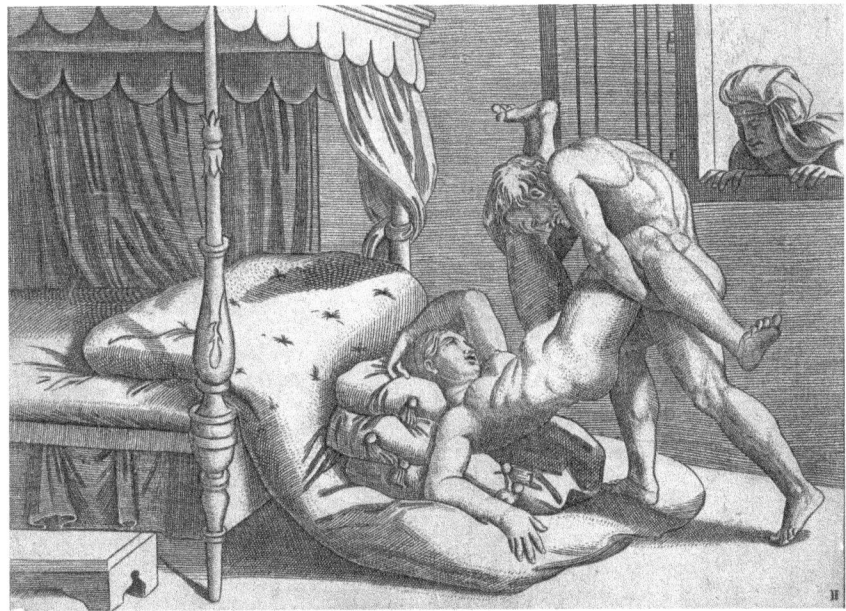

Fig. 3.1. *I modi*, position 11. Marcantonio Raimondi, after Giulio
Romano. Cred. Graphische Sammlung Albertina, Vienna.

you, whore: prepare yourself / For I will break two ribs from your spine."[29] Leontes' response is less violent, but no less conclusive. In his version, the friendly conversation he observes between his wife and friend metamorphoses first into a flirtation, then into a carefully masked performance, and concludes with an audible orgasm: "paddling palms, pinching fingers, / As now they are, and making practised smiles / As in a looking-glass; and then to sigh, as 'twere / The mort o' th' deer—*O!*, that is entertainment / My bosom likes not, nor my brows" (1.2.115–19, my italic and exclamation point). The preposterous conclusion thus signified is explained in Leontes' opening aphorism: "To mingle friendship far is mingling bloods" (1.2.109); that is, "mingling body fluids," as his phantasia informs him.

Less than 170 lines later these indexical *visiones* have themselves become amplified into an Italian graphic novella shaped by telltale signs of clandestine love as he speaks to Camillo:

> Is whispering nothing?
> Is leaning cheek to cheek? Is meeting noses?
> Kissing with inside lip? stopping the career
> Of laughter with a sigh (a note infallible
> Of breaking honesty)? horsing foot on foot?
> Skulking in corners? wishing clocks more swift?
> Hours, minutes? noon, midnight? and all eyes
> Blind with the pin and web, but theirs; theirs only (1.2.282–9)

Leontes is not only fabricating a multiply detailed, extended ekphrasis of a brief episode observed earlier in the scene—ostensibly to persuade Camillo of his conviction—he is actually recapitulating the practice of Aretino himself when *he* provided glosses for Marcantonio's engravings of Giulio's drawings. In contrast to Aretino's complementary verses, notes Manfredo Tafuri,

> the personages of *I modi* express a sense of seriousness rather singular, given the theme of the engravings. The multiplex variations of sexual intercourse come to be executed in the form of a ritual series: the evident aura of affecting the antique of the compositions thus has a precise role. It is what renders the same compositions neither erotic nor pornographic: in them there rather dwells a subtle distinction between subject and representation.[30]

This is not to say that in the eyes of their original beholders the images were not arousing and therefore potentially scandalous. Vasari notes that "some of these sheets were found in places where they were least expected"—a remark that recent historians have interpreted as referring to chambers of the Vatican clergy, for whom, presumably, they were not intended. However, as Bette Talvacchia points out, when Aretino came along he took Giulio's classicized images and made them even more scandalous than the engravings alone had appeared to papal officials. "Several of the sonnets have contemporary names," she writes,

> including those of well-known courtesans in the Roman curia, and thus place the action recounted in the sonnet, and by extension depicted in the image the sonnet accompanies, in the same ambiance ... Aretino's seditious practice operates to infuse the verses with a topicality that was lacking in the much more neutral engraving, adding slander and offense by virtue of its specific protagonists and their setting.[31]

He further contemporizes that setting by using common colloquial expressions. In the same way that Aretino modernizes and localizes Giulio's classicized pictures, Leontes idiosyncratically radicalizes through his lewd ekphrases what must have been seen by the theater audience and Camillo as decorous, if animated and affectionate, courtly gestures exchanged by his wife and friend.

Now there is an obvious difference between the relationship of Aretino's verses to Giulio's pictures and that of Leontes' verses to the living image of Hermione and Polixenes. Giulio's pictures show a naked man and woman assuming a variety of sexual postures, however much they may affect the antique. Hermione and Polixenes are both fully clothed and are not engaged in sexual activity. Yet Leontes evidently sees through their garments and postures and invents erotic interactions not unlike those we find informing the images of *I modi*. For example, "kissing with inside lip" certainly seems to be going on in position 13 (Fig. 3.2), whose sonnet begins "*Dammi la lingua, e apponto i piedi al muro*" ("Give me your tongue, and prop your feet on the wall"). "Leaning cheek to cheek" is clearly gestured in the full horizontal embrace of position 1 (Fig. 3.3): "*Fottiamci anima mia, fottiamci presto / Poi che tutti per fotter nati siamo*" ("Let's fuck, my beloved, let's fuck right away since we are all born for fucking"). And "meeting noses" appears in position 2 (Fig. 3.4): "*Mettimi un ditto in cul caro vecchione / E spingi dentro il cazzo apoco apoco*" ("Put a finger up my ass, dear old man, and push your cock in, little by little") and in position 12 (Fig. 3.5): "*Marte malatestissimo poltrone, / Cosi sotto una donna non si reca*" ("Mars, most damned sluggard, a woman can't bear up underneath like this").[32] Depending on how one interprets "horsing foot on

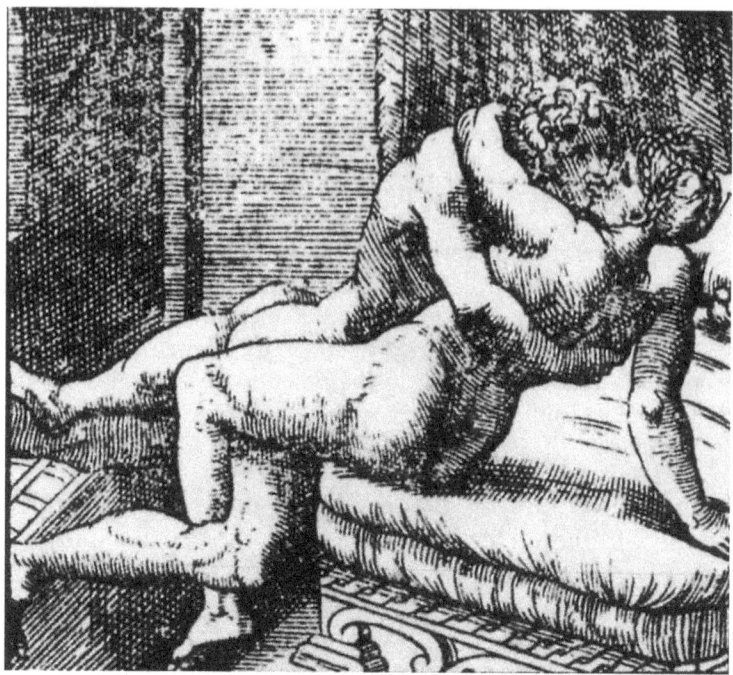

Fig. 3.2. *I modi*, position 13. Anonymous sixteenth-century woodcut after Marcantonio Raimondi, after Giulio Romano.

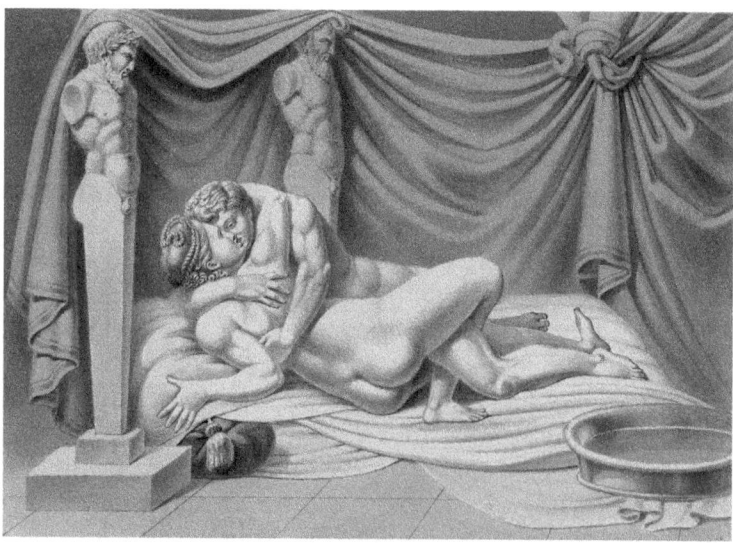

Fig. 3.3. *I modi*, position 1. Nineteenth-century drawing by Jean-Frédéric Maximilien Waldeck, after Marcantonio Raimondi, after Giulio Romano. The British Museum, London.

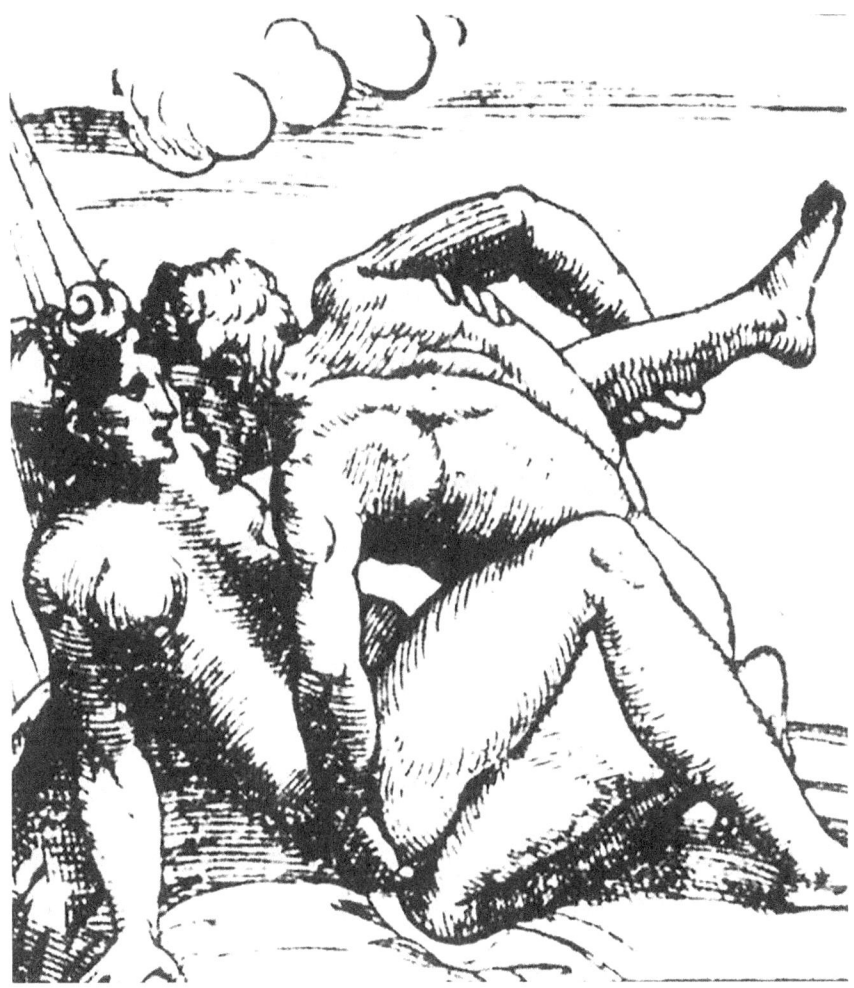

Fig. 3.4. *I modi*, position 2. Anonymous sixteenth-century
woodcut after Marcantonio Raimondi, after Giulio Romano.

foot," its counterpart in *I modi* might be position 7 (Fig. 3.6), which
shows a man perched on a cassone at mattress end, half-kneeling,
half-standing, behind a woman whose right foot adjoins his left foot
on the floor and who has reached behind her to grab his penis while
he asks where she'll put it: "O 'l metterete voi? Ditel di gratia, /
Dietro, o dinanzi?" ("Where will you put it? Tell me most kindly,
behind or in front?").[33] With the man backing the woman and ready
to mount, the image is highly suggestive of animal coupling. Leontes'
choice of words might well recall these images to those who had
looked them over.[34]

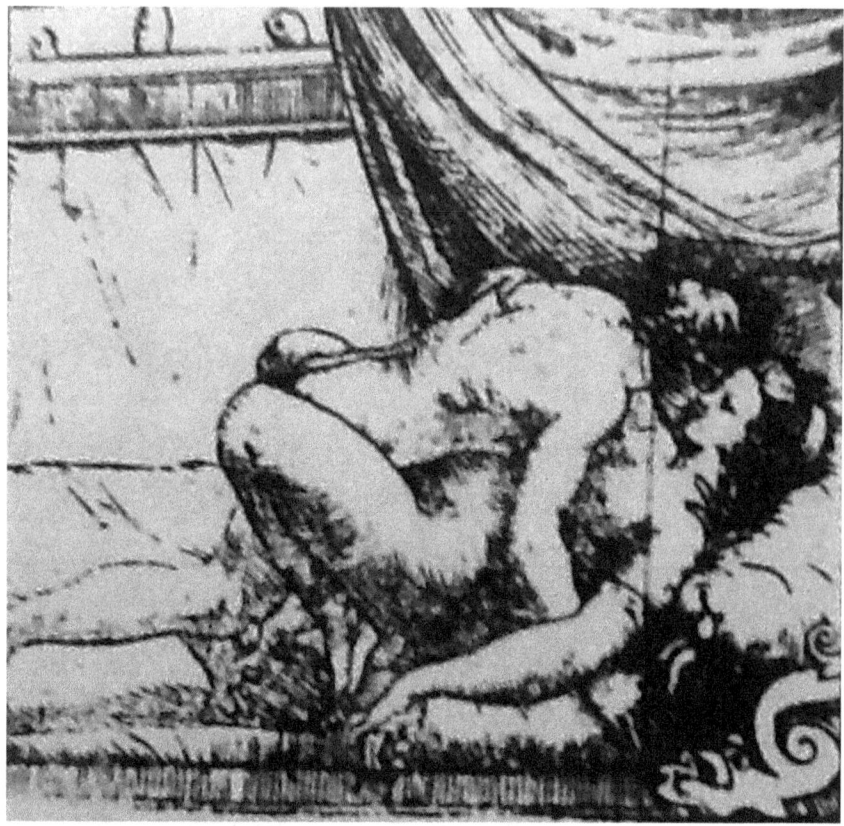

Fig. 3.5. *I modi*, position 12. Anonymous sixteenth-century woodcut after Giulio Romano.

It must be admitted that Shakespeare's familiarity with *I modi* is not a prerequisite for Leontes' lascivious imaginings. As suggested in the previous chapter, his palimpsestic geminal fantasies, as he hears and watches Hermione and Polixenes amiably conversing, might be sufficient. Moreover, Iago had scattered obscene images before Brabantio's and Othello's receptive *phantasiai* years before without the nominal presence of Giulio in the play (*Oth.* 1.1.88–9, 111–16; 2.3.179–84; 3.3.416–26)—though these tend to be metaphorical rather than literal. Indeed, Jacobean drama is filled with lurid evocations of furtive sexual activity in the nooks and crannies of Italian Renaissance palaces.[35] Nonetheless, Giulio's touted authorship of Hermione's statue in 5.2, and—as we shall see presently—the deliberate way in which details of his religious painting enter allusively into the dialogic description of the reunion of the families in that same scene, offer a strong presumption that Shakespeare's acquaint-

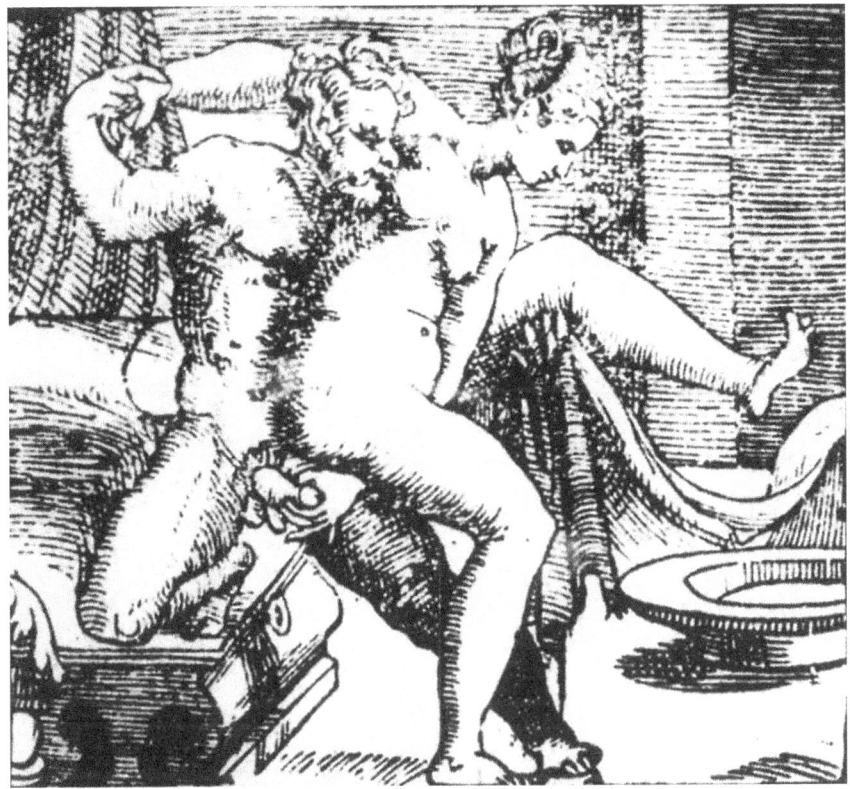

Fig. 3.6. *I modi*, position 7. Sixteenth-century woodcut after Giulio Romano.

ance with Giulio's pictures and Aretino's verses contributed to Leontes' self-deluding ekphrases in Act 1, Scene 2. This helps to account for the concrete nature of the lustful gestures he projects upon the couple, which—reinforcing the overheard language of their dialogue and the geminal phantasmata[36] that already contaminate their words—function as a further overlay on the actual images he sees to expedite his plot against the life of Polixenes later in the scene; the brutal casting-off of his newborn daughter in Act 2; and his ruthless prosecution of Hermione, until she apparently faints away dead in open court, in Act 3. If that is the case, then Giulio Romano was actively contributing to the language and action of *The Winter's Tale*—not just as the alleged creator of a lifelike statue to be introduced in the fifth act, but quite early in the play, as the author of obscene pictures that inform the erotic fantasies of its protagonist. Many in his audiences may have experienced an "Aha!" moment at the mention of his name in 5.2.[37]

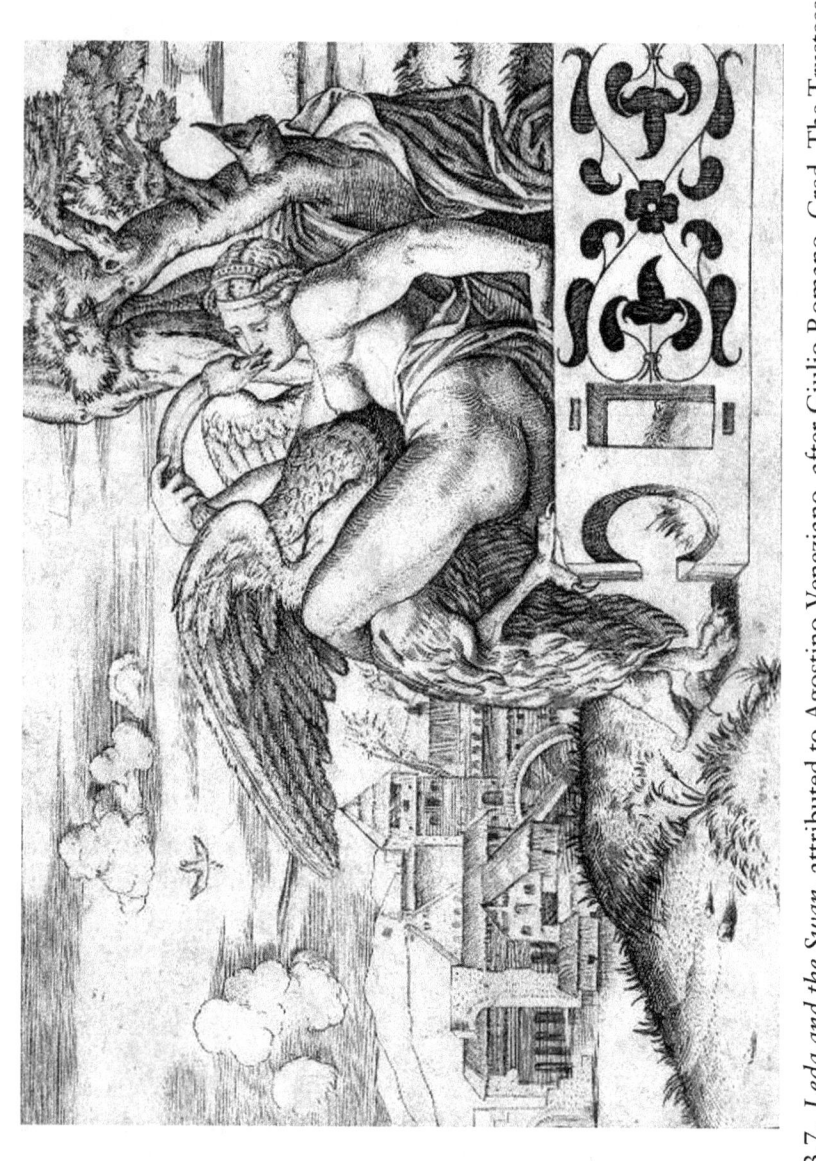

Fig. 3.7. *Leda and the Swan*, attributed to Agostino Veneziano, after Giulio Romano. Cred. The Trustees of the British Museum.

But this begs a question that we have not yet addressed. It is one thing to argue that *Shakespeare* was familiar with *I modi*. Is there any textual support for the hypothesis that *Leontes* has pored over Giulio's pictures?[38] For this we must look to the curious exchange between the king and Camillo later in the scene, just before he piles up those damning images of his wife and friend quoted earlier. It occurs when Camillo explains why he believes Polixenes has agreed to stay longer in Sicilia at Hermione's request:

> *Camillo*: To satisfy your highness, and the entreaties
> Of our most gracious mistress.
> *Leontes*:   Satisfy?
> Th' entreaties of your mistress? Satisfy?
> Let that suffice. I have trusted, thee, Camillo,
> With all the nearest things to my heart, as well
> My chamber-counsels, wherein, priest-like, thou
> Hast cleansed my bosom; aye, from thee departed
> Thy penitent reformed. But we have been
> Deceived in thy integrity, deceived
> In that which seems so. (1.2.230–9)

Othello-like, Leontes starts at the word "satisfy," hearing in it Hermione's longing for sexual pleasure.[39] And that leads him to recall intimate thoughts or acts that he has shared with Camillo, who seems to have served him in the role of father confessor as well as political counselor, *cleansing* and *reforming* him, and leading him to *penitence*. For what offenses did he have to repent? It is far more hazardous, I realize, to attempt to infer the reading habits of a *dramatis persona-cum-character* than those of his dramatist; nevertheless, Shakespeare's words indicate that there is a guilty back-story to Leontes that is hinted at just at the time that his imagination is flooded with "dirty pictures" of his own or of Giulio's devising. This makes those words worth adding to our circumstantial evidence. Vasari, after all, had reported that "some of these sheets were found in places where they were least expected." In this instance, the king's privy chamber?

If this is an acceptable reading of the etiology of Leontes' lewd descriptions of the behavior of his wife and old friend, it greatly enriches our sense of Shakespeare as bodger. It is one thing to bodge up a blank verse (or a passage of prose) from someone's literary work and quite another to bodge a visual work of art into your text through ekphrasis. In the first case, you are writing a play and reading another's material to "see" how it might enrich your own work, then stitching it in with appropriate changes—as when Greene's Foist in St. Paul's becomes Autolycus. You are operating in the same medium, and changing words, setting, and action to suit your purposes. In the second case, you are engaged in an intermedial transaction. You have seen Giulio's pictures of *I modi*, explicated by Aretino, and silently grafted these images into your text to serve as a pair of lenses through which Leontes views the scene in his own court. Though its function in character portrayal is not different in effect from Romeo's Petrarchan projections upon the reviving Juliet, its more arcane origin introduces a degree of subtlety that we and its original audiences might not have appreciated until Giulio's name is announced in the fifth act. The same can be said of the major ekphrasis that we encounter in the next section.

Whether my larger argument passes the touchstone of probability must be judged by the reader. Not least of the challenges in tracking the association is the fact that picture and verse tend to be conflated in contemporary English references to *I modi*. As Ian Frederick Moulton observes, "While the existence of the sonnets and engravings was well known in Elizabethan London, there is little proof that any English person owned or had even seen a copy. Thus the notion that Aretino was the artist as well as author of the volume circulated widely."[40] Talvacchia, however, argues that when Leontes marvels at how Hermione's statue exhibits "her natural posture" (5.3.23), Shakespeare deliberately uses the English singular form of *I modi* to "convey erotic longing. The figure's stance is itself alluring, so that it recalls to Leontes the early days of the couple's love: 'O, thus she stood . . . when first I wooed her!'" (5.3.34–6).[41] In this way, she suggests, Shakespeare brings the name "Julio Romano" into dialogue with Aretino's "postures." In her reading, the Giulian subtext of Act 1, Scene 2 for which I have been arguing comes to the surface as Leontes responds ardently to the apparently Giulian statue of Act 5, Scene 3.[42]

III

But now I wish to return to that crossroads and pursue the path more sacred. There is a psycholinguistic phenomenon in *The Winter's Tale* that is placed in deep relief by the invocation of "that rare Italian master" in Act 5. As we saw in the two previous chapters, it is the play's recurrent rhetoric of visual representation. By this phrase I mean that Shakespeare's language thematizes representation, often using terms drawn from the visual arts to describe a natural phenomenon (image, copy, print); it displays the act of representation, exhibiting both an object and its refashioning by someone ("kissing with inside lip" etc.); and it frequently employs, in a strict and a liberal sense, the rhetorical device of ekphrasis to "place before the eyes" an exotic location, a dream, or (as we have seen above) works of visual art.

The ekphrasis of location is expressed in an awed travelogue as Dion and Cleomenes return from their errand to Delphos with the oracle's response. They take turns praising the shrine of Apollo and its ambiance. "The climate's delicate, the air most sweet, / Fertile the isle," exclaims Cleomenes. Not to be outdone, Dion replies, "I shall report, / For most it caught me, the celestial habits— / Methinks I so should term them—and the reverence / Of the grave wearers" (3.1.1–6). Notice that this is carefully worded as a future "report"— a messenger speech in rehearsal, if you will. But the peculiar thing about their joint message is that it refrains from being specific. We don't know exactly what the "celestial habits" looked like, or what forms the reverent manner of the wearers assumed. This is because even as they praise the shrine the speakers admit the increasing ineffability of their experience. Its climax is stated outright by Cleomenes:

> But of all, the burst
> And ear-deafening voice o'th'oracle,
> Kin to Jove's thunder, so surprised my sense
> That I was nothing. (3.1.8–11)

Shakespeare is adapting the ekphrasis, with its emphasis on detailed description, to a situation in which the speaker is nearly incapable of describing what he has seen and heard because he has encountered the divine. Ultimately, his perceptive faculties have been overwhelmed and his subjectivity annihilated. To put it another way, he has temporarily lost any "subject position" from which he might interpret his experience, however idiosyncratically. It is a foretaste of the loss of critical faculty that is demanded at the end of the play when Paulina tells Leontes and the other bystanders in her chapel, who have been studying the lifelike qualities of the statue: "It is required / You do awake your faith" (5.3.94–5).

At another serious moment in the play where a *dramatis persona-*cum-character believes he has encountered a spiritual being, Shakespeare deploys an ekphrasis, but in this instance it is grotesque in its abundance of detail. His motive is perhaps to warn the audience to receive the description with a measure of skepticism. It is when Antigonus arrives on the coast of Bohemia bearing the babe wrapped in swaddling clothes and tells the infant that her mother had appeared to him on the previous night:

> To me comes a creature,
> Sometimes her head on one side, some another;
> I never saw a vessel of like sorrow,
> So filled and so becoming. In pure white robes,
> Like very sanctity, she did approach
> My cabin where I lay, thrice bowed before me,
> And, gasping to begin some speech, her eyes
> Became two spouts; the fury spent, anon
> Did this break from her: 'Good Antigonus,
> Since fate, against thy better disposition,
> Hath made thy person for the thrower-out
> Of my poor babe according to thine oath,
> Places remote enough are in Bohemia;
> There weep and leave it crying, and for the babe,
> Is counted lost for ever, Perdita
> I prithee call't. For this ungentle business
> Put on thee by my lord, thou ne'er shalt see
> Thy wife Paulina more.' And so, with shrieks,
> She melted into air. (3.3.18–36)

These are not the words of a man who has encountered the ineffable. The images are vivid, the actions are described with specificity, and the message is recalled at length. We hear of a female figure whose mourning is conveyed by a disconsolate wagging of her head from left to right and right to left, whose spotless robes made her seem to be the personification of sainthood or holiness itself, who out of nowhere in particular came to Antigonus's cabin ritually bowing her head three times, and who could not speak until she had turned into a virtual conduit, gushing water from her eyes until the "vessel" was empty.[43] This last detail flirts dangerously with Ovid's well-known description of the dying Pyramus who has plunged his sword into his body, from which "the spouting blood leaped high; just as when a pipe has broken in a weak spot in the lead and through the small hissing aperture sends spurting forth long streams of water, cleaving the air with its jets."[44] Robert Miola has noted that "Shakespeare imitates Ovid in his sudden shifts of style, particularly in the unpredictable change from high seriousness to bathetic humour."[45] Though Miola did not have this passage from *The Winter's Tale* in mind, the effect he describes fits its purportedly tragic description of the behavior of the apparition. After seriously counseling Antigonus to leave the lost babe crying and to call it Perdita, "for the babe / Is counted lost for ever," she informs him of his own fate and suddenly disappears, shrieking (3.3.31–6). While it is true that ghosts were thought to shriek (cf. 5.1.65–6), for "very sanctity" to exit shrieking smacks of bathos in the Ovidian manner.

Preceding his ekphrasis Antigonus had expressed Protestant skepticism that "the spirits o'th'dead / May walk again" (3.3.15–16). By the end of the description he has persuaded himself that they can. "Dreams are toys," he says dismissively, embracing the alternative idea that he has met a spiritual revenant: "Yet for this once, yea superstitiously, / I will be squared by this" (5.3.38–40). Unlike Hamlet, who had faced a similar ambiguity (*Ham.* 1.4.21–5), he then rationalizes the cause of the ghost's appearance: "I do believe / Hermione hath suffered death, and that / Apollo would—this being indeed the issue / Of King Polixenes—it should here be laid, / Either for life or death, upon the earth / Of its right father" (3.3.40–5). For his apostasy he is "torn to pieces with a bear" (5.2.62), following the most undignified exit in all of Shakespeare. It is an appropriate transition to the tragicomic tonic mingling we hear when the Shepherd and his son enter only moments later. Yet Shakespeare is doing something else as well. By means of Antigonus's vivid recollection of what he insists "was no slumber" but a "spirit of the dead," and his subsequent analysis of the significance of the visitation, Shakespeare is obliquely informing his audience that this was not an encounter with the supernatural. Antigonus has remained in full possession of his critical faculties. He leaves the scene not with Cleomenes' confession of egoistic loss ("I was nothing") but with a clear-eyed appraisal of his dire physical situation: "I am gone forever!" (3.3.57).[46]

Understanding Shakespeare's representation of these two meetings with divine and allegedly holy powers enables us to better understand the ekphrasis that turns up on our sacred way. It is heard in Act 5, Scene 2, just before the Third Gentleman's announcement of a statue "newly performed by that rare Italian master." As excitement quickens, first on the arrival of Florizel and Perdita, fleeing an irate Polixenes, determined to prevent the marriage of his son to a shepherd's daughter, then on the announcement that Polixenes himself has arrived in the city, accompanied by Camillo, and that they have apprehended the Shepherd and the Clown, Shakespeare makes a notable dramaturgic choice. He *shows* the sympathetic reception of the young couple in Leontes' court before Polixenes and his party appear and Perdita's true identity is revealed (5.1), and merely *describes* the reunion of Polixenes and Leontes and the revelation of Perdita's identity (5.2). This can be explained as an act of rhetorical economy, whereby Shakespeare reserves the audience's emotional energy for release in the final scene when the statue "comes to life." To fully appreciate the artfulness of Shakespeare's dramaturgic plan, however, we mustn't fail to notice the complex descriptive structure and style of Act 5, Scene 2, which is even more self-consciously "visual" than the first, dramatized episode, for Shakespeare has chosen to convey the scene of reunion and revelation ekphrastically—as a *painting*, a *dumb show*, and a *staged play*, described and eagerly discussed by a clutch of courtly connoisseurs.

When asked by Autolycus if he were present at this "relation," the First Gentleman says that he *was* there at the beginning, when the Shepherd explained how he had found the infant and opened the fardle containing tokens of its identity. But then, he admits, he had been commanded out of the room, and could only *see* what happened next:

> I make a broken delivery of the business; but the changes I perceived in the King and Camillo were very notes of admiration. They seemed almost with staring on one another to tear the cases of their eyes. There was speech in their dumbness, language in their very gesture; *they looked as they had heard of a world transformed, or one destroyed.* A notable passion of wonder appeared in them, but the wisest beholder that knew no more but seeing could not say if th'importance were joy or sorrow—but in the extremity of the one it must needs be. (5.2.9–19, italics mine)

The scene described puts one in mind of sixteenth-century paintings of such miraculous events as the Assumption of the Virgin or the Transfiguration of Christ—not only because of the arrested physical gestures of the participants but also because of its eschatological allusions. Despite the early iconoclasm of the English Reformation, paintings of such scenes were on display in the households of both Protestant and Catholic aristocracy and gentry from the middle of the sixteenth century—and increasingly so in the Jacobean and Caroline periods, when they became decorative objects in their own right—so references of this kind were not likely to be lost on audiences in 1610 and 1611.[47]

These become even more explicit when a Second Gentleman arrives to ask if it is true that the king has found his heir, and on his heels a Third Gentleman, Paulina's steward, confirms the rumor— "if ever truth were pregnant by circumstance" (5.2.30–1). At first he merely fills in those circumstances, directing their imaginations to translate sounds into sights: "That which you hear you'll swear you see, there is such unity in the proofs," then he goes on to enumerate those proofs—Hermione's mantle, her jewel, Antigonus's letters, the girl's resemblance to her dead mother, her noble demeanor. Then, pluming himself on having been an eyewitness, he asks the Second Gentleman if *he* saw the reunion of the two kings, and when answered in the negative, he boasts:

> Then you have lost a sight which was to be seen, cannot be spoken of. There might you have beheld one joy crown another so and in such manner that it seemed sorrow wept to take leave of them, for their joy waded in tears. There was casting up of eyes, holding up of hands, and with countenance of such distraction that they were to be known by garment, not by favour. (5.3.42–9)

The Third Gentleman has done the First one better. He picturesquely commingles the contrary emotions (which the First had insisted must be one or the other), even as he emphasizes the incapacity of mere words to convey the intensity of the pathos of the scene—invoking the modesty topos in a *paragone* of painter and poet. As we shall see, Shakespeare seems to be revisiting the problematic issue of representing the hieratic that was voiced by Cleon and Diomedes earlier in the play, and resolves it this time by referring the auditor to conventional pictorial gestures with which he or she would be familiar.

The ekphrastic intention of the Third Gentleman's report becomes virtually palpable when he remarks to his companions,

> *One of the prettiest touches of all*, and that which angled for mine eyes—caught the water, though not the fish—was when at the relation of the Queen's death, with the manner how she came to't bravely confessed and lamented by the King, how attentiveness wounded his daughter; till from one sign of dolour to another, she did, with an "Alas!", I would fain say bleed tears, for I am sure I wept blood. Who was most marble there changed colour. Some swooned, all sorrowed; if all the world could have seen't, the woe would have been universal. (5.3.80–90, italics mine)[48]

The aestheticism that has motivated the Gentlemen's descriptions all along is fully evident in the Third Gentleman's reference to "one of the prettiest touches of all," as though he were commending an artist's rendering of the event, and he records his own emotional response to it twice, unable to suppress a self-indulgent turn of wit. But notice that the object described *is* and *is not* a painting. Nor is it any longer even a dumb show. For it contains not only temporality and movement, but vocality: "Alas!" and, earlier, "O, thy mother, thy mother!" In its capacity to incorporate these kinetic and aural elements, ekphrasis comes very close to performance itself, though its images are experienced only in the mind's eye. Through its *energeia* and quotation, the *paragone* of poet and painter thematized by the Third Gentleman turns out to be not a binary contest but a dialectical one, passing via ekphrastic description to celebrate the medium that combines word, image, motion, and temporality: staged drama. Fittingly. For immediately following this passage is the inquiry as to what the royal families did next, and the Third Gentleman's answer. They've gone to see Giulio Romano's statue, but they actually participate in a theater of resurrection.

Now why is Giulio to be found along this ekphrastic path? Because its language of religious miracle points to the creator of *I modi*. The most celebrated Renaissance rendering of the biblical episode known as the Transfiguration of Christ—recorded in Matthew, Mark, and Luke—was painted by Raphael of Urbino (Fig. 3.8). It was his last commission. Some thirty years after the fact Vasari writes that Raphael had completed it with his own hand before his death, but recent art historians have attributed much of the work in the lower right half of the painting—showing an incident immediately following in all three Gospels, in which a possessed boy is brought by his father to be cured by Jesus's disciples—to Giulio Romano, who had prepared figure studies for the painting.[49] The style of the upper half, where Christ appears in radiance flanked by Elijah and Moses, floating above the startled apostles Peter, James, and John, who are shielding their eyes from the dazzling hieratic apparition,[50] is very different from the mannerist drama of the lower half, where eyes indeed bulge out of sockets, expressions of wonder are seen, and hands stretch in many directions. In fact, three of them point to the scene above, where, in Matthew, God has declared, "This is my beloved Son, in whom I am well pleased; hear ye him" (17: 5). It is a strange painting. In the Gospels the two episodes are temporally distinct, but Raphael's unique synchronic composition stresses the connection between the illness and the cure.[51] This, as Jesus explains to the perplexed disciples who could not heal the boy, is faith: "If ye have faith as a grain of mustard seed, ye shall say unto this mountain, Remove hence to yonder place; and it shall remove: and nothing shall be impossible to you" (17: 20). The thematic relation between the painting and the climax of the play is clear enough—"I'll make the statue move indeed," says Paulina to Leontes, who imagines he

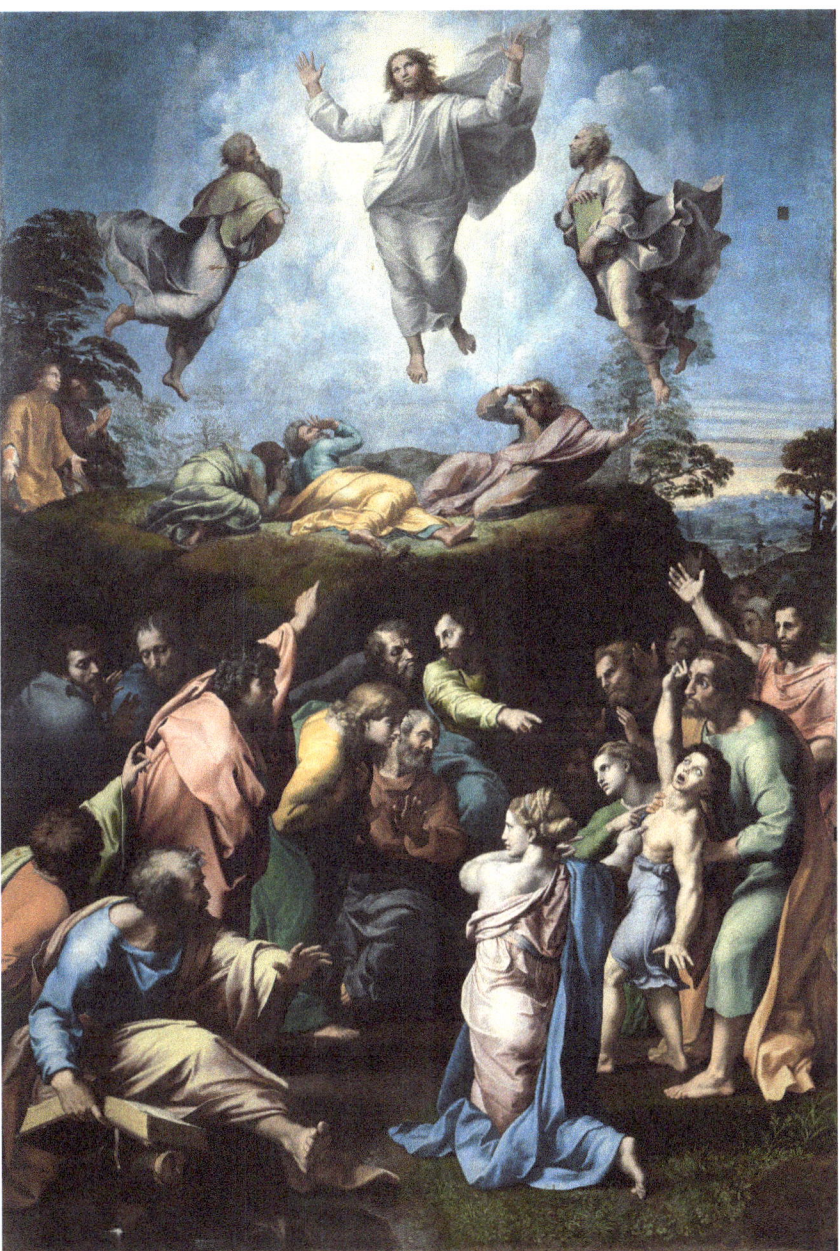

Fig. 3.8. Raphael of Urbino, *The Transfiguration of Christ.*
Copyright Governate of the Vatican City State-Directorate of the
Vatican Museums.

sees motion in its eyes and blood in its veins: "It is required / You do awake your faith" (5.3.88, 94–5). And when Leontes yields his agency to Paulina's priestly authority, the statue does remove: it descends from its pedestal and embraces him.

But more than theme connects play and painting. As Christian K. Kleinbub has persuasively argued, Raphael juxtaposes two contrasting modes of vision in the condensed narrative of *The Transfiguration*—fleshly and spiritual seeing.[52] There is even a suggestion of that intermediate mode, the imaginative vision of the *phantasia*. In the lower half of the painting, showing the possessed boy and his family—and the disciples left behind when Jesus climbed to the summit of Mt. Tabor with Peter, John, and James—we find a striking contrast in the treatment of the figures' eyes. On the right-hand side, the eyes of the party seeking help are wide open, with the exception of one woman in the shadows behind the father's head, who seems absorbed in prayer. The boy's and the father's eyes do indeed bulge from their sockets—the boy's wildly pointing in opposite directions, the father's staring straight ahead at the apostles. In the background at far right, a man dressed in red holds up his right arm, the fingers of his hand spread apart in an attitude of extreme consternation. The diagonal of his arm leads the viewer's eye to the scene at the top of the mountain, but the man himself seems unaware of what is happening there. In the foreground of the left-hand side of the painting, however, an apostle also dressed in red answers his gesture by deliberately pointing with his left hand to the Transfiguration above, yet his eyes are closed and his right hand rests on his breast.[53] Just to his right on the picture plane, a young apostle leans sympathetically toward the family. His eyes seem open, but both hands rest on his breast as if to say that his vision lies in his heart, and two other figures behind the red-robed disciple cast their eyes downward in contemplation. The contrast is not schematic, but, as Kleinbub argues, it does appear to draw upon a venerable Christian tradition expounded by Augustine and Thomas Aquinas, among others, in which the vision of the faithful must not remain fixed on visible objects but must read through those objects to the spiritual content within by means of the mixed mode of the *phantasia*—physical insofar that it "sees" by means of images; spiritual in that it partakes of the intellect, which can contemplate invisible reality.[54] Purely spiritual, beatific vision is experienced by the intellect alone, through faith, and is represented by Christ in the upper half of the painting. Ironically, the figure whose eyes most resemble those of the lunatic boy is that of the transfigured Christ: his eyes roll upward, no longer focused on the physical world, but gaze upon the invisible deity, who declares, "This is my beloved son, in whom I am well pleased." The boy, however, still looks downward with his left eye, as though drawn to earth by his demonic possessor.[55]

Physical, imaginative, spiritual vision. The process is discernible in the last scene of *The Winter's Tale*, as Leontes, Polixenes, Perdita, and the others stand in admiration before the alleged workmanship of Giulio Romano, examine its surface in detail, attempt to touch it, "imagine" that the statue breathes, moves its eyes, and that blood courses through its marbled veins—then yield to Paulina's insistence that they either presently quit the chapel or awake their faith and stand still, thus imitating the synchronic outward-to-inward narrative represented in the painting.[56]

IV

But could Shakespeare have known of Giulio's putative role in painting "a world transformed, or one destroyed"? To begin answering this question it is required not that we awake our faith but that we take on the difficult task of determining whether a copy of the work existed in England when Shakespeare was composing *The Winter's Tale*, and whether it was possible for him to have seen it and remembered it.

In the chapel of the College of God's Gift in Dulwich, founded by Edward Alleyn in 1619, there hangs a nearly full-sized copy of Raphael's *Transfiguration*.[57] There is no evidence that it was ever owned by Alleyn, but it was evidently well known among art collectors in the eighteenth century. It was given to Dulwich Chapel in 1796 by Thomas Mills of Great Saxham Hall in Suffolk, who had purchased it for £42 at a Christie's auction in March of that year, its last owner being Benjamin Vandergucht.[58] Vandergucht was the third descendant of an Anglo-Flemish family of London artists and art dealers, a Royal Academician, and an esteemed collector and connoisseur. The preface to Christie's catalogue praises him as a man concerning "whose Taste and Judgement the Public has had sufficient Testimonials."[59] In Lot 92 of the catalogue the description of his painting echoes that of the man:

> RAFFAELLO SANTI. The Transfiguration. The original has ever been the admiration of all men of taste and judgment, admitted as the finest of all his works; more need not be said in the illustration. This

copy, *which is visibly the hand of Julio Romano*, has been judged to rival if not excel even the original in point of spirit and expression; such a masterly picture by his best scholar becomes a very valuable acquisition.[60]

Fifty-nine years earlier, we find similar language, evidently describing the same painting, in a 1737 auction catalogue of the collections of Sir Thomas Sebright, Bart. and Thomas Sclater-Bacon, Esq.—Christopher Cock of Covent Garden, auctioneer. After listing for sale the works of Claude Lorrain, Titian, and Nicholas Poussin, among others, the advertising copy on the cover adds in a separate paragraph: "Particularly that celebrated Picture the Transfiguration by *Julio Romano*, after Raphael."[61] It is shown as Lot 101 of the second day's sale on May 18, where it is described as "The Transfiguration, after *Raphael*, a most Capital Picture."[62] In the eighteenth century, it seems, the attribution of this copy of Raphael's painting was secure. Whether or not it is truly from the hand of Giulio is less important for our purposes than the fact that it was believed to be, and if its reputation was known in England in the earlier eighteenth century, it might have been known in England in the seventeenth century. The question, however, is whether that reputation can be traced back to the time of Shakespeare. This is a more difficult matter.

A copy of Raphael's *Transfiguration* was among the paintings in the storied collection of Charles I. From there it may have passed into the collection of Sclater-Bacon, who was an MP from Cambridge during the last fourteen years of his life, and a connoisseur of prints and drawings as well as a serious book collector. His prints and drawings were auctioned by Cock in February of 1737 and included "The Works of Raphael, Julio Romano, Ann. Carracci, Titian, Paul Veronese" and other masters.[63] His considerable library, auctioned by Cock the following March, included Vitruvius's *De architectura* translated into French and an Italian edition of Palladio's *L'architettura*. On the other hand, the "Julio" copy of the *Transfiguration* may have passed into the possession of the Sebright family, for there exists in the British Library an early eighteenth-century copy of the Parliamentary inventories and evaluations made for the sale of "The Late King's Goods" in 1651–53, which was in the Sebrights' possession. They may have acquired it as documentary evidence of the provenance of their painting.[64] This manuscript records that "The Transfiguracon . . . after Raphael" was "sold" to Major Edward Bass. Bass served as the leader of three

Dividends—those syndicates of creditors who accepted goods in lieu of cash as payment of debts owed them by the Crown. He was also an informer against those who had acquired royal goods illegally.[65] He purchased this painting for £15—a low sum when compared to what he paid for Raphael's *St. George*, whose value is shown as £150, perhaps because at that time a copy of a masterpiece, even a good one, had not acquired the cachet it possessed in the eighteenth century.[66] However, a self-portrait by Rubens' own hand was appraised at only £16, and a *Mary Magdalen* by Titian went for just £25.8s.[67]

Two questions follow: is this painting the copy that descended to Dulwich College Chapel and, if so, how did King Charles acquire it in the first place? The answer to the first question remains uncertain in the absence of direct evidence of when, how, and from whom either Sclater-Bacon or Sebright came into possession of the work.[68] The answer to the second is problematic because of conflicting accounts of its provenance. In the year 1639, Abraham van der Doort, the beleaguered Keeper of the Cabinet Room at St. James's Palace, began to assemble an inventory of the king's collections. He lists "a little alter peece being the assention of Christ wth manie Appostles by, and one possessed youth, the Oridginall being an alter Peece in a Church at Roome done by Rafell Urbin." In the margin he notes, "This peece was given to the king by my Lord Lumley in Jorney into the North."[69] Oliver Millar, the modern editor of the catalogue, believed this donor was Richard, First Viscount Lumley, and conjectured that Charles acquired the painting during a journey to Scotland in 1633.[70] More recently Kathryn Barron, studying the Lumley family inventories, has suggested that the Lord Lumley referred to is actually John, Lord Lumley, who died in 1609, when Charles was too young to be given the painting, and that the king referred to is James I, who visited Lumley Castle on his journey to London in 1603.[71] Whichever Lumley was the donor, the epithet "little" must give us pause, though in van der Doort's uncertain English the word may simply have signified "reduced in size."[72]

There is, however, a later, variant manuscript of van der Doort's inventory in the National Art Library at the Victoria and Albert Museum with a different description and attribution. Here, without indicating size, the painting is listed more familiarly as follows: "A peece wherin is the Ascension and the young man possessed with an—evill spirit brought to the Apostles this sett in a gilt frame, and given by my Lord of Exeter."[73] This V&A manuscript is described as "A Catalogue of the works of art in the Long Gallery, Chair

Room and Cabinet Room . . . at Whitehall and . . . of pictures in the Gallery at St James's Palace . . . Written in a contemporary hand, not to be identified with any of the scribes of Van der Doort's MSS."[74] Observes Millar: "It will be seen at a glance that the entries are much briefer and less elaborate than those compiled by Van der Doort, but the occasional changes in attribution, the different wording of the descriptions, the appearance of a few works of art that do not seem to be recorded by Van der Doort . . . render the manuscript an important addendum to Van der Doort's catalogue." He then adds, "The manuscript seems to have been written by an Englishman, possibly with access to Van der Doort's catalogue, although not entirely dependent on it, and probably by one of the members of the King's circle."[75] Van der Doort, a Dutchman whose command of English was idiosyncratic at best, was a long-time royal servant. He had been hired by Prince Henry in 1611 as Keeper of his new Cabinet, designed by Inigo Jones, and remained after Henry's death as Keeper of Prince—later King—Charles's royal collection. At this point in his tenure, van der Doort's records may not be entirely reliable, for his position was being undermined by courtiers close to Charles I, whom he suspected of preventing him from doing his job properly and of purloining objects under his care. His obsessive insecurity evidently led him to hang himself in 1640.[76]

We are left, then, with four "documented" donors of Charles I's copy of *The Transfiguration*: (1) Richard Lumley, Viscount of Waterford (1589–1661); (2) his older cousin, Baron John Lumley (1533–1609), a great collector of books and works of art; (3) Thomas Cecil, elder son of William Cecil, Queen Elizabeth's Lord Burghley, who became the second Lord Burghley and first Lord Exeter (1542–1623); and (4) his son William Cecil, third Lord Burghley and second Lord Exeter (1566–1640). The first of these, Richard Lumley, is not known to have been an art collector, but he did inherit Lumley Castle, the family seat in Durham, where James I stopped to visit John Lumley on his journey south to his coronation in April 1603. John Lumley was a well-known art and book collector. The Lumleys were an old Catholic family, and John was son-in-law and heir to the Catholic courtier and sympathizer Henry Fitzalan, the 12th Earl of Arundel. (Both were involved in the Ridolfi plot of 1571.) Not surprisingly, the Lumley inventory of 1590 reveals an interest in religious art and includes "A Speciall picture of Christ cast in mould by Raphael de Urbino, brought into England from Rome by Cardynall Poole." A second entry includes a painting "Of Raphael de Urbino, the great paynter," but does not otherwise identify the work.[77] The

1609 inventory of Lumley Castle lists only "Raphael Orbines his picture."[78]

As to the 1st Earl of Exeter, Thomas Cecil, there is no evidence that he had any interest in art, though he did travel to Italy in his early years. His elder son William, however, 2nd Earl of Exeter, was an avid continental traveler who made at least four trips to Rome between 1586 and 1609, and became something of a connoisseur of Italian art. On one occasion he stayed with Cardinal Alessandro Farnese, the notable collector of antiquities whose galleries included paintings by Raphael and Titian. On a subsequent trip William was entertained by Virginio Orsini, Duke of Bracciano, who was feasted in return by Thomas Cecil when visiting London on January 8, 1601.[79] During that visit, Orsini attended the queen several times and was entertained at court on Twelfth Night by a performance of the Lord Chamberlain's Men. It was argued many years ago by Leslie Hotson that the play he saw there was *Twelfth Night*, in keeping with the occasion, and that he was the namesake of Shakespeare's Orsino—a perhaps dubious honor regarding which subsequent editors have registered skepticism.[80] If, however, the Chamberlain's Men also performed at Thomas Cecil's house at Wimbledon or at Exeter House on the Strand during the same season, that would have also provided a possible link between the younger William Cecil and Shakespeare. Though in the current state of our knowledge hard evidence is lacking, Lord John Lumley and the second Lord Exeter seem to have the greater claims to be the donor of Charles I's copy of *The Transfiguration*.[81]

Now 1601 is somewhat early for details of the painting to be readily called to mind while Shakespeare was composing *The Winter's Tale*, and one might expect that it would take more than a single viewing for it to live in his memory. So it also makes sense to look to the period of 1608–11, when Shakespeare's company performed at court at least thirty-six times[82] and yet another person may have been involved in the transactions. Prince Henry was forming his own picture collection at St. James's Palace in the years just preceding his early death and was the heir to the bulk of John Lumley's library when Lumley died in April of 1609.[83] It has been long recognized that *The Winter's Tale* refers to Jonson and Jones's investiture masque *Oberon*, featuring the prince and presented to the king on January 1, 1611 in the Banqueting House at Whitehall. In the fourth act a Servant, introducing twelve dancing men, says, "One three of them by their own report, sir, hath danced before the King" (4.4.332–3). The Exchequer records indicate £15 paid to "players imployed in the maske,"[84] and they probably were the King's Men. So the performance spaces at Whitehall, Richmond, and St. James's Palace—the latter two residences of the Prince—are likely to have been familiar venues to Shakespeare. Was there a copy of Raphael's *Transfiguration* in one of the royal collections? Were this the case, the ekphrases in Act 5, Scene 2 of *The Winter's Tale* would have had a special resonance for the audience when it was performed at court. To the question posed at the beginning of this section—could Shakespeare have known of Giulio's putative role in painting "a world transformed, or one destroyed"?—we can therefore offer a provisional answer: "Yes."

Notes

1. *The Winter's Tale*, First Folio, TLN 3102–3111. In designating the Gentlemen by number, I depart from Pitcher and follow the Folio's Gent. 1, Gent. 2, Gent. 3.
2. Richard Meek cites further examples of generic references to painting and sculpture in *Venus and Adonis, The Rape of Lucrece, Hamlet*, and the sonnets (*Narrating the Visual in Shakespeare*). The most nuanced account of Shakespeare's interest in the visual arts is provided by Keir Elam, who, in analyses of *The Taming of the Shrew, The Merchant of Venice, Hamlet*, and *Twelfth Night*, persuasively demonstrates "the extraordinary iconographic richness and density of Shakespeare's language, replete as it is with references to visual representation of all kinds." *Shakespeare's Pictures: Visual Objects in the Drama* (London: Bloomsbury, 2017), p. 41.
3. I include here the last two lines of the reported epitaph omitted in n. 43 of Chapter 2: ROMANUS MORIENS SECUM TRES JULIUS ARTEIS / ABSTULIT (HAUD MIRUM): QUATTUOR UNUS ERAT. Vasari, *Le vite*, vol. 2, p. 837. Under the name "Giulio Romano" at the beginning of his *Vita* are the words "Pittore et architetto"; the epitaph, however, suggests that the third art with which Giulio absconded was sculpture, as befitting the title of Vasari's work. Vasari actually writes that Giulio designed sculpture, specifying two caryatids for a building near the Old Mint in Rome (ibid. p. 831). But the language of the epitaph alone suggests how Giulio, acclaimed for his painting and architecture, could have become the sculptor of Shakespeare's play.
4. There is no evidence that Shakespeare ever traveled to Italy and saw Giulio's tomb, so textual or verbal reports must be hypothesized. Oxfordians have argued that Edward de Vere, 17th Earl of Oxford, their "Shakespeare," did, which would account for so many references in the plays to places in northern Italy. See, e.g., John Hamill, "The

Ten Restless Ghosts of Mantua: Shakespeare's Specter Lingers over the Italian City," *Shakespeare Oxford Newsletter* 39.3 (2003): 1, 12–16. Mantua, however, is not among the known cities he visited.

5. *Lives of the Most Eminent Painters, Sculptors, and Architects by Giorgio Vasari*, trans. Gaston du C. de Vere, 10 vols. (London: Medici Society, 1912–14), vol. 3, p. 149, slightly modified. The 1568 edition of *Le vite* omits the epitaph.

6. For details of Giulio's professional emphasis on *disegna*, *schizzo*, *studio*, and *modello*—the early stages in the development of a commission, as opposed to its "performance" or completion, which was usually carried out by his assistants—see Janet Cox-Rearick, ed., *Giulio Romano, Master Designer* (New York: Hunter College of the City University of New York, 1999), pp. 17–24.

7. De Vere, vol. 3, pp. 152, 155, 158, 160. The same examples are present in the shorter 1550 edition, but are not so detailed, nor is their emphasis on Giulio's illusionism as fully articulated.

8. In the context of imitation theory, these are yet further examples of the techniques prescribed by Roger Ascham, as we observed in Chapter 1.

9. Jones heavily annotated Vasari's chapter on Giulio, and seems to have used it as a guide when he visited the Palazzo Te during his second trip to Italy in 1613–14. See Jeremy Wood, "Taste and Connoisseurship at the Court of Charles I: Inigo Jones and the Work of Giulio Romano," in *The Stuart Courts*, ed. Eveline Cruickshanks (Stroud: Sutton Publishing, 2000), pp. 118–40.

10. Mario Praz, "Shakespeare's Italy," in *The Flaming Heart: Essays on Crashaw, Machiavelli, and Other Studies of the Relations between Italian and English Literature from Chaucer to T. S. Eliot* (New York: Norton Library, 1973; rpt. of 1958 original), p. 164.

11. Keir Elam, "'At the cubiculo': Shakespeare's Problems with Italian Language and Culture," in *Italian Culture in the Drama of Shakespeare and his Contemporaries*, ed. M. Marrapodi (Burlington, VT: Ashgate, 2007), p. 100. Among many other likely inspirations Shakespeare may have found in Florio, *Second Frutes* contains a scene of travel advice between an older man and a younger that strongly resembles Polonius's advice to the departing Laertes.

12. Lawrence, *"Who the devil"*.

13. Cf. *Antonio and Mellida*, 2.1.200; 3.2.178–9, 181–2, 222, 265–6; 4.1.191–208. The last passage is a long, excited dialogue between Antonio and Mellida, reunited after losing each other a second time, and their lapse into Italian is remarked by Antonio's page—"I think confusion of Babel is fall'n upon these lovers, that they change their language" (4.1.219–27)—who then defers to the audience's judgment of its appropriateness. Citations are to G. K. Hunter's edition (Lincoln: University of Nebraska Press, 1965).

14. Lawrence, *"Who the devil"*, p. 123, n. 21.

15. Charlotte Carmichael Stopes, *The Life of Henry, Third Earl of Southampton, Shakepeare's Patron* (Cambridge: Cambridge University Press, 1922); Frances A. Yates, *John Florio: The Life of an Italian in Shakespeare's England* (Cambridge: Cambridge University Press, 1934); G. P. V. Akrigg, *Shakespeare and the Earl of Southampton* (London: Hamish Hamilton, 1968).

16. Lawrence's argument does not obviate the possibility that Shakespeare used other sources as well, including Alexander Sylvayn's *Orator*, trans. Lazarus Piot, as Quentin Skinner suggests in *Forensic Shakespeare* (Oxford: Oxford University Press, 2014), pp. 145–6.

17. See Louise George Clubb, *Pollastra and the Origins of "Twelfth Night"* (Burlington, VT: Ashgate, 2010), pp. 54–5.

18. On the former, see Pietro Aretino's letters on Titian, which circulated in sixteenth-century England; the second volume of the *Lettere* was dedicated to Henry VIII. On Raphael, see Vasari's report of the epitaph written by Pietro Bembo, which culminates in this passage: ILLE HIC EST RAPHAEL,TIMVIT QUO SOSPITE VINCI / RERUM MAGNA PARENS, ET MORIENTE MORI: "This is that Raphael, by whom in health the Great Mother of All Things feared defeat / And in whose death did fear herself to die" (1550, vol. 2, p. 641).

19. Vasari reports that within a few years Giulio separated himself from Gianfrancesco in order to perform work in his own style (1550, vol. 2, p. 831).

20. De Vere, vol. 3, pp. 104–5.

21. See Manfredo Tafuri, "Giulio Romano: linguaggio, mentalita, committenti," in *Giulio Romano: Saggi di Ernst H. Gombrich, Manfredo Tafuri, Sylvia Ferino Pagden, Christoph L. Frommel, Konrad Oberhuber, Amedeo Belluzzi e Kurt W. Forster, Howard Burns* (Milan: Electa, 1989), p. 18.

22. For the probable sequence of events, the cultural context, and the motives behind the conception, execution, and consequences of publishing Giulio's drawings as engravings, see Richard Aste, "Giulio Romano as Designer of Erotica: *I modi*, 1524–25," in *Giulio Romano, Master Designer*, pp. 44–53; Tafuri, "Giulio Romano"; Bette Talvacchia, *Taking Positions: On the Erotic in Renaissance Culture* (Princeton: Princeton University Press, 1999); Ian Frederick Moulton, *Before Pornography: Erotic Writing in Early Modern England* (Oxford: Oxford University Press, 2000); Waddington, *Aretino's Satyr*.

23. Bette Talvacchia, "That Rare Italian Master and the Posture of Hermione in *The Winter's Tale*," *Literature, Interpretation, Theory* 3 (1992): 170.

24. *Timber: or, Discoveries*, in *Ben Jonson*, vol. 8, pp. 583–4.

25. See *Volpone*, 3.4.96–7, and *The Alchemist*, 2.2.42–5, in *Ben Jonson*, vol. 5. Corvino's threat to Celia in *Volpone* also alludes to *I modi* and Aretino's emphasis on buggery in the *sonetti*: "And now I think on't,

I will keep thee backwards: / Thy lodging shall be backwards, thy walks backwards, / Thy prospect—all be backwards; and no pleasure, / That thou shalt know, but backwards" (2.5.58–61). Later he reassures her that "to sleep by" Volpone is no sin because he is not some "hot Tuscane blood / That had read Aretine, / Conn'd all his printes" and "Knew every quirke in lust's labyrinth" (3.7.60–2). See also Greene, *The Black Book's Messenger* (1592); Nashe, *Christ's Tears Over Jerusalem* (1593); Donne, *Ignatius His Conclave* (1611); and Middleton, *A Game at Chess* (1624), as discussed by Elam in *Shakespeare's Pictures*, pp. 130–5. For a wide-ranging analysis of "Italian sex" in the drama of the period, with reference to *I modi*, see Celia R. Daileader, "Back Door Sex: Renaissance Gynosodomy, Aretino, and the Exotic," *ELH* 69.2 (2002): 303–34.

26. *Supposes*, Prol. 11–13, in *Drama of the English Renaissance*, ed. Fraser and Rabkin, vol. 1; *The Alchemist*, 2.2.41–5.

27. Elam, *Shakespeare's Pictures*, p. 128; the translation is Elam's, modified by me. See also James G. Turner's extraordinary study, *Eros Visible: Art, Sexuality and Antiquity in Renaissance Italy* (New Haven and London: Yale University Press, 2017), pp. 68–9. The allusion to *I modi* in the later version of *I suppositi* (pub. 1551) and the reference to "wanton pictures" in the Induction to *The Taming of the Shrew* support Lawrence's argument that Shakespeare often consulted more than one version of his source, as he is also likely to have done with Vasari's *Vite*.

28. A reference to *I modi* in *The New Metamorphosis* by "J. M. Gent" (c. 1600) indicates that the book in a woodcut edition was available at bookstalls in London at the time (Elam, *Shakespeare's Pictures*, p. 131).

29. "Ahi ribalda, ahi ribaldo, in terra, & in letto / Io ti veggio puttana, è t' apparecchia / Ch'io ti rompa due costole del petto." Aretino, Sonnet 11, in Talvacchia, *Taking Positions*, p. 215, translation mine; subsequent translations of Aretino are Talvacchia's, with occasional emendation by me.

30. Tafuri, "Giulio Romano," p. 15, translation mine.

31. *Taking Positions*, p. 92.

32. Turner brilliantly connects this outburst with the lively pictorial tradition of the adultery of Mars and Venus, which had recently been represented by Baldassare Peruzzi at the Villa Chigi, where Giulio worked as Raphael's assistant in decorating the interior (*Eros Visible*, pp. 112–21). The exchange continues: "And you can't make love to Venus blindly, with a lot of haste and little discernment," to which the man replies: "I am not Mars, I am Hercole Rangone, and I am screwing you, who are Angela Greca" (Talvacchia, *Taking Positions*, p. 217). Rangone is a soldier serving the Este family and Greca a well-known Roman courtesan. He wants none of her mythologizing.

33. The images shown are sixteenth-century woodcuts (except for the engraving of position 11) after Marcantonio Raimondi after Giulio Romano and the nineteenth-century drawing of position 1 by Jean-Frédéric Maximilien de Waldeck, after Marcantonio Raimondi.

34. Recollection of this Giulio image may have been provoked by Hermione's own language earlier in the scene (1.2.94–6). There is a further animalistic Giulian allusion at 1.2.181–4, as Leontes walks off with Mamillius and glances back at Hermione and Polixenes: "Go to, go to! / How she holds up the neb, the bill to him, / And arms herself with the boldness of a wife / To her allowing husband." Suddenly Hermione is a bird nuzzling her mate with her beak. Where did this come from? Giulio had produced a *disegno a stampa* of Leda and the Swan, engraved by Agostino Veneziano, in which Jupiter-as-swan stands between Leda's naked, embracing legs as she clutches his arched neck with her right hand, supporting herself with her left arm, and he enters his upper beak into her mouth, holding her lower lip down with his lower beak. It is a weird transposition, in which the woman raped is seen as provoking and enjoying the assault. Turner suggests that this engraving may have been included among the original *Modi* (*Eros Visible*, pp. 377–8). See Fig. 3.7.

35. See, e.g., John Marston, *The Malcontent*, 1.5.20–50, 1.7.16–49, 3.2.25–51; Thomas Middleton, *The Revenger's Tragedy*, 1.2.180–92, 1.4.27–44. Citations are to *English Renaissance Drama*, ed. David Bevington et al. (New York: Norton, 2002).

36. I am trying to be precise here, not to confuse: as specified in the previous chapter, in the Aristotelian psychology underlying the use of ekphrasis, the phantasia is the entity that receives external sensory presentations and passes them on to the memory, while the phantasma (pl. phantasmata) is the product of the confluence of old and recent presentations in the memory and becomes the "screen," as it were, through which new presentations are observed, interpreted, and passed on to other observers.

37. Many years ago Andrew Gurr offered a modest but provocative argument that I would like to adduce in support of this last claim. Though it was not directed at the source of Leontes' imaginings, it raised the issue of the *lusis* or "tease" that may have informed the name "Giulio Romano" when it was uttered in Act 5. Gurr's point was that, like Jonson and Webster, who enjoyed indulging in recondite allusions for the more sophisticated "understanders" of their plays, Shakespeare probably expected some members of his audiences to recall that Giulio Romano was the creator of *I modi*. See "The Many-Headed Audience," *Essays in Theatre* 1.1 (1982): 52–62. Elam's observation is perhaps even more apposite: "The recurrent references in the English drama to the *Sonetti* and *Modi* and their classical models confirm the fact that knowledge of their existence was widespread not only among

dramatists and poets but also among their audiences, since nothing falls flatter onstage than a learned reference to an unknown text or art work" (*Shakespeare's Pictures*, p. 135).

38. This would further distinguish him from the Chorus of *Henry V* discussed in Chapter 2 and enable us to specify the etiology of the sexual fascination and disgust Leontes expresses in this scene.

39. Cf. *Othello*, 3.3.395–406.

40. Moulton, *Before Pornography*, p. 123. If Shakespeare had read Vasari, however, as evidently he had, he would have known of Giulio's role in drawing "the various ways, attitudes, and positions in which licentious men have intercourse with women"—and so would his "more sophisticated 'understanders'" (cf. Gurr, n. 37 above).

41. "That Rare Italian Master," p. 168. Shakespeare's infrequent use of the word (only six times in the canon, plus the plural), she notes, "makes reference to artifice and a contrived presentation of the human form" (*JC* 5.1.33; *Cym.* 3.3.94, 5.5.165; *H8* 3.2.118), or is "linked to physical allure that comes by means of divine intervention" (*Cor.* 2.1.210), or "reverberates with salacious overtones, and its setting has to do with the stage" (*AC* 5.2.221). For Shakespeare the term "posture" thus conflates a sense of falsification or "imposture" and erotic attractiveness. Cf. Daileader, "Back Door Sex," pp. 329–30; and François Laroque, "'Rare Italian Master(s)': Roman Art in *Romeo and Juliet*, *Antony and Cleopatra*, and *The Winter's Tale*," in *Shakespeare, Italy, and Intertextuality*, ed. Michele Marrapodi (Manchester: Manchester University Press, 2004), pp. 234–5.

42. There is an ancient history concerning the power of a female sculpture to arouse desire. Behind Pygmalion's passion for the form he has sculpted himself is the story of the Cnidian Aphrodite by Praxiteles, with whom an avid admirer attempted to enjoy sexual intercourse and left the statue stained. For the tradition and its development in the early modern period, see Turner, *Eros Visible*, pp. 223–69.

43. Shakespeare had used this simile before, when Marcus likens the blood issuing from Lavinia's hacked tongue and hands to "a conduit with three issuing spouts" to emphasize the enormous loss of blood he sees (*Titus Andronicus*, 2.4.30).

44. *Metamorphoses*, 4.121–4; trans. Frank Justus Miller, Loeb Classical Library (London: Heinemann, 1921–22). Shakespeare had parodied this episode in *A Midsummer Night's Dream*, when Bottom as Pyramus, believing his Thisbe dead, draws his weapon and exclaims, "Come tears, confound; / Out sword, and wound / The pap of Pyramus. / Ay, that left pap, / Where heart doth hop. / Thus die I: thus, thus, thus!" (5.1.284–9).

45. *Shakespeare's Reading*, p. 21.

46. In the syncretic religious ambiance of *The Winter's Tale*, Antigonus is an unwitting apostate. Having departed from Sicilia before the oracle

was read at court, he cannot know that Apollo has declared Hermione chaste and Polixenes blameless, but his belief that "Apollo would—this being indeed the issue / Of King Polixenes—it should here be laid, / Either for life or death, upon the earth / Of its right father" (3.3.42–5) further cues the audience that he is an unreliable interpreter of things supernatural.

47. See Richard L. Williams, "Collecting and Religion in Late Sixteenth-Century England," in *The Evolution of English Collecting: Receptions of Italian Art in the Tudor and Stuart Periods*, ed. Edward Chaney (New Haven and London: Yale University Press, 2003), pp. 159–200.

48. Note the subtle preview of the mollification of the statue in the final scene.

49. See Frederick Hartt, *Giulio Romano*, 2 vols. (New Haven: Yale University Press, 1958; rpt. 1981): "Critics have generally accepted the sublime upper portion of the picture as by Raphael at his greatest, and as his also the design of the lower portion. But the demoniac boy and the men and women about him are so unparalleled in all Raphael's work for their cold violence that most scholars ascribe this section to Giulio Romano" (vol. 1, p. 34). Tom Henry and Paul Joannides, in *Late Raphael* (New York: Thames & Hudson, 2013), pp. 160–77, include a chalk study by Giulio of the possessed boy and his father (p. 171) and offer a detailed analysis of the issues involved in the composition of the painting and their progressive solutions. Ippolita Di Majo attributes the composition of the bottom half of the painting to Raphael's imitation of Leonardo's *Adoration of the Magi*, to which it bears a resemblance, and the contrasts in tone to Raphael's late style. See *Raffaello e la sua scuola* (Florence: Il Sole 24 ORE, E-ducation.It, 2007), pp. 276–83.

50. In Luke, they are sleeping (9: 32).

51. In the preceding 200 years, the Transfiguration was painted by Duccio di Buoninsegna (1311), Fra Angelico (c. 1440), Giovanni Bellini (c. 1455), Lorenzo Lotto (c. 1510), and Pietro Perugino (1517). In none of these is the second episode represented.

52. *Vision and the Visionary in Raphael* (University Park: Pennsylvania State University Press, 2011), pp. 120–45.

53. Of Raphael's painting of St. Catherine of Alexandria (c. 1506–7), Kleinbub notes, "To signal the vision embedded in her body, Catherine touches her left breast with her right hand, indicating how she sees the vision not with her physical eyes but with her heart, a seat of spiritual vision" (ibid. p. 20).

54. *The Transfiguration*, writes Kleinbub, "is an image in which the goal of knowing God through faith is represented metaphorically as the choice between external and internal vision. Faith, defined as belief in unseen things, is equated here with internal vision; faithlessness, in contrast, is associated with the delusions of the bodily eyes as well as disorderly and materially inclined imagination. In the contest of

internal and external vision, portrayed in the altarpiece as the struggle of the apostles to heal the possessed boy, the prize is the vision of the transfigured Christ on the mountain, a vision believed to anticipate the beatific vision of the divine essence" (ibid. p. 123).

55. Phantasia in the demonically possessed can work in ways that parody that of the divinely inspired (ibid. p. 132).

56. It would seem that Shakespeare's theatrical ekphrasis of the Transfiguration in 5.2 participates in that aestheticization of religious art described by Williams, "Collecting and Religion," pp. 170–1, even as it leads him to invoke the lingering spiritual message of the painting to bring about the dramatic resolution of 5.3.

57. Copies of this famous painting are to be expected, though I had not anticipated finding one in England ascribed to Giulio. Vasari records in his life of Penni that Pope Clement VII, who had commissioned the original *Transfiguration* for his episcopal seat in Narbonne when still cardinal, decided after Raphael's death to place it in San Pietro a Montorio in Rome. He then asked Giulio and Penni to make a copy that he could send to Narbonne. They began to work on it together, but Penni alone brought it to completion when Giulio left for Mantua. The copy never arrived in Narbonne because Penni, then in the service of the Marchese del Vasto, Alfonso d'Avalos, traveled to Ischia in his train, along with the completed work, whence it was installed in the church of the Santo Spirito degli Incurabili in Naples. Today it may be seen at the Prado in Madrid. For a useful recent discussion of the original painting and the copy, see Henry and Joannides, *Late Raphael*, pp. 173–7.

58. This is the price shown in the Dulwich College acquisition records. According to William Harnett Blanch, the sum was £60. See *Dulwich College and Edward Alleyn: A Short History of the Foundation of God's Gift College at Dulwich, Together with a Memoir of the Founder* (London: E. W. Allen, 1877), p. 6.

59. Bénédicte Miyamoto, "'Making Pictures Marketable': Expertise and the Georgian Art Market," in *Marketing Art in the British Isles, 1700 to the Present: A Cultural History*, ed. Charlotte Gould and Sophie Mesplède (Burlington, VT: Ashgate, 2012), p. 129.

60. Copyright © J. Paul Getty Trust, italics mine.

61. It is not clear from the language whose painting it was—Sebright's or Sclater-Bacon's. Bärbel Küster believes it belonged to the Sclater-Bacon collection ("Copies on the Market in Eighteenth-Century Britain," in *Marketing Art in the British Isles*, p. 183), but she relies on George Redford's undocumented entry of 1888 (see n. 68). As I mention below, there is separate evidence suggesting it may have belonged to Sebright (n. 63).

62. As Miyamoto notes, "The term 'capital' is used in eighteenth-century auction catalogues as a qualitative adjective meaning 'first-rate, standing at the head.'" This evaluation is reflected in the lot number assigned

to the painting in both auctions, for auctioneers had established, and the buying public had come to expect, a rhythmic fluctuation in each day's prices, and the most highly esteemed paintings were usually reserved for the end of the day's bidding.

63. BL Shelf 381.45 in Rare Books and Manuscripts.

64. In his edition of *The Inventories and Valuations of the King's Goods, 1649–1651* (Glasgow: Walpole Society, 1972), p. xxvi, Oliver Millar refers to a typescript of this manuscript. In correspondence held by the Office of the Surveyor of the Queen's Pictures at St. James's Palace, Millar identifies the manuscript in a letter of 1981 as B.L. Loan Ms. #78, which is written in an early eighteenth-century hand.

65. See W. L. F. Nuttall, "King Charles I's Pictures and the Commonwealth Sale," *Apollo* (October 1965): 302–9, esp. 307.

66. On the growing respectability of copies of paintings in the eighteenth century and the theory behind it, see Küster, "Copies on the Market," esp. pp. 188–90.

67. Another, more detailed copy of the inventory and evaluations records the evaluation of *The Transfiguration* at £15 and specifies that it was "Sold Mj. Bass & Others in a Dividend as Apprised," 19 December 1651 (BL Ms. 4898). For the Rubens and Titian, see Millar, *The Inventories and Valuations*, pp. 272 and 190.

68. In *Art Sales: A History of the Sales of Pictures and Other Works of Art*, 2 vols. (London: Whitefriars, 1888), vol. 1, p. 27, George Redford attributes ownership of the painting to Sclater-Bacon, but gives no supporting evidence for the choice. Though he lists "Seabright" in his Index of Sales as selling pictures on May 17, 1737, and Cock as the auctioneer, there is no entry in his text indicating the content of the sale.

69. *Abraham van der Doort's Catalogue of the Collections of Charles I*, ed. Oliver Millar (Glasgow: Walpole Society, 1960), p. 69.

70. Ibid. p. 232.

71. Kathryn Barron, "The Collecting and Patronage of John, Lord Lumley (c. 1535–1609)," in *The Evolution of English Collecting*, ed. Chaney, p. 158, n. 108.

72. Raphael's painting measures 15 feet, 1½ inches by 9 feet, 1½ inches; the Dulwich copy is just under 12½ feet high, so it is about 20 per cent smaller than the original, but not "little." Of perhaps more significance is that the extant paintings showing the two scenes van der Doort mentions contain twenty-six human figures. These would be very difficult to render on a "little" canvas, especially considering the importance of the expressions on their faces.

73. V&A Shelf No. MSL/1907/1753. This manuscript is dated by reference on p. 58 to the Earl of Strafford as Lord Lieutenant of Ireland. The title was conferred on Strafford in 1640, and he was executed in 1641, so it post-dates van der Doort's 1639 manuscript.

74. Millar, *Van der Doort*, p. xxiii.

75. Ibid. p. xxiv. Exeter is also entered in van der Doort's catalogue as the donor of "a very greate Booke in folio of Prints. being of several Antiquities of statues and Roman buildings" (p. 126).

76. Details of van der Doort's career as a royal servant are given by Millar, *Van der Doort*. Van der Doort made other errors concerning donors and recipients in his catalogue. See Timothy Wilks, "Art Collecting at the English Court from the Death of Henry, Prince of Wales to the Death of Anne of Denmark (November 1612—March 1619)," in *Journal of the History of Collections* 9.1 (1997): 35. For a useful account of the copies in the royal collection, see Susan Bracken, "Copies of Old Master Paintings in Charles I's Collection: The Role of Michael Cross (*fl.* 1632–60)," *British Art Journal* 3.2 (Spring 2002): 28–31.

77. Lionel Cust, "The Lumley Inventories," *Walpole Society* 6 (1918): 27, 25. The 1590 inventory includes goods located not only at Lumley Castle but also at Nonsuch Palace and at Lumley's London residence, Tower Hill.

78. Mary F. S. Hervey, "A Lumley Inventory of 1609," *Walpole Society* 6 (1918): 42.

79. On the Thomas Cecil festivity, see *The Letters of John Chamberlain*, ed. N. E. McClure, 2 vols. (Philadelphia, 1939), vol. 1, p. 115 (3 February 1601, Chamberlain to Carlton).

80. For a review of the possible dates of the play's first performance, see Stanley Wells and Gary Taylor, *William Shakespeare: A Textual Companion* (New York: Norton, 1997), p. 123. Keir Elam, editor of the Arden 3 *Twelfth Night* (2008), offers a balanced assessment of the case for Orsini's attendance at a Whitehall performance in 1601 (pp. 93–6). It should be noted, however, that one of the possible Italian sources of the play, Curzio Gonzaga's *Gl'inganni*, was bound together in the sixteenth century with Girolamo Parabosco's *Il viluppo*, which "contains a lovesick character called Orsino" (Lawrence, "*Who the devil*", p. 168, n. 35), so the name was ready to hand before news of Orsini's visit arrived the previous December. Indeed, it might have been considered a complimentary act of welcome to present to the visiting duke an English play whose Italian sources he must have been familiar with, since *Gl'ingannati* spawned numerous imitations and was "the single most popular Italian comedy of the century, celebrated throughout Europe." See Clubb, *Pollastra and the Origins of "Twelfth Night"*, p. 1; Robert Melzi, "From Lelia to Viola," *RenD* 9 (1966): 67–81; Leslie Hotson, *The First Night of Twelfth Night* (New York: Macmillan, 1954), pp. 120–1.

81. On Exeter's interest in Italian art, and his correspondence with Gilbert Talbot, 7th Earl of Shrewsbury, the father-in-law of Thomas Norfolk, Earl of Arundel, the great collector, see J. Irene Whalley, "Italian Art and English Taste: An Early Seventeenth Century Letter," *Apollo*

(September 1971): 184–91, and Susan Bracken, "The Early Cecils and Italianate Taste," in *The Evolution of English Collecting*, ed. Chaney, p. 204. According to Bracken, "William's appreciation of the finer points of painting continued throughout his life" (ibid.).

82. E. K. Chambers, *William Shakespeare*, 2 vols. (Oxford: Clarendon Press, 1930), vol. 2, pp. 335–6.

83. See Roy Strong, *Henry, Prince of Wales, and England's Lost Renaissance* (London: Thames & Hudson, 1986), pp. 200–12, and Timothy Wilks, "'Paying Special Attention to the Adornment of a Most Beautiful Gallery': The Pictures in St. James's Palace, 1609–49," *The Court Historian* 10.2 (2005): 149–72.

84. E. K. Chambers, *The Elizabethan Stage*, 4 vols. (Oxford: Clarendon Press, 1923), vol. 3, pp. 385–6.

Chapter 4

What Did Hermione's Statue Look Like? The Four Ladies of Mantua and the Science of True Opinion

I

We have seen Shakespeare's ingenuity at work bodging two of the visual arts—engraving (or woodcut) and painting—into the text of *The Winter's Tale* by means of ekphrastic dialogue. I now want to explore his incorporation of a third—sculpture—by examining the text to determine what it can tell us about the play's onstage presentation. I shall begin by asking what we know about the appearance of Hermione's "statue" when it is revealed in Act 5, Scene 3. Next, I will inquire into a related matter: is there any historical evidence to support Shakespeare's attribution of the supposed sculpture to Giulio Romano, beyond Vasari's report that Giulio's epitaph claimed that he made "*sculpted and painted* bodies breathe"? Finally, I shall propose a reader's ekphrasis of Hermione's statue, based on the evidence gathered. Let us address these three issues in the order of their appearance.

More than 400 years after the original production of the play, and with no contemporary eyewitness accounts save that of Simon Forman, who says nothing about the statue, we must glean what we can from the text's first printing. The Folio provides scenic facts concerning the statue's authorship, state of finish, substance, and posture, which can be gathered from dialogue that supplies oblique stage directions.[1] Our first piece of evidence addresses its provenance and verisimilitude: it is "a Peece many yeeres in doing, and now newly perform'd, by that rare Italian Master, *Julio Romano*," who "so neere *Hermione*, hath done *Hermione*, that they say one would speake to her, and stand in hope of answer" (5.2.93–5, 98–9).[2] The

Third Gentleman has identified the statue as the work of a sixteenth-century artist who—fictionally—is still living, but who actually died sixty-five years before *The Winter's Tale* was produced. He has labored over it for a very long time and just recently put the finishing touches to it. Among its other functions, the line serves to reinforce the early modern setting of a play whose historical context Shakespeare shifts in accordance with the thematic value he wishes to emphasize. Recall, for example, the journey to the oracle of Apollo at Delphos by Dion and Cleomenes in 3.1, followed two scenes later by Antigonus's Protestant hesitation before interpreting his vision of Hermione in Catholic eschatological terms. Now we are in a world of mingled Cinquecento Italian art and Seicento English art appreciation, and Shakespeare freely makes the appropriate moves.

Given his own newly performed ekphrasis of the reunion of the royal families (5.2.41–90), the Gentleman evidently fancies himself a connoisseur obliged to display his learning for the benefit of his fellow courtiers. This impression is strengthened by the fact that he not only emphasizes the effect of Giulio's skill but clearly speaks from the position of an insider—he is, after all, "the lady Paulina's steward" (26)—for he reports the reaction of certain privileged viewers—"they say" (98–9)—even as he inadvertently suggests that he himself has not seen the statue. Who are the "they" who remark upon the statue's potential responsiveness? Creatures of his self-aggrandizing fantasy, it would seem, for in the very next scene Paulina says of the statue, "I keep it / Lonely, apart" (5.3.17–18), implying that the statue is her secret and not a subject for household gossip—not to mention the fact that the statue qua statue is non-existent and therefore could not have been seen by *any* viewers. Thus the Gentleman's passage is an audible *trompe l'oreille*—intended gently to satirize the speaker and to prepare his audiences, onstage and off, to expect an extraordinary work of art.[3]

In order actually to *see* Hermione's statue, the royal party must pass through Paulina's gallery—by 1611 a not-unfamiliar appurtenance in aristocratic households—which contains "many singularities" (5.3.12).[4] Despite such *comparanda*, claims Paulina, "her dead likeness I do well believe / Excels whatever yet you looked upon / Or hand of man hath done" (5.3.15–17). The theater audience then shares with her guests a direct view of the statue. "But here it is," she says; "prepare / To see the life as lively mocked as ever / Still sleep mocked death. Behold and say 'tis well" (5.3.18–20). Following this encomium, she must then disclose the statue. There is no stage direction, though modern editors adopt Rowe's "Paulina draws a curtain, and reveals Hermione standing like a statue."[5] As readers, however, we don't yet know that she is standing at all.

How does the statue of Hermione comport itself? "Her natural posture," declares Leontes, after silently viewing it. What does that tell us? Nothing specific, for the figure may be reclining; but if it is standing the words suggest an informal pose, perhaps following the contrapposto "S-curve" of Greek and Roman figures popularized by Italian sculptors and painters in the sixteenth century—among them, as we shall see, Giulio Romano himself. Often such poses entailed asymmetrical positioning of the arms and hands—one arm crooked, wrist bent on hip, for example, the other extended outward or downward, as in Paul van Somer's 1617 portrait of Anne of Denmark before Oatfields (Fig. 4.1).[6] That the statue is not recumbent, in the manner of a funeral monument, is evident from Leontes' further remark: "O, thus she stood, / Even with such life of majesty—warm life / As now it coldly stands—when first I wooed her" (5.3.34–6).[7] But there is a problem: the statue's face is wrinkled. "Hermione was ... nothing / So aged as this seems," Leontes interjects (5.3.28–9). Paulina then makes defect perfection, as she explains it as testimony to "the carver's excellence, / Which lets go by some sixteen years, and makes her / As she lived now" (5.3.30–2). This Giulio Romano, true to his epitaph, goes hand in hand with nature.[8]

An even more significant detail is soon heard. Caught up in the naturalness of the figure before her, Perdita asks, "Dear Queen, that ended when I but began, / Give me that hand of yours to kiss," and must be reminded by Paulina of what it is she's addressing: "O, patience! / The statue is but newly fixed; the colour's / Not dry" (5.3.45–8). Modern editors inform their readers that, in the words of Stephen Orgel, "Elizabethan and Jacobean effigies (like ancient Greek statues) were invariably painted to look lifelike."[9] This should be qualified, however, for the practice was followed with considerable latitude, which, if acknowledged, opens an intriguing window onto the statue's appearance. We find, for example, that the recumbent figures of John Manners, 4th Earl of Rutland, and his wife Elizabeth on Gerard Johnson's monument of 1591 are more lightly polychromed than those of their kneeling children (Figs. 4.2 and 4.3)—especially on hands and face—while the images of Sir Roger Aston, his wife Mary, and their five children on William Cure's monument of 1612 are all fully colored (Fig. 4.4). Yet in the latter year Maximilian Colt, commissioned in 1605 to fashion the elaborately painted monument of Elizabeth I, completed the tomb of Robert Cecil, 1st Earl of Salisbury, where "the gaudy colouring

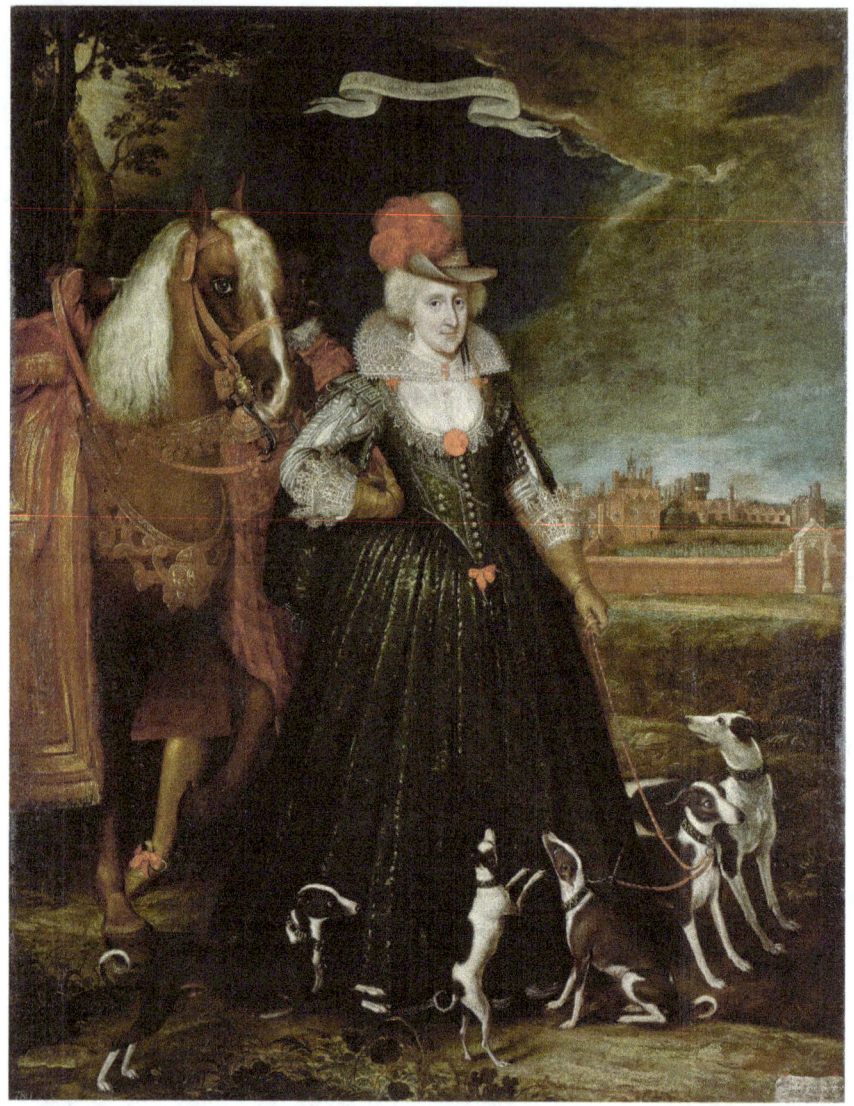

Fig. 4.1. Paul van Somer, Anne of Denmark. Royal Collection Trust, Her Majesty Queen Elizabeth II.

of Elizabethan and early Jacobean tombs is replaced by a simple contrast of black and white marble" (Fig. 4.5).[10] Thus it is not self-evident just how much paint was used or in what manner it was applied to make Hermione's statue "lifelike."[11]

Further complicating the issue is the growing influence of European practice regarding paint. Roberta Panzanelli and Marco

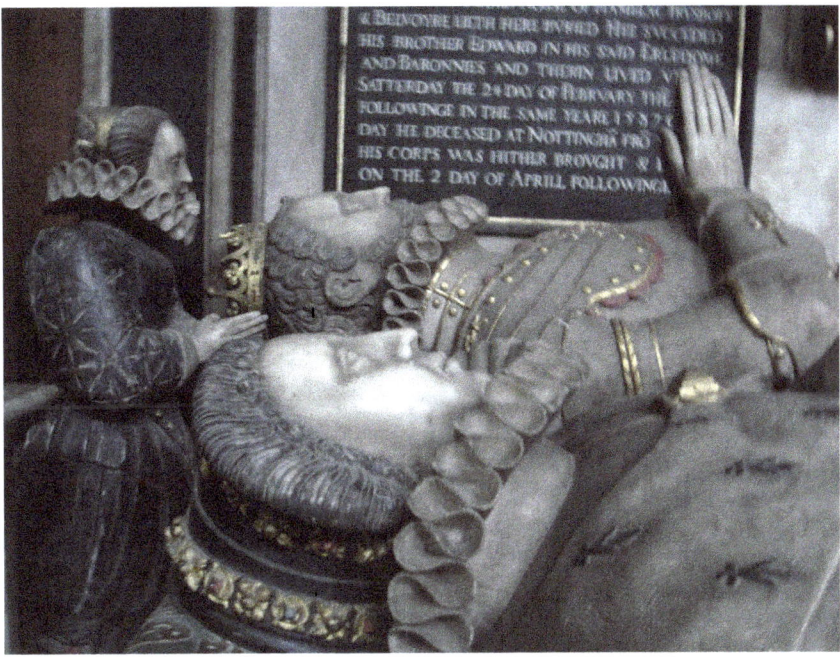

Fig. 4.2. Monument of John Manners, 4th Earl of Rutland, by Gerard Johnson, in the Church of St. Mary the Virgin in Bottesford, UK (1591), detail. Photograph by author.

Collareta have shown that continental statues in the early modern period also bore differing degrees of coloration, ranging from the colorless—in imitation of what was deemed to be the classical manner—to the fully polychromed, a practice lingering from the Middle Ages, when it was believed that color elicited strong affect in the viewer.[12] In the very year the King's Men presented *The Winter's Tale* they performed a macabre version of this belief concerning the power of color to arouse passion in Thomas Middleton's *The Second Maiden's* [or *Lady's*] *Tragedy*, as the Tyrant removes the mouldering body of his beloved from her tomb and hires an artist to paint her face so he can make love to her. "Our arms and lips," he says, "Shall labour life into her" (5.2.104–5).[13] This perverse example should put us in mind of the possibility that the statue of Hermione may have worn more "natural" paint on hands and face—the potential points of touch for her daughter and husband (5.3.45–8, 79–83)—while other parts of her figure, whether in classicizing or contemporary garb, may have simulated the marbling of stone beneath their coloration. Indeed, her "coming to life" would be all the more startling if

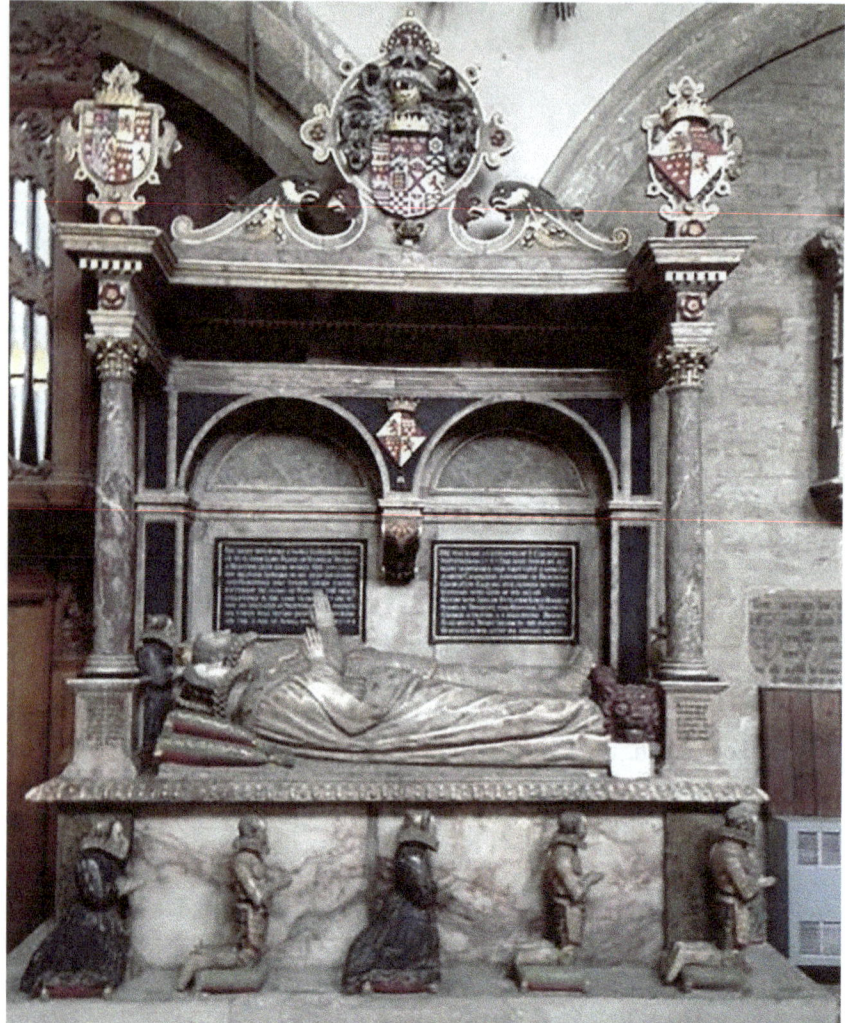

Fig. 4.3. Monument of John Manners, full view.

this were so. For her stoniness is adverted to five times (5.3.24, 37, 38, 42, 58) before Paulina commands, "Be stone no more" (99)—at which point not only her posture but the marble-streaked surface of her costume would soften and become mobile.[14]

In support of this hypothesis, we should note another scenic fact. Gazing at the statue, Leontes asks Polixenes, "Would you not deem it breathed, and that those veins / Did verily bear blood?" (5.3.64–5). What veins? we may be prompted to ask. Jacobean painted statues did not normally show veins. But Polixenes sees them, too: "Masterly

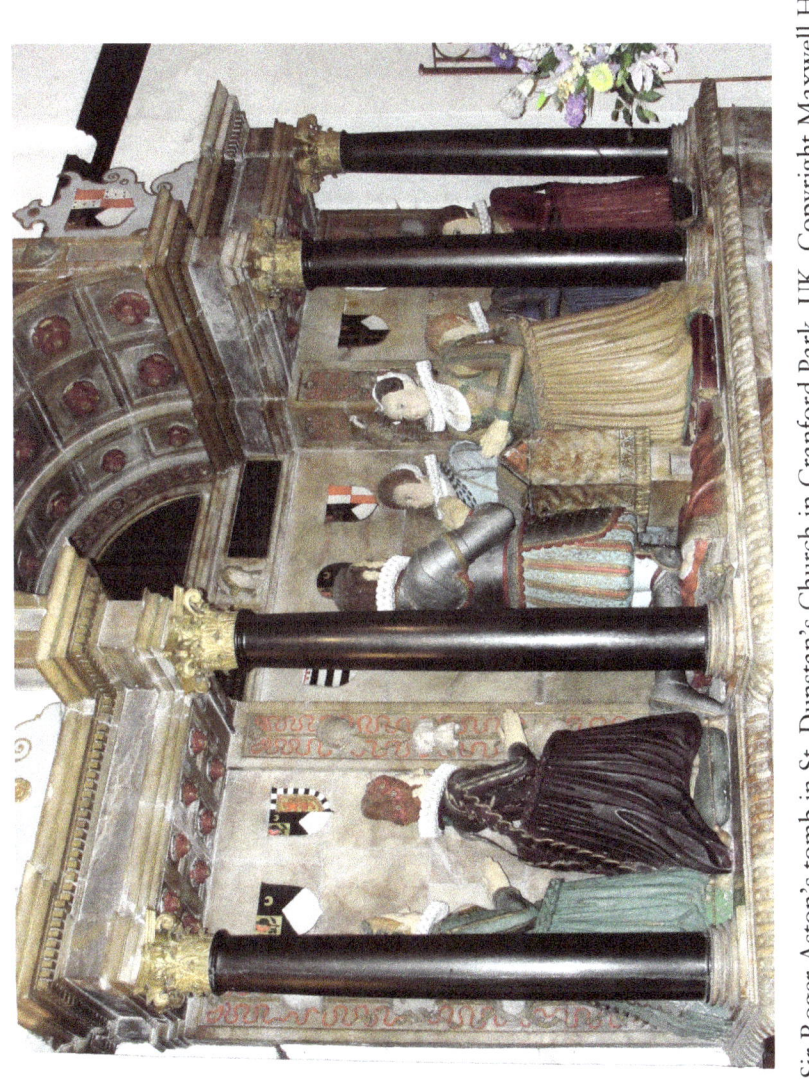

Fig. 4.4. Sir Roger Aston's tomb in St. Dunstan's Church in Cranford Park, UK. Copyright Maxwell Hamilton. Used under an Attribution-ShareAlike 2.0 Generic License.

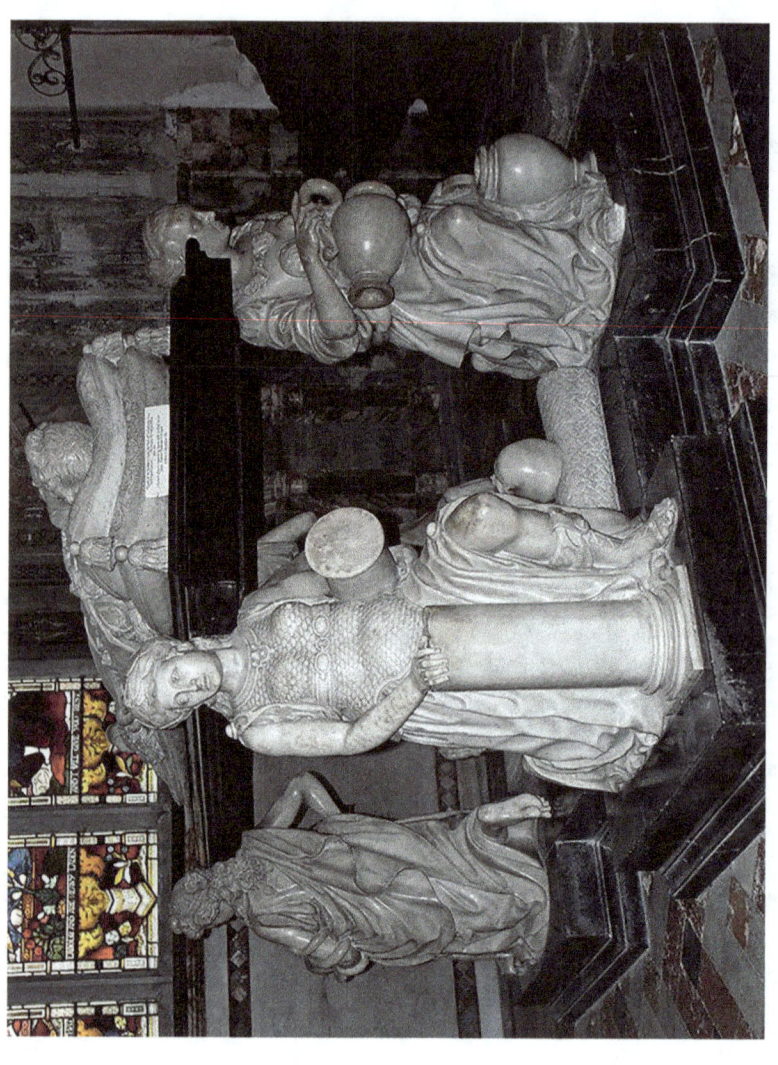

Fig. 4.5. Sir Robert Cecil's monument by Maximilian Colt (1612) in the Church of St. Etheldreda, Hatfield, Hertfordshire, UK. Shown with permission by B. Thomas Curtis, photographer.

done!" he replies. In this act of ekphrastic connoisseurship, are they actually describing the living Hermione's veins or veins of marble painted on the exposed parts of her throat, forearms, wrists, and hands?[15]

Where is the statue standing? And is it attached to a supporting prop? Again, we have to rely on dialogue to learn that the statue is elevated. "I'll make the statue move indeed, descend / And take you by the hand," says Paulina to Leontes (5.3.88–9), and then commands it to do just that. Still, all we know is that it stands above the footing of the onstage spectators, and we can only speculate as to where it stands. A theatrically effective location would be the discovery space at the Globe, where Simon Forman saw the play on May 15, 1611, and its equivalent in the screen of the Banqueting House at Whitehall (its other specified early venue), which would permit concealment behind an arras, then a gentle thrusting-forth when the curtain is drawn aside. Eighteenth- and nineteenth-century productions included a column of sorts, so that the actress would not have to remain immobile and unsupported for eighty-four lines,[16] but as we know from contemporary street performers this is not impossible to those who are trained in mime. For the young seventeenth-century actor who played Hermione it would not have been difficult; on the other hand, he might have used his free arm to steady himself on an entablature or plinth, in the classical manner.

The question that I pose in my chapter title, then, is answered by a number of *scenic* if not *actual* facts that raise further questions left unexplained by onstage speakers who enjoy the advantage—not shared by readers—of seeing the statue. But the text does contain one singularly important clue that we have not yet examined in detail: the attribution of the finished statue to Giulio Romano. While generations of editors have pointed out that Giulio—heir to Raphael's workshop in Rome and supervisor of public works for Federico Gonzaga, 1st Duke of Mantua—was known as a painter and an architect, not a sculptor, the epitaph quoted by Vasari is sufficiently ambiguous to give rise to the belief that he was a sculptor as well.[17] In what follows I will present evidence that he was certainly a designer of sculpture, if not a sculptor himself, and that his work may have inspired the statue of Hermione in *The Winter's Tale*. And if a designer, then easily the painter who put the finishing touches ("newly performed") to the statue. That is to say, Shakespeare may well have known what he was talking about.

II

Adjoining the wall of the north transept of the Church of Sant'
Andrea at Mantua in the Petrozzani Chapel is a strangely evocative
funerary monument. Made for Pietro Strozzi, a wealthy Mantuan
citizen, in 1529—following his instructions that it be fashioned
of marble at the cost of 400 gold scudi and supervised by three
friends—it was originally installed in the Church of San Domenico
and moved to Sant' Andrea in 1805 after the former church had
been suppressed.[18] Its placement in San Domenico is unknown, but
its peculiar design suggests that it was located against a wall, as it is
in Sant' Andrea.

It is divided into four distinct sections (Fig. 4.6).[19] The lowest is a
rectilinear base of white marble elaborately carved into metopes of
animals, cupids, and bearded masks. The topmost section consists
of a black marble sarcophagus carved with garlands, grotesques,
and the Strozzi crescent moons, surmounted by a white marble slab
on which rests the full-length effigy of Pietro Strozzi himself, made
of similar material (Fig. 4.7). His head turns slightly toward us on a
pillow; his near shoulder—the right—is bare, as is his chest, though
a drapery descending in heavy folds from his left shoulder discreetly
covers his body below the chest. With his naked right arm at his
side bending to rest his hand on his abdomen, and his sandaled feet
extending beyond his garment, he looks as though he were asleep.
The bier rests on a massive corniced entablature of white marble,
embellished by a floral frieze and several courses of decorative
molding (Fig. 4.6). Supporting it are four caryatids, who may remind
the modern viewer of those standing in the Erechtheion in Athens.[20]

There is, of course, a major difference. It is a difference not only
of number but also of posture and style.[21] Supporting each of the
four corners of the entablature, the Strozzi caryatids are disposed in
contrasting positions (Fig. 4.8). The figure at the left, as one views
the monument, stands frontally, her right arm bent as she reaches up
to the base of the entablature, which her hand grasps firmly, while
her left arm reaches diagonally down to a plinth where her hand
rests, which states in Latin: "For Pietro Strozzi, the just and well-
deserved affections of friends have placed this majestic monument,
MDXXIX."[22] She is rendered in the style of archaic Greek sculpture:
she stands erect, legs parallel to one another, her weight equally distributed on each. Her arms, though reaching in opposite directions,
do not pull the torso from its rigid upright posture. Most strikingly,

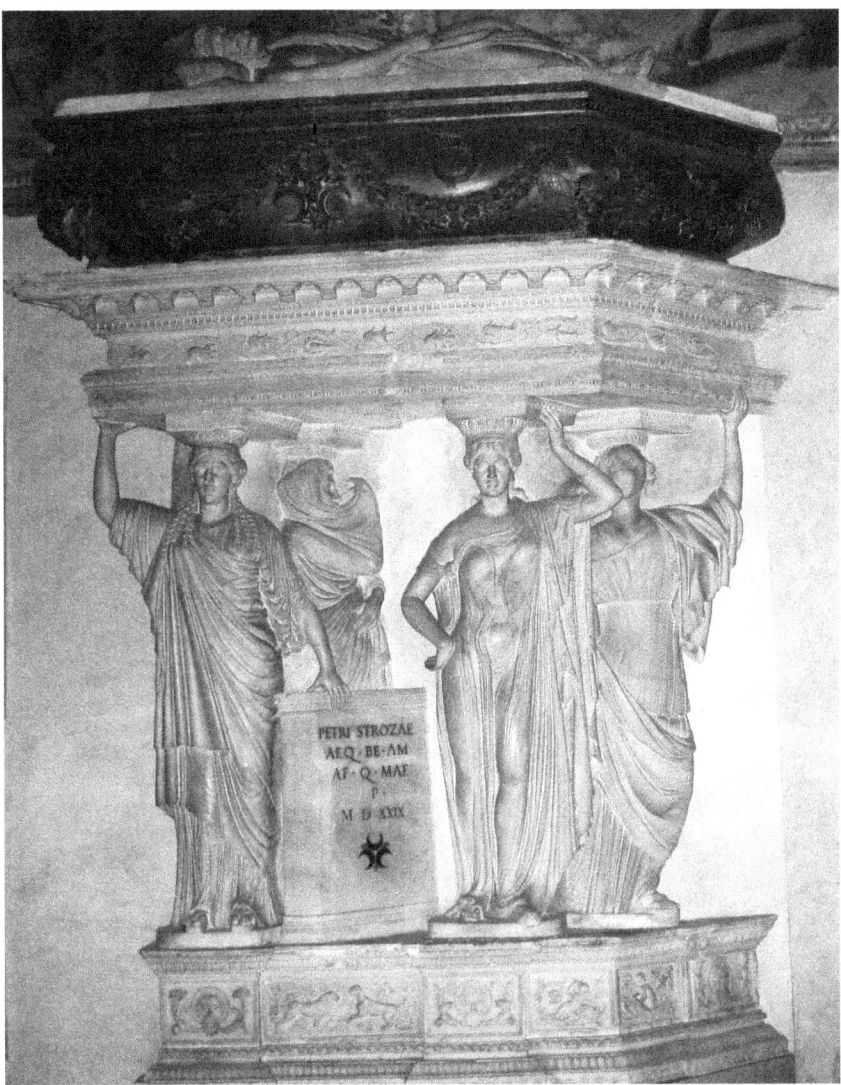

Fig. 4.6. The monument of Pietro Strozzi, full view. Design attributed to Giulio Romano. Photograph by author.

her hair is formally arranged, with long curls falling from the back of her neck, which are cut symmetrically with a rolling drill and draped over the front of her shoulders, while the himation and long Ionic chiton she wears suggest heavy material covering virtually all her body except for the forearms and her toes.

In contrast, the figure to her left (and to the viewer's right) is carved in the later Hellenistic style, even though with some

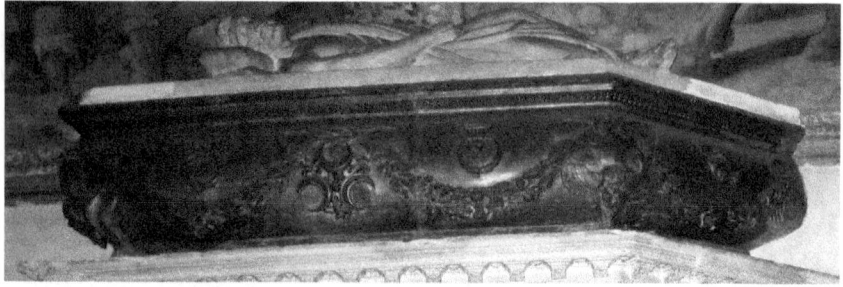

Fig. 4.7. Strozzi monument, detail of effigy.

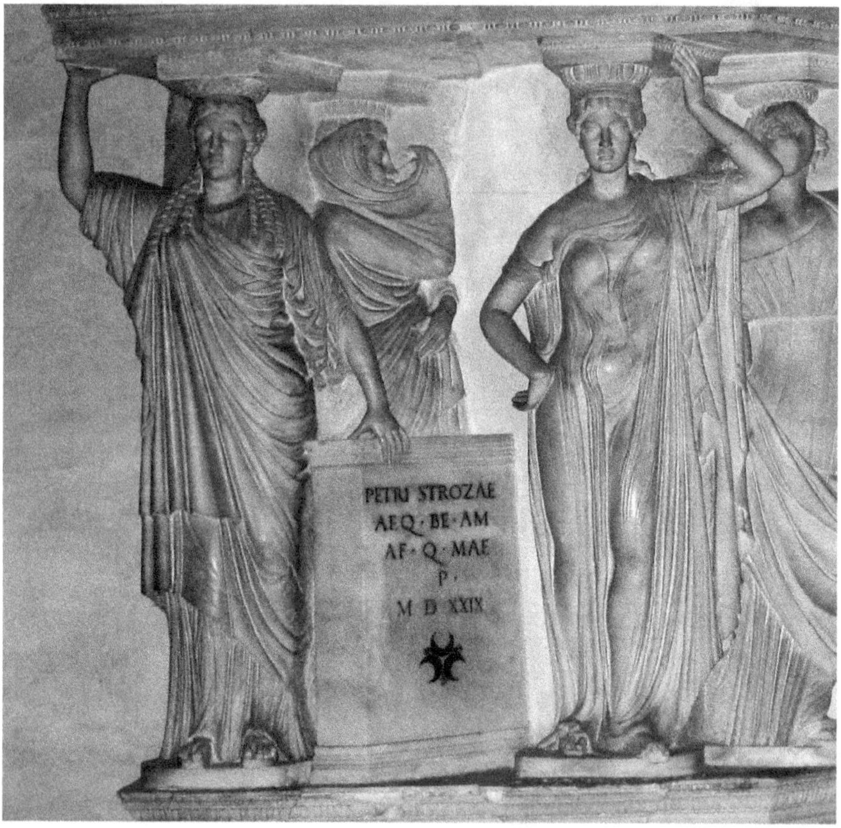

Fig. 4.8. Strozzi monument, close-up of caryatids.

significant variants her position mirrors that of the first caryatid. Her right arm is again bent but this time turns downward, and the back of her hand sits firmly on her own slightly elevated right hip, hinting at a certain independence from place and task, while her left arm, also bent at the elbow, reaches up not to the entablature, but to the capital beneath it that bears down on the echinus above her head. There her fingers lightly rest. She, too, gazes frontally, but her body follows a contrapposto "S" curve, her right leg bearing more of her weight than her left, which is turned so that her toes point outward. Her hair, parted in the middle and finely combed, flows freely down the back of her neck. Like Strozzi above her, her right shoulder is bare, and she is largely bare-armed. And unlike her archaic sister, she wears a single garment—a very light chiton, with no concealing himation. Indeed, beneath the hand placed on her hip, the garment has parted, revealing nearly the whole length of her nude right leg. Loosely knotted below her armpit, and carved in such a way that not only is the swelling of her breasts evident but the nipples press forward under the seemingly transparent cloth, the chiton fully reveals the contours of waist, belly, and thigh. The effect, as is often the case in Hellenistic sculpture, is that of a living creature caught in a passing moment. Even the blue veins of the marble hint at real blood vessels beneath.

If we stand before the monument and read it from right to left, then from front to back and left to right, we are confronted by a demonstration of stylistic virtuosity and also by what seems to be an allegory of womanhood. The Hellenistic figure, though clearly not a very young girl, does appear to be a maiden. Her informal hair arrangement, the freedom of her garment, and the nubile sexuality she exhibits all point to readiness for marriage. The archaic, heavily robed figure bears the marks of modest and dignified domesticity. Behind her a third figure—vaguely but not distinctly classical—stands in front of her assigned capital, supporting it only by association, for she is carved in deep relief, not quite free of the supporting rear wall of the monument. She is turned to the right, her head, shoulders, and arms covered by a large shawl. Her right arm extends forward and bends up vertically within the shawl, forming a hollow into which her partially exposed face peers. It is a protective gesture, as if a baby were within, yet no child can be seen. Stranger yet, her profile suggests the backward tilt of a pregnant woman, and her left hand is placed on her belly. Thus she appears to be the image of a child-bearing matron, with one babe literally in hand and another on the way—more absorbed in her maternity than in supporting a sarcophagus.

The fourth figure is more mysterious still (Fig. 4.6). All we can see of her is the back of her head, neck, and body. For she is literally disappearing into the wall from which she seems carved. She is still doing her job: her head supports the capital and echinus beneath the entablature and her right arm is bent up so she can grasp the entablature with her hand. Her hair is tied in a chignon at the back of her head, with loose curls about her ears. The upper left portion of her back is exposed, though she is wearing an otherwise closely fitted full-length garment covered by a heavily draped himation. Yet in her anonymity—her very facelessness—she gives the unmistakable impression that she is departing the scene, a woman who has spent enough time supporting a man. What might the designer of the sculpture have intended to convey? Is she taking leave to repossess herself—or is she vanishing into the selflessness of death?

Neither the designer nor the sculptor (or sculptors) is documented. The only recorded information about the origin of the monument is Strozzi's will, which specifies cost and materials, supervision by his friends, and San Domenico as its destination. He is to be buried in the large chapel reserved to the Strozzi family at San Domenico, and asks the widow Polissena Boschetti, his cousin Tommaso Strozzi, and his dear friend Lodovico Maynoldi, doctor of law, to commission the construction of a marble sepulchre to be completed within a year and a half following his death, for which they are to pay 400 scudi in gold—instructing his heir and executor, Francisco Strozzi, to make that sum available to Lodovico immediately after he, Pietro, dies.[23] Nothing is said about the monument's design.

Models for the caryatids, however, are not lacking, nor are informed conjectures as to their author. The late art historian Roberto Longhi cited as the model for the archaic figure a statue once in the Museo d'Antichità di Mantova, which it faithfully reproduces except for the naked part of the right arm and the hand resting on the incised plinth, and he found another in a statue of the tragic muse Melpomene in the Palazzo Ducale in Venice.[24] He linked the Hellenistic figure to a headless Aphrodite that had existed in Rome before it was purchased for the ducal collection in Mantua (Fig. 4.9).[25] It reappears in the form of two sibyls in the Sala di Costantino in the Vatican, painted by Giulio Romano in the 1520s (Fig. 4.10), "among which one was lifted for the sepulchre, with the movements of the Gonzaga Venus reversed, precisely as in the second Strozzi caryatid."[26] Longhi refers here, as do Vittorio Matteuchi and Carlo d'Arco before him, and Alda Spinazzola Levi afterwards, to a tradition connecting Giulio Romano with the project of the monument.[27] Re-examining this tradition in the 1980s, the late Richard Harprath noted that the headless figure in Mantua, a copy "originating in the age of the Antonini, of the fifth caryatid of the Erechtheion, with a tragic mask adjoined like the muse Melpomene . . . must have

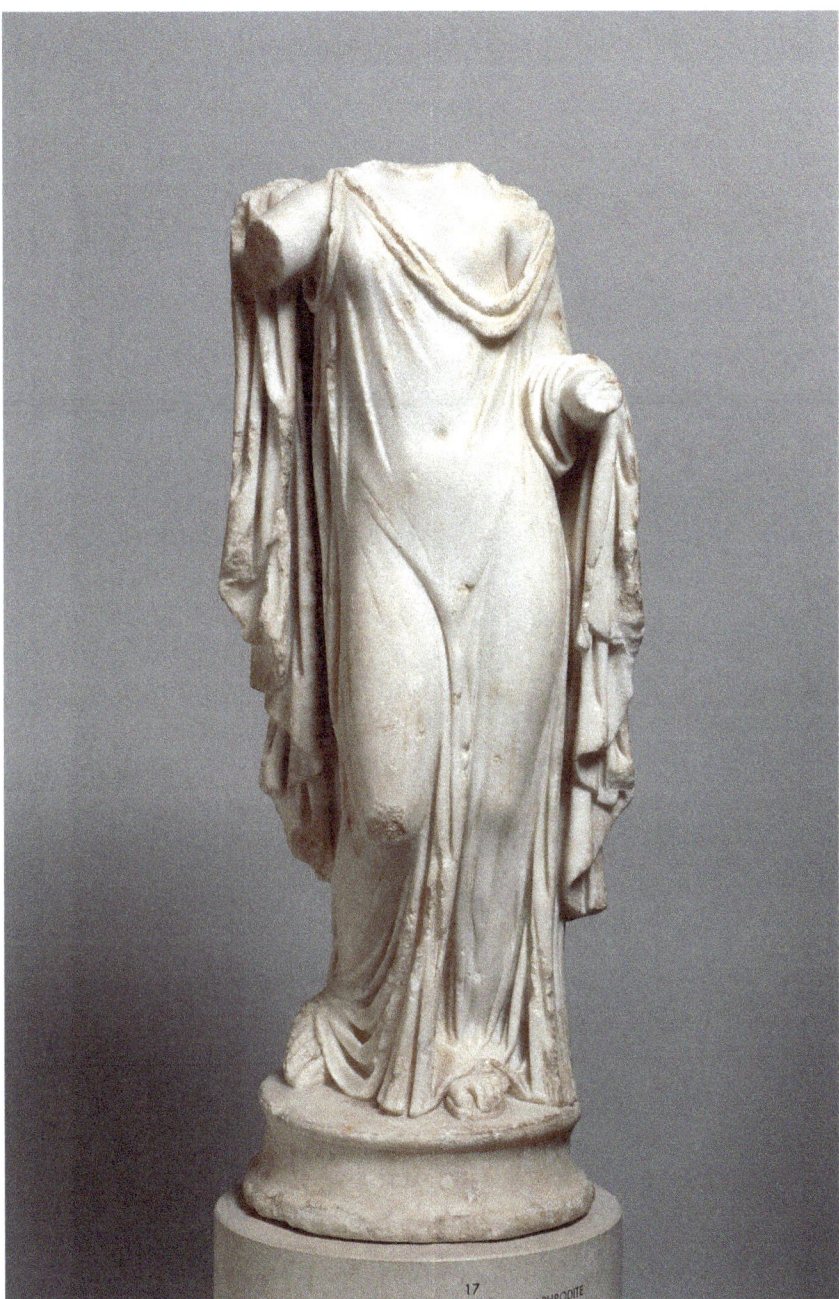

Fig. 4.9. "Venus Genetrix." Kunsthistorisches Museum, Vienna.

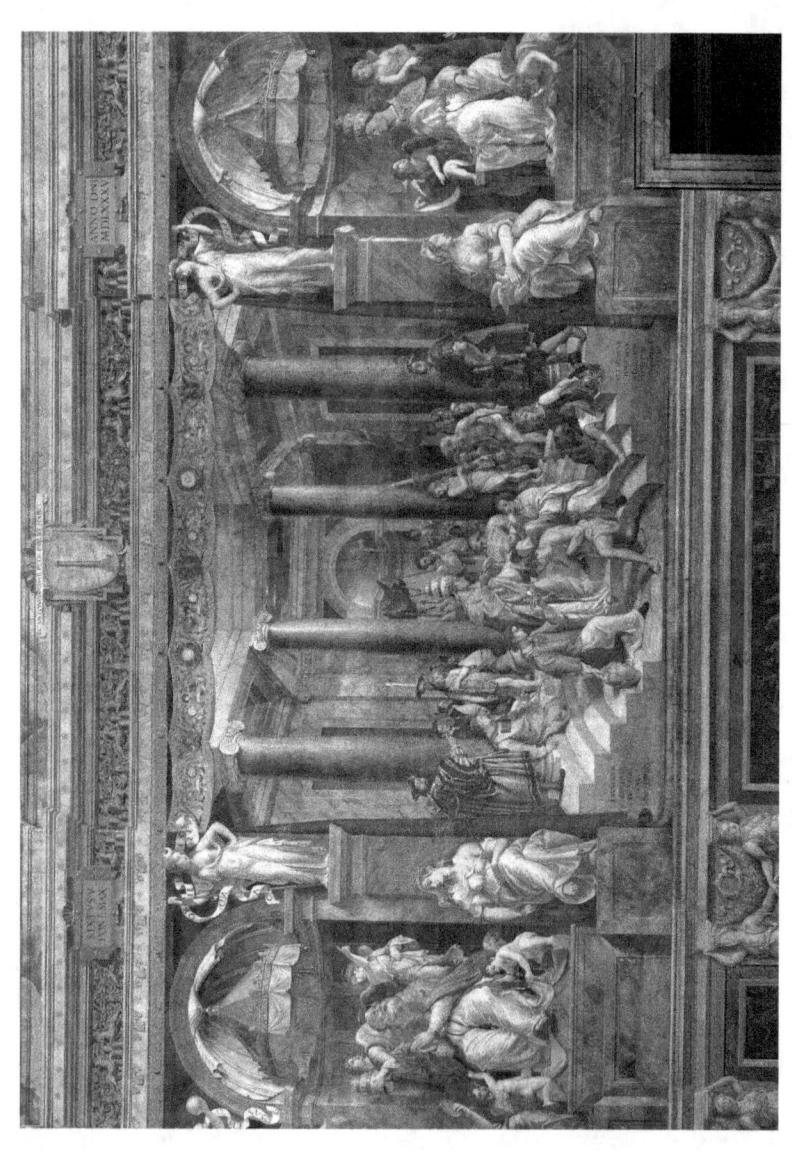

Fig. 4.10. The Baptism of Constantine. Copyright Governate of the Vatican City State-Directorate of the Vatican Museums.

arrived there from the Roman collection of G. Ciampolini through the agency of Giulio Romano."[28]

Caryatids seem to have interested Giulio. In addition to those painted in the Sala di Costantino, we are told by Vasari that he designed two for a building near the Old Mint in Rome.[29] In the Louvre there is a painting of Ceres made circa 1518 for Bernardo Dovizi, Cardinal Bibbiena, that is attributed to Giulio, though it bears the name "Raphael Urbinas," to whom he was then apprenticed (Fig. 4.11). While not a caryatid, the grisaille goddess has the hand-on-hip posture and diaphanous chiton of those in the Sala di Costantino and of the Hellenistic figure on the monument.[30] Finally, two more images of caryatids with connections to Giulio have survived. The first appears to be based on knowledge of the Erechtheion or its Roman copies (Fig. 4.12).[31] Drawn in black pencil and dated 1535, it shows four maidens standing on heavy stylobates along one length of a loggia, the two central figures positioned frontally, the two extreme figures turned toward them, the one at the left possessing a second face at the back of her head. A fifth figure is seen between the two figures at the right, along the other axis of the loggia, echoing one so placed in the Erechtheion. Because it is so crudely rendered, Harprath believed it is a copy of Giulio's work by a member of his circle at Mantua and presented in evidence a second, composite image believed to have belonged at one time to Vasari (Fig. 4.13).[32] This one shows two heads of caryatids from the other drawing, more delicately rendered in Giulio's characteristic media,[33] and may have come from one of those sheets Vasari reports Giulio to have shown him during his visit to Mantua in 1541.[34] Concerning the Strozzi monument Harprath concluded, "The ideation arose without doubt from Giulio Romano, given that the inscription carries a date following by only 5 years his arrival in Mantua, where nearly no one would have been capable of such a realization."[35]

Let me sum up my argument thus far in addressing the question, "What did Hermione's statue look like?" The scenic facts described above indicate that the statue is standing in a relaxed yet regal posture. She is placed on a pedestal. Her skin bears visible traces of paint, probably more so on face, neck, arms, and hands—and bluish veins of simulated marble are visible on her exposed flesh. Additionally, she may be using a support of some kind, perhaps a column or plinth. That the statue is "newly performed by that rare Italian master Giulio Romano" is fully consonant with the labile fictional setting of the play and the facts concerning the artist's activities revealed by modern art historical research—reflecting

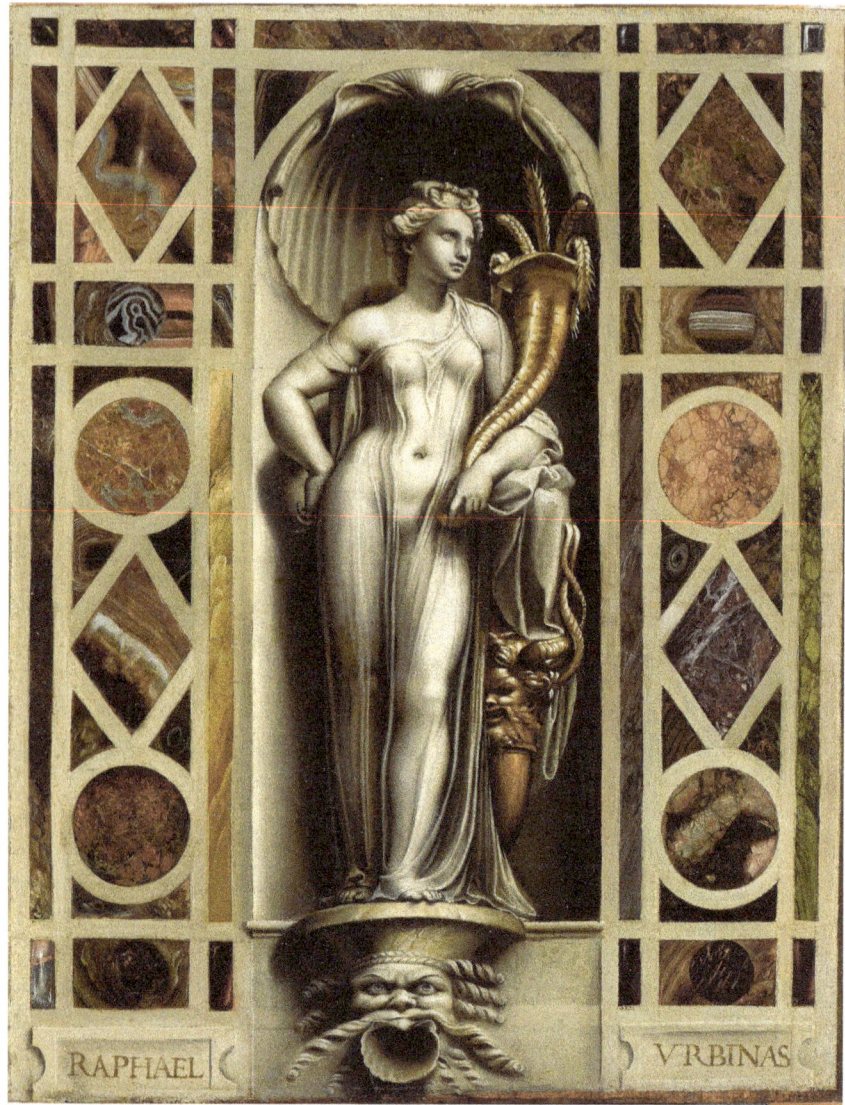

Fig. 4.11. "Ceres," by Giulio Romano. Musée du Louvre, Paris.

Giulio's interest in painted and carved figural sculpture, supported by Vasari's encomium that he made "sculpted and painted bodies breathe."

But there are also close connections between Polissena Boschetti, one of the overseers of the monument, and Giulio Romano. Polissena was the sister of Baldassare Castiglione, who knew Giulio well. In 1523 he consulted Giulio about the purchase of antique

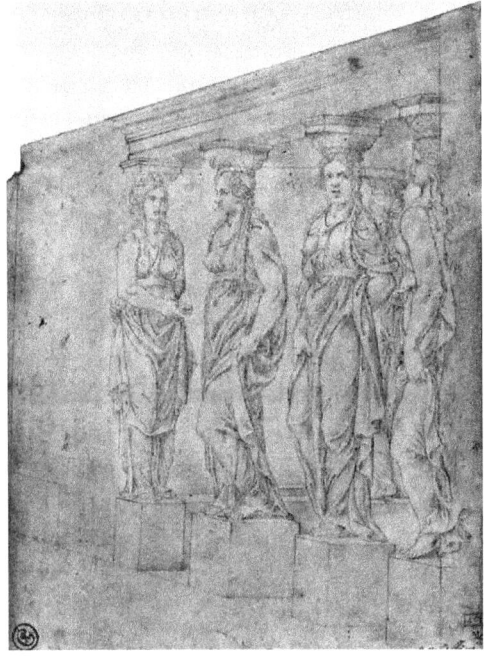

Fig. 4.12. Sketch of Erechtheion caryatids attributed to workshop of Giulio Romano.

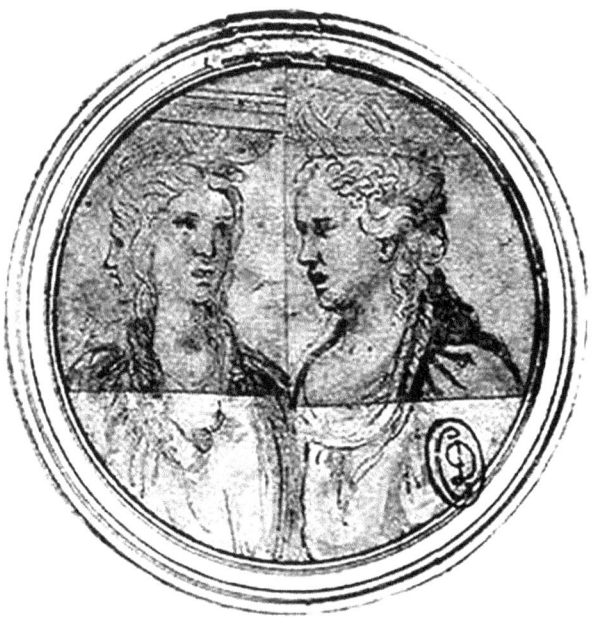

Fig. 4.13. Vasari's pastiche of Giulio Romano's caryatid sketches.

marbles offered for sale by Gianfrancesco Penni, Giulio's colleague in Raphael's workshop. On being told that they were not of good quality, he decided to forgo the purchase.[36] In 1524, after some years of conducting negotiations between Federico II Gonzaga and Giulio, Castiglione accompanied the latter from Rome to Mantua, where Giulio assumed the duties of court artist and ultimately surveyor of public works for Gonzaga. When Castiglione died in 1529, his mother Aloisa Gonzaga and his heir Ludovico Strozzi commissioned Giulio to design his monument for Santa Maria delle Grazie in Curtatone, outside of Mantua. In 1536, Polissena commissioned Giulio to decorate the Chapel of San Longino in the Church of Sant' Andrea, where the relics of Longinus, San Gregorio Nazianzeno, and Beato Adalberto were to be gathered, and she herself was eventually buried there.[37] If not conclusive proof of Giulio's authorship of Strozzi's monument, all this evidence constitutes a very strong presumption.

III

Given our inability to place Shakespeare before the Giulian monument in San Domenico, its residence during the dramatist's lifetime, by what paths might we trace its thematic and synecdochic reappearance in *The Winter's Tale*?[38] One way would examine the reports of English travelers to Mantua that might have attracted his attention.[39] Another would lead us in search of print renderings, like that of the Mantuan engraver Giorgio Ghisi (Fig. 4.14), which may have circulated in England in the late sixteenth and early seventeenth centuries.[40] A still more persuasive route would take us into Shakespeare's social and professional milieu, to inquire who, among his theatrical acquaintance, might have visited the monument and described it—or sketched it—so vividly that it took root in his imagination and there blossomed. That way lies Inigo Jones, who traveled to Italy around 1599, probably in the entourage of Francis Manners, younger brother of Roger, the 5th Earl of Rutland (for whom Shakespeare worked in 1613),[41] and again, it is believed, in 1605, well before his famous tour with Thomas Howard, Earl of Arundel, and his wife, in 1613–14.[42]

A further possibility is Shakespeare's likely encounter with Italian *commedia* players in England.[43] Mantua was an important center of theatrical activity in the later sixteenth and early seventeenth centuries. The Gelosi company of Franceso and Isabella Andreini,

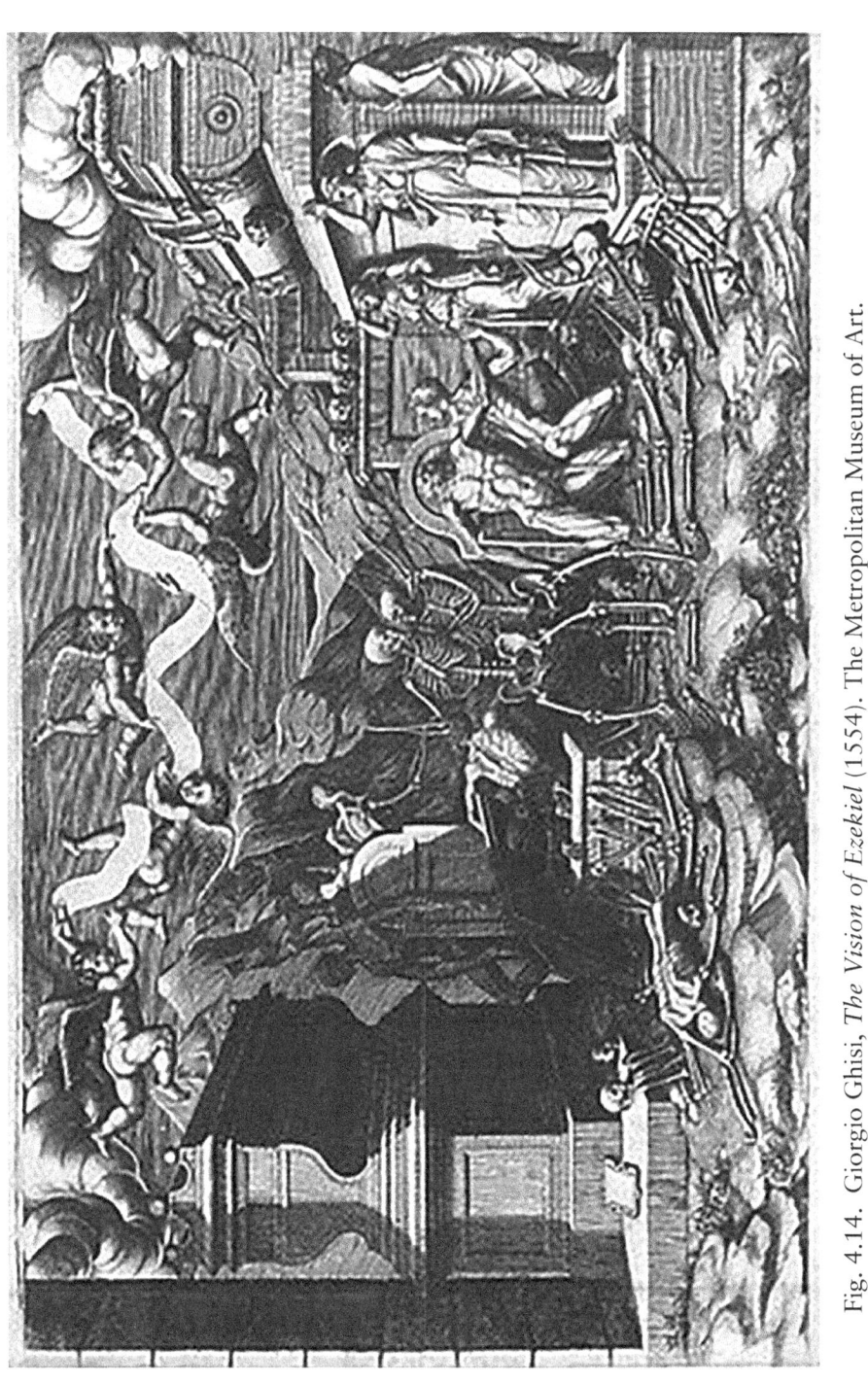

Fig. 4.14. Giorgio Ghisi, *The Vision of Ezekiel* (1554). The Metropolitan Museum of Art.

the Confidenti of Giovanni Pellesini and Vittoria Piissimi, and the company of Tristano Martinelli (the original Arlecchino) and his brother Drusiano enjoyed the protection of Guglielmo Gonzaga, 3rd Duke of Mantua, and of his successor, Vincenzo I, 4th Duke. The latter also patronized the *Uniti*, and in 1598–99 established an official ducal company led by the Martinelli brothers, which featured some of the best actors then exercising their profession in Italy.[44] These actors were not just entertainers but instruments of foreign policy in Mantua, as the Gonzaga realized that they could compete theatrically and festively, if not financially and militarily, with their more powerful neighbors.[45] Although *commedia* players are known to have performed in England in the 1570s and 1580s, a 1591 letter to Francis Bacon concerning Italian spies who came to England disguised as acrobats suggests that Italian players were still common enough to offer protective cover. There are also literary references to Italian actors, indicating their familiarity to English readers—like that of Thomas Nashe, who writes in 1590 that he met "that famous Francatrip' Harlicken" in Bergamo on his way home from Venice, "who asked me many particulars of the order and maner of our plays and enquired of me if I knew any such Parabolano here in London as Signior Chiarlatano Kempino."[46] The famous mountebank Scoto of Mantua, whose persona is appropriated by Jonson's *Volpone*, performed before the queen in the late 1570s or early 1580s, evidently leaving a communal memory in England to be tapped by Shakespeare's company in 1606.[47] As Lea points out, Jonson develops the jealous Corvino's lines in a manner that casts Scoto as an actor in a *commedia* performance.[48] This indicates that Jonson, who, like Shakespeare, seems never to have visited the continent—except for a stint as a soldier in the Netherlands—was certainly familiar with the masks and scenes of the *commedia dell'arte* and was still able to exploit public awareness of Italian players many years after their known visits to England were documented.[49]

Taken together, all of the above constitutes a web of data outlining the likely routes by which reports might have traveled from the Church of San Domenico in Mantua into Shakespeare's imagination. There are, however, no positive connections. This raises a larger scholarly question. In an early modern culture where dramatists and performers were literally dependent on word of mouth to catch news of what their colleagues and competitors were bringing to the marketplace they all shared, and were also influenced by the verbal reports of travelers returning from abroad, what kind of evidence should we find acceptable when attempting to account for Shakespeare's awareness that Giulio Romano was a designer of sculpture, and even for the possibility that he was familiar with Giulio's caryatids on the Strozzi monument? Hypothesizing his knowing is attractive because it helps to explain the deep embedment of the Italian artist in the play text, yet it is obviously risky. Absent any trace of external proof, what will suffice, for oneself and one's readers, to reason our way to accepting the internal evidence supplied by the scenic facts and supported by art historical research? There are two approaches that seem tenable to me: one is theoretical, the other practical—and they are found in Shakespeare's own reflections on the very problem we are considering. Together they license a humbling of expectations concerning the availability of positive historical evidence and acceptance, where that is lacking, of an approach that I shall call a methodology of the lost circumstance, capable of producing an ekphrastic scenario that will persuade.

This is a reasonable approach that merits consideration in research conditions where material documentation is wanting. It is based on known historical practices, is psychologically compelling, and is also intellectually respectable. Indeed, it has an august pedigree, originating in Aristotle's opening reflections in the *Nichomachean Ethics* on the kinds of measurement one should apply to different objects of study and, consequently, on the degree of cognitive precision that may be expected. The knowledge we seek, he argues, must be in accordance with the nature of the object. "For a well-schooled man is one who searches for that degree of precision in each kind of study which the nature of the subject at hand admits: it is obviously just as foolish to accept arguments of probability from a mathematician as to demand strict demonstrations from an orator," who deals not with things which cannot be other than they are but with the variable material of human actions.[50] In attempting to determine what Hermione's statue looked like and why it looked that way, the very process of analysis, therefore, must mediate between the conditions manifested in the play text itself, *statuefication* and *mollification*—between, that is, the fixity with which sculptures or printed words disguise the fluid human interactions that precede their being "newly performed" or typographically imposed on the press and their *soft* ontologies, consisting of many variable, sometimes irretrievable shaping circumstances that must be reconstructed. Both processes, as we have seen, are deeply implicated in *The Winter's Tale*—represented in the visible mollification of the rigid statue at the end of 5.3 and in the printed textual references that offer hints about the etiology of Giulio's presence in Shakespeare's imagination even before his name is uttered in 5.2.

That Shakespeare himself was interested in the way *soft*, often fortuitous, human interactions become rigid data in need of mollification so as to enable equitable judgment is evident in the way he often thematizes the issue in his plays. Consider Juliet, the pseudo-corpse whose color is just returning to her cheeks when Romeo unwittingly reverses the process through his phantasmatic Petrarchan heroics before she awakens from Friar Laurence's sleeping potion, as discussed in Chapter 2. Returning to consciousness, she discovers he has taken poison and joins him in actual death by stabbing herself. Members of the Watch then enter: "We see the ground whereon these woes do lie, / But the true ground of all these piteous woes / We cannot without circumstance descry" (5.3.179–81). This is a call for a verbal reconstruction of the elements that have been conducive to the lovers' deaths. The events leading to the shocking display of their inert bodies are then serially related to the Duke and the elder Montague and the Capulets by the Friar, Balthasar, and Paris's Page, to the best of their knowledge. But only the theater audience knows the full circumstances of the more complicated back-story—including the sheer accident of Friar John's imprisonment as he bears a letter to Romeo in Mantua—having witnessed the motives, emotions, misprisions, hesitations, words, and actions of the two lovers. Ironically, the result of the attempted mollification by Friar Laurence, Balthasar, and the Page is literally statuefication—as Montague vows to raise a "statue in pure gold" of Juliet, and Capulet promises the same for Romeo: "There shall no figure at such rate be set / As that of true and faithful Juliet. / As rich shall Romeo's by his lady's lie, / Poor sacrifices of our enmity!" (5.3.301–4). Genuine though the families' grief may be, Shakespeare makes it clear that the lovers will have lost whatever distinctive qualities that made them so engaging and led them to do what they did—in the way that they did—as they are transformed into cautionary monuments to the dire effects of civil discord.

With less obvious irony, at the conclusion of *Hamlet* Horatio promises to explain to the astonished audience of Fortinbras and the English ambassadors the quarry of dead bodies they see heaped before them:

> Give order that these bodies
> High on a stage be placed to the view,
> And let me speak to [th'] yet unknowing world
> How these things came about. So shall you hear

Of carnal, bloody, and unnatural acts,
Of accidental judgments, casual slaughters,
Of deaths put on by cunning and [forc'd] cause,
And in this upshot, purposes mistook
Fall'n on th' inventors' heads: all this can I
Truly deliver. (*Ham.* 5.2.377–86)

Though it is spoken at the end of the tragedy, Horatio's offer to fill in the circumstances that have led to the visible debacle sounds very much like an *argumentum* that usually precedes the action of a play.[51] As such it functions as a plot outline, and though it is nominally "circumstantial" insofar as it lists the *kinds* of event that have led to the scene of slaughter, and thus inform its content, it, too, will fail to render the *particular* qualities of agents, their thoughts and their actions, which only the theater audience has witnessed. Speech, character, and complex, visible behavior will succumb to the art of narrative.[52]

A similar process occurs, this time with tragicomic consequences, in *Much Ado About Nothing*. Claudio's denunciation of Hero at their marriage ceremony, notes Friar Francis, has caused "A thousand blushing apparitions / To start into her face, a thousand innocent shames / In angel whiteness to beat away those blushes" (4.1.158–60), before her spirits were "smothered up" by "these things, come thus to light," according to Don John the Bastard (4.1.111–12). However, by means of the therapeutic scheme devised by the Friar, Hero publicly dies to the world so that Claudio may reflect upon every circumstance of her life, and even amplify her virtues under the pressure of his guilt. In this way he will resurrect the innocent Hero:

When he shall hear she died upon his words,
Th'idea of her life shall sweetly creep
Into his study of imagination,
And every lovely organ of her life
Shall come apparell'd in more precious habit,
More moving, delicate, and full of life,
Into the eye and prospect of his soul,
Than when she liv'd indeed. (4.1.223–30)[53]

Friar Francis's prediction proves to be correct. On hearing Borachio's confession, Claudio exclaims, "Sweet Hero, now thy image doth appear / In the rare semblance that I lov'd it first" (5.1.251–2). He mourns her at Leonato's family monument and composes a hymn imploring Diana, "goddess of the night," to pardon "Those that slew thy virgin knight." The next morning, thinking to wed her cousin in recompense, he finds the living Hero to be his bride. "The former Hero," cries Don Pedro. "The Hero that is dead!" A repentant Leonato corrects him: "She died, my lord, but whiles her slander lived" (5.4.66–7).

In this instance the comic agency of a wise friar releases the powers of mollification in Hero's betrothed, whose public confession prevents her from becoming a monument, to either female deception or mythic chastity. Cressida is not so fortunate. Shakespeare's most voluble heroine before Cleopatra, she understands how a powerless woman can retain some measure of agency in a world ever ready to instrumentalize her. It is by living as fully as she can in the medium of possibility and acting to her advantage according to the decorum of the moment while concealing her inward desires. On the walls of Ilium in 1.2 she is a witty Beatrice, punning with Alexander, teasing Pandarus and engaging him in naughty parlor talk; but alone at the end of the scene she unexpectedly reveals her love for Troilus to the audience, and explains her *modus vivendi*:

> Things won are done, joy's soul lies in the doing.
> That she belov'd knows nought that knows not this:
> Men prize the thing ungain'd more than it is.
> That she was never yet that ever knew
> Love got so sweet as when desire did sue.
> Therefore this maxim out of love I teach:
> Achievement is command, ungain'd beseech;
> Then, though my heart's content firm love doth bear,
> Nothing of that from mine eyes appear. (1.2.287–95)

"Things won are done, joy's soul lies in the doing." Cressida is caught up in the soft ontology of a play that values the circumstantial continuity of a fluid present in its fear of coming to a reified ending. The clearest expression of this need to keep open the medium of possibility is Agamemnon's greeting to Hector:

> Worthy all arms! As welcome as to one
> That would be rid of such an enemy.
> But that's no welcome. Understand more clear,
> What's past and what's to come is strew'd with husks
> And formless ruin of oblivion;
> But in this extant moment, faith and troth,
> Strain'd purely from all hollow bias-drawing,
> Bids thee, with most divine integrity,
> From heart of very heart, great Hector, welcome. (4.5.163–71)[54]

With these words Shakespeare allows Agamemnon to recapture from the teleology of history the heroic agency in which two men can appear to one another as they are and not as events have made them: conqueror and victim. Similarly, Cressida, even though she loves Troilus, fears becoming a consumable product of his desire. To avoid this, she must practice the defensive art of living "in this extant moment" and acting circumstantially, for it is the only way she can continue to be herself while remaining loyal to the man she loves. As if to confirm the validity of her fear, Shakespeare shows how she is indeed instrumentalized after warily succumbing to Troilus's assurance that the only "monstruosity in love" is "that the desire is boundless and the act a slave to limit" (3.2.83). For him, sexual pleasure ends in bathos; for her, it ends in statuefication. On the morning following their night of lovemaking, Cressida is traded to the Greeks for Antenor, and thence becomes the fixed image of deception in both Greek and Trojan eyes as she tries to sustain her limited agency. When we see her in 4.2, both her fear and devotion are apparent, yet as she passes helplessly into the Greek camp in 4.5, exchanging graceful compliments and kisses with the assembled generals, her chosen decorum invites Ulysses to designate her a daughter of the game whose "wanton spirits look out / At every joint and motive of her body" (56–7). She is still trying to keep things in motion at her final appearance in 5.2—so much so, in fact, that modern editors usually slow down the repeated exchange of Troilus's sleeve between Diomed and herself by giving her the part-line (81) assigned to him in both Quarto and Folio and eliminating two apparently authorial speech prefixes. Thus the Folio:

> *Cres.*: O all you gods! O prettie, prettie pledge;
> Thy Maister now lies thinking on his bed
> Of thee and me, and sighs, and takes my Glove,
> And gives memorial dainty kisses to it;
> As I kiss thee.
> *Dio.*: Nay, doe not snatch it from me (81)
> *Cres.*: He that takes that [doth take] my heart withal.
> *Dio.*: I had your heart before, this follows it. (F 3063–70;
>   5.2.77–83)

What the old texts indicate is that the pledge passes to Diomed even as Cressida apostrophizes it, and when she attempts to kiss it, Diomed holds onto it firmly, ending the game. Her next line then comes as a partial realization that the sleeve has become a talisman betokening her investment in love rather than her commitment to

Troilus, so that Diomed's response—"I had your heart before"—is another misreading that fixes what had been only potential. After that, Cressida's attempts to remain faithful to Troilus seem increasingly elegiac—"'tis done, 'tis past; And yet it is not" (96)—and though she fails to appoint an hour for her next meeting with Diomed, it is evident that he is now her lover. Her last full line before he exits traces in its abrupt disjunctions the end to her waverings: "Ay, come—O Jove!—do come.—I shall be plagued" (105). With this she has become Robert Henryson's Cresseid—the byword that will "stick the heart of falsehood": "As false as Cressid'" (3.2.195–6).[55]

Shakespeare was clearly fascinated by the interplay of the qualities of *character*, which manifest themselves in the myriad changing circumstances in which an individual makes decisions and acts, and what I have called in Chapter 2 *dramatis persona*, a reproducible type, more or less fixed in time. With these examples in mind, let us return to the scene of our inquiry by questioning the Strozzi monument.

IV

What was written between the lines of Pietro Strozzi's will? Was he envisioning the design of his monument when he specified 400 gold scudi, marble, and friends to supervise its construction? From the evidence of Robert Cecil's monument some eighty years later, probably not. But if Strozzi, like Cecil, saw a model before he died and approved it, the resulting monument can be considered an expression of his wishes. Cecil lies clad in his Garter robes, the Principal Secretary's seal bag clutched in his left hand, the Lord Treasurer's staff of office in his right—all symbols of his worldly distinction (Fig. 4.5). He is supported by four kneeling women, personifications of Prudence, Temperance, Justice, and Fortitude, the interior qualities for which he apparently wished to be remembered. Strozzi cuts a different figure. He wears a Roman fillet on his brow; his shroud resembles a toga in its drapery; and sandals complete the picture of a citizen in the classical mode devoted to public service. Not kneeling virtues, but four standing caryatids hold him up on his entablature. Did he request them of his friends, off the record, as a salute to a revered past, or were they the idea of the designer, who knew from Vitruvius that they represented the conquered women of ancient Carya?[56]

Whatever answer the extant record conceals, the monument declares that Strozzi reposes utmost confidence in these four stone bearers, reinvented from Roman copies of Greek originals and given pride of place. Unlike Cecil's virtues, they do not *represent* him, they *pay homage* to him. He has assigned them the role of loyal supporters in a sense quite different from Cecil's virtues. Yet whether they are material emanations of ideas that Strozzi conveyed into words for his friends or that the designer shaped from his own mind into a model for his or their approval, they embody the process of statuefication. Ideas, words, stone. The process seems benign—how else can one order one's tomb?—and therefore quite natural. But that is just the point: the natural can harbor unanticipated implications, especially in the case of a last will and testament. In Renaissance psychology "natural" thoughts are not pristine, as Shakespeare, and perhaps Strozzi, well knew. Prompted by experience, they are infused with the passions that accompany perception, retained in their saturated form by the memory, and shaped in the imagination as phantasmata.[57] Once uttered, they assume material form, whether as reverberating currents of air, printed letters, or carved statues. Kenneth Gross offers a suggestive observation about statues that has relevance to both Pietro Strozzi's monument and *The Winter's Tale*:

> The statue represents an idea that has been silenced, restricted, or censored, even by virtue of its formal eloquence. Such a fate is partly the result of the bondage of ideas to the unstable yet reifying domain of the word. But their petrifying transformation could also be read as a result of our imperfect *reception* of ideas and words. Language may make ideas into statues, but that they remain statues may depend on our failure to reanimate the language we inherit, our failure of desire or tact, a submission to the contingent priority of our words; it may also be the result of a need to lend an illusory stability to ideas, even at the cost of emptying them out.[58]

In the case of a last will and testament, the ideas that were given words, which were then put into writing in a legal document—perhaps supplemented in remarks to friends—are especially inflexible, since by the time the will is executed the thinker and speaker is no longer capable of changing his mind. What he thought at the time he spoke is now literally irrevocable. Translated into the language of our monument, Strozzi has declared himself a model of classical civic virtue and the Four Ladies exemplars of female decorum circulating within his orbit—and does so in a manner that exhibits his appreciation of Greco-Roman aesthetics. Through these, he has transmitted to posterity what might, at the time he approved the project, have revealed the distinctive qualities of character that shaped his decision but which, in the course of time, have become, to borrow the theatrical term I have used earlier, his *dramatis persona*.

The process would be the same, albeit further inflected, even if these decisions were not initially—or ever—his. Suppose they were interpretations of his wishes by his friends, who then conveyed them to the designer they commissioned, in this case Giulio Romano. Vasari reports that Giulio could hear a client describe what he wanted and instantly realize it: "no sooner had one opened his mouth to explain to him his conception than he had understood and drawn it."[59] As encomiast and ekphrast, Vasari is not disposed to analyze the transformations that must inevitably occur as the client's conception passes to his tongue, thence to the artist's ear and imagination, whence it informs his hand; but we may safely assume such changes did occur, though with sufficient fidelity to the client's wishes as to gain his approval. The facility Vasari describes was developed during Giulio's years in Raphael's workshop, where it was standard practice for the master to provide a *schizzo* to be completed by his most talented *garzone*, whose distinctive touches would often enhance his master's idea.[60] In a world where faithful mimesis of the actual was highly valued, this talent to render what was merely imagined as though it were actually seen earned high praise from his younger contemporary Giovanni Battista Armenini, who writes that Giulio "was so gifted and dexterous . . . that when he drew something extemporaneously, one could say that he was copying a subject in front of his eyes rather than composing it from his own ideas."[61] Such was his facility at invention that whatever object he saw or merely heard about also became *his own*.[62] And when he turned over his drawings to the sculptors who executed them—probably artists in his workshop—it was inevitable that Strozzi's monument would undergo further modifications, however slight, in accordance with the individual talents and skills of the workmen involved.[63]

Thus words are not as fixed as Gross implies. They do indeed tend to reification, but they are subject to the mediation of listener or reader, who perceives and understands them according to his or her own preconceptions, his or her present emotional disposition, his or her shaping fantasy. One might say that fantasy adapts fantasy. When Hermione declares at her trial, "My life stands in the level of your dreams" (3.2.81), responding to Leontes' charge of conspiring with Polixenes to murder him (3.2.77–8), she makes explicit the reifying trajectory taken by Leontes' thoughts and words, which aim to fix her as an adulteress and traitor. But her apparent death and burial, which elicit Leontes' avowed (and reportedly fulfilled) repentance, followed by her reappearance as a living statue, reveal her resistance to his reification. She has taken his intention and—with the collaboration of Paulina, that collector of "many singularities"— has adapted it to the new purpose of redemption. Yet how she did this—with the myriad circumstances that form the content of her statuefication—remains concealed.[64]

Which suggests that there is a further analogy between Strozzi's monument and Shakespeare's play. For if Strozzi had envisioned a tomb in which he would be supported by four faithful caryatids, something curious has occurred in the process of realization. As we have seen, the marble women do perform their assigned tasks, but each figure has become individuated in such a way as to suggest that she also has something on her mind unrelated to Strozzi's service. The archaic figure at front left presents herself as a powerful image of mature domesticity. The Hellenistic figure at front right strikes a seductive pose that seems designed to attract the male gaze.[65] The figure at rear left is preoccupied with motherhood. And the figure at rear right looks as though she's had enough.

So statuefication had undergone mollification—both psychologically and physically—in the representation of the four caryatids by the time the monument was completed. They have become, in Vasari's words, both "anticamente moderna e modernamente antica." How might this process occur in written plays, "modernizing" their "antiquity" by revealing that the poet's conceit harbored unanticipated possibilities? The obvious answer is by performing them. Some onstage discoveries will be recorded in the rehearsal manuscripts (actors' roles or playbook), in the form of stage directions or revised lines of dialogue, but many will not, such as voice, gesture, and blocking. Nevertheless, that performed script—whether in the author's hand or in a fair copy—will move on to the printer's shop, be imposed on the press, and emerge as a typographical cousin to the Strozzi monument: a *textus receptus*. In the case of *The Winter's Tale*, we have a posthumous document that has passed before many interpretive eyes en route to its fixed public space, the 1623 Folio edition of *Mr. William / Shakespeares / Comedies, / Histories, & / Tragedies. / Published according to the True Originall Copies*. The task of editors, scholars, and critics is to take up that transformative process where their predecessors left off. They must ingeniously, then (it is to be hoped) rationally, methodically, and transparently address the Folio pages and redeem the author's words, if typographically corrupt; their possible meanings, where obscure or ambiguous; their references and allusions, if retrievable; and their rhetorical relationships with their original audiences—that is, the reciprocal interaction of text and performative context—insofar as that can be determined; and infer the appearances and movements implied by the dialogue, an invisible semiotic spectacle in need of visualization.[66]

Central to this task of retrieval is the question posed by the present chapter—"What did Hermione's statue look like?"—and its ancillary: is there any value in investigating the claim that the statue has been "newly performed by that rare Italian master Julio Romano"? However intriguing and illuminating the answers to these questions may be, they cannot be called the retrieval of *fact*. In the matter of the statue's appearance, until another witness to a pre-Folio performance adds words to Simon Forman's silence, we must rely on such inferences as are invited by the dialogue—those textual clues that I have called "scenic facts." These inferences, however, are strengthened intellectually and given visual reinforcement by adducing the known history of Giulio's activity as a designer of sculpture and the scholarship concerning the Strozzi monument. With the lack of documentary evidence that Shakespeare ever gazed upon the monument in San Domenico at Mantua, or examined a detailed engraving of the structure and its statues, read about them, or even heard them vividly described, truth is simply not to be had. Instead, the result will only be "true opinion" at best, however rigorously we pursue the work of recovery.

This oxymoronic phrase is enough to make a reasonable person shudder. It is what Leontes claims he possesses when he discovers that Polixenes and his train, led by Camillo, have slipped, in evident guiltiness, through the city's posterns and fled Sicilia: "How blest am I / In my just censure, in my true opinion!" (2.1.38–9). *The Winter's Tale* foregrounds the fallibility of such a measure, its "interestedness," hence its ineluctable bias. Why apply a demonstrably deceptive standard of measurement to the study of a play that focuses on its insufficiency?

First a bit of explication, then a disclaimer. In his assertion, Leontes is arrogating to himself a Platonic prerogative. For "true opinion," Socrates maintains in the *Meno*, "is as good a guide as knowledge for the purpose of acting rightly"—where "rightly" means justly, rationally, appropriately, and correctly.[67] In this context "true opinion" is related to Plato's doctrine that all knowledge is a form of recollection, "true opinion" being an intimation of that knowledge—yet not a full grasp of it. A Christian version of this belief is found in Juan Luis Vives' *De instrumento proba-bilitatis*, where the humanist describes certain native *anticipationes* implanted in humans by God, through which truth may be actualized by collecting and judging verisimilitudes and probabilities. This religious inflection of a secular rhetorical tradition is repeated by Thomas Wilson in *The Art of Rhetoric* and inspires Hieronimo in *The Spanish Tragedy* and (more comically) Polonius in *Hamlet*, so it is by no means recondite.[68] But Leontes' literally preposterous course of reasoning, originating in an imagined conflation of his boyhood friend and himself, and infused by what seems to be more recent, if unacknowledged, sexual stimulation, presents a textbook lesson in the risks that can be incurred in attempting to achieve a "true opinion." Moreover, his insistence that his is a "just censure" as well as a "true opinion" carries a certain legal resonance that might make an audience wary. For the late sixteenth and early seventeenth centuries saw a gradual refinement in the concept of evidence, as scientists, historians, lawyers, and philosophers developed a scale of credibility ranging from conviction achieved by demonstration, to belief secured by sifting higher and lower probabilities (weighing the number, consistency, and trustworthiness of testimonies), to doubt concerning unlikelihoods, to outright rejection of impossibilities—a scale on which "opinion" stood in the lower ranks.[69] In examining questions where demonstration could not be had, there developed the criterion of moral certainty, notably in the case of jury trials. As one writer remarks, echoing Aristotle, since most contested acts are not capable of "infallible Mathematical demonstration," juries "often find that which in their Conscience, doth fully persuade them that the accused person is guilty . . . They don't swear the Bill is True, but that they in their Consciences believe that it is so."[70] It is in this self-limiting sense that I propose a "science of true opinion." A science, yes, insofar as it follows a rigorous, transparent, repeatable procedure. But more modest than Leontes' "true opinion," as it abjures Platonic and Christian warranties. And therefore fallible. Yet if we keep a critical eye on our inborn tendentiousness as we sift the probabilities, we may arrive at a "true opinion" that happens to be true, though incapable of demonstration, and that can bear the scrutiny—perhaps even earn the "just censure"—of more skeptical eyes, until further evidence comes to light.

So what did Hermione's statue look like? For the present, I propose that we put together the "scenic facts" of Act 5, Scene 3 discussed earlier in this chapter and the evidence we have examined of Giulio's known ventures in the medium of sculpture, including the paintings and drawings of sculpture ascribed to him. This procedure will allow us to compose an ekphrasis such as this: "When Paulina draws the curtain, she reveals the statue of Hermione standing on a low pedestal. She is posed in the natural but dignified manner of a Hellenistic caryatid without an entablature to support—one arm bent, hand on hip, the other cast downward, her fore-arm resting on a waist-high plinth with her hand extended in welcome, as 'when first I wooed her.' The white stone from which she appears to be carved is seen mainly in the areas of face, neck, and hands. They are lightly colored in flesh tones to make her look natural—a bit ruddier about the lips—and some thin streaks of blue, which often occur in veiny marble, are visible on her neck and wrists. Her contemporary attire is colored in a manner that resembles the costumes of the other players onstage—'as she lived now'—and her hair is arranged formally as befits her rank. Her friendly eyes look straight ahead, meeting the gaze of her observers."

Notes

1. By "scenic facts" I mean printed evidence of what was described onstage, which, unless contradicted, represents what at least some pre-Folio audiences are likely to have seen.
2. *The Winter's Tale*, First Folio, TLN 3103–5, 3108–9, with act, scene, and line numbers from Pitcher, as before.
3. These deliberate cues and miscues are consistent with Shakespeare's finely tuned manipulation of audience response, as we shall see in greater detail in the next two chapters.
4. The galleries of the Howards, Wriothesleys, Lumleys, Cecils, and other prominent families—to say nothing of those of Prince Henry—were an increasing source of social prestige as art collecting became a sign of cultural sophistication in early seventeenth-century England. See the essays in Chaney, *The Evolution of English Collecting*. "Many singularities" may also suggest that Paulina's gallery shares the features of a *wunderkammer*, as Peter Platt argues in *Shakespeare and the Culture of Paradox* (Burlington, VT: Ashgate, 2009), p. 200.
5. The Folio's massed entrance direction at the beginning of the scene reads, "Enter Leontes, Polixenes, Florizell, Perdita, Camillo, Paulina: Hermione (like a Statue:) Lords, etc." No further clue here.
6. A good source of variants on this pose is *Dynasties: Painting in Tudor and Jacobean England 1530–1630*, ed. Karen Hearn (Peterborough: Tate Gallery, 1995), esp. figs. 107, 109, 110, 121, 125, 129, 135, 139.
7. This is admittedly a stumbling block in Catherine Belsey's argument

that the statue is a funerary effigy. See *Shakespeare and the Loss of Eden* (New Brunswick, NJ: Rutgers University Press, 1999), pp. 85–127. The phrase "life of majesty," however, does suggest that her "natural posture" has what we might call a "regal" informality about it.

8. No matter that the theater audience may not be able to see the wrinkles; ekphrasis will persuade them they do, especially since Polixenes confirms Leontes' observation.

9. *The Winter's Tale*, ed. Stephen Orgel (Oxford: Oxford University Press, 1996), p. 226, n. 47.

10. Margaret Whinney, *Sculpture in Britain, 1530 to 1830* (Harmondsworth: Penguin, 1964), p. 20.

11. Unusual, too, for English monuments is the design of four female figures, representing the classical virtues, supporting the slab on which the effigy of Cecil rests. In his will of 1604 he had arranged that a monument be fashioned and placed in the parish church of Hatfield, and in 1609 Colt presented a model for his approval, so presumably the completed monument is in conformity with his wishes—though it cost more than twice the stipulated £200. Its design may reflect European influence, for the slab with effigy supported by human shapes is usually traced to the tomb of Count Engelbert of Nassau at Breda, made in 1520 by an Italian, Romasco Vincidor. Katherine Esdaile, in *English Church Monuments 1510–1840* (London: Batsford, 1946), claims, however, that there are English variants of independent origin (p. 50).

12. *The Color of Life: Polychromy in Sculpture from Antiquity to the Present*, ed. Roberta Panzanelli (Los Angeles: J. Paul Getty Museum, 2008), pp. 4–15, 67–75. Arguing that even in the first decade of the seventeenth century sophisticated English taste was turning away from painted statues, B. J. Sokol invokes Truewit's satirical remarks linking the Collegiate Ladies' face-painting in Jonson's *Epicoene* (1609) to the newly unveiled painted statues of Peace and Charity on the refurbished Aldgate (*Art and Illusion*, pp. 58–61). He reprises the argument in *Shakespeare's Artists* (London: Bloomsbury, 2018), pp. 87–8.

13. *Thomas Middleton: The Collected Works*, ed. Gary Taylor and John Lavagnino (Oxford: Clarendon Press, 2007).

14. In her study of painted bodies on the early modern stage, Andrea Stevens observes that "There is no way of knowing . . . whether statue-Hermione is painted differently from how she appeared before—more vividly, or with more thickly applied colour, or with more whiteface underneath to simulate her 'stoniness'; perhaps not," she concludes, "since those who see her insist that she is uncannily life-like for a statue" (*Inventions of the Skin: The Painted Body in Early English Drama, 1400–1642* [Edinburgh: Edinburgh University Press, 2013], p. 151, n. 45). Yet there must have been some touches of "stone" in her "lifelikeness," else she would not have been "life-like" and the players would have given the game away.

15. If the former, the line is an example of what I call the "tragicomic cue" in Chapter 5 below. But they could just as easily be seeing painted veins of marble, exaggerated to further stage the illusion of statuary.

16. *The Winter's Tale*, ed. Orgel, figs. 7–10, 13, 14.

17. This was first argued by Karl Elze in the nineteenth century. See *Essays on Shakespeare*, trans. L. Dora Schmitz (London: Macmillan, 1874), pp. 284–9.

18. See Vincenzo Farinella and Giovanni Agosti, "Su Roberto Longhi, la scultura e il Classicismo," *Quaderni di Palazzo Te* 2.3 (1985): 37.

19. All images of the Strozzi monument are photographs taken by the author.

20. In the sixteenth century, few Italian viewers would have made the connection, given the difficulty of access to Athens after the Turks occupied Greece in the mid-fifteenth century. The more likely associations would have been to various ancient copies seen in Rome and in Mantua. On this, see below.

21. None of the six Erechtheion maidens used their arms to support the entablature. Their right hands, at their sides, held phiales, or shallow ritual bowls; their left hands lightly held their skirts. See Martin Robertson, *A History of Greek Art*, 2 vols. (Cambridge: Cambridge University Press, 1975), vol. 1, p. 346.

22. PETRI STROZZAE / AEQ(UA) BE(NEMERENTIA) AM(ICORUM) / AF(FECTUS) Q(UE) MAE(STITIA) / P(OSUERUNT) / MDXXIX. My translation from Farinella and Agosti's conjectural reconstruction of the abbreviated Latin epitaph, "Su Roberto Longhi," p. 38, n. 26.

23. See *Giulio Romano: Repertorio di fonti documentarie*, ed. Daniela Ferrari, intro. Amedeo Belluzi, 2 vols. (Mantua: Ministerio per I Beni Culturale e Ambientali Ufficio Centrale per I Beni Archivisitici, 1992), vol. 1, p. 313.

24. Roberto Longhi, "Le Cariatidi della sepultura Strozzi in S. Andrea di Mantova sono imitate dall'antico," *Quaderni di Palazzo Te* 2.3 (1985): 31–2. Longhi's notes on this subject apparently date from the first third of the twentieth century, according to Vincenzo Farinella and Giovanni Agosti, "Su Roberto Longhi," pp. 33–8. They are amplified in considerable detail by Alda Spinazzola Levi, "Monumenti inediti di Mantova in rapporto con l'arte di Giulio Romano," *Atti della Pontificia Accademia Romana di Archeologia* 21 (1944–45): 213–39, esp. 232–9. Levi offers a meticulous comparison of the archaic caryatid with its apparent model in the Gonzaga collection. She argues that it follows the characteristic Giulian mingling of the antique with the Cinquecento, and she offers further identification of the models for the Hellenistic caryatid at the front right and the fourth figure behind her.

25. This is the "Venus Genetrix," now in the Vienna Kunsthistorisches Museum, which Giulio Romano brought from Rome and presented to Federico II Gonzaga after he had entered his employ. See Guido

Rebecchini, *Private Collectors in Mantua, 1500–1630* (Rome: Edizioni di Storia e Letteratura, 2002), pp. 216–17.

26. Longhi, "Le Cariatidi," p. 31, translation mine.

27. Vittorio Matteuchi, *Le chiese artistiche del Mantovano* (Mantua, 1902), p. 142; Carlo d'Arco, *Monumenti di pittura e scultura tras-celti in Mantova e nel suo territorio* (Mantua, 1827), pp. 11–12; Alda Spinazzola Levi, "Monumenti inediti di Mantova in rapporto con l'arte di Giulio Romano," *Atti della Pontificia Accademia Romana di Archeologia* 21 (1944–45): 213–39.

28. Richard Harprath, "Giulio Romano e la conoscenza della Loggia delle Cariatidi dell'Eretteo," *Quaderni di Palazzo Te* 2.3 (1985): 39, all translations mine.

29. *Le vite*, vol. 2, p. 831.

30. Ceres or *Dovizia* (Abundance) was a play on the Cardinal's surname. The image covered the *Small Holy Family*, also in the Louvre, which Raphael delegated to Giulio to prepare as a gift for the Cardinal. See Linda Wolk-Simon, "Raphael, Giulio Romano, and the Business of Love," in *Giulio Romano: Art and Desire*, ed. Barbara Furlotti, Guido Rebecchini, and Linda Wolk-Simon (Milan: Electa, 2019), p. 34; Henry and Joannides, *Late Raphael*, pp. 74, 252.

31. Harprath, "Giulio Romano," p. 40.

32. Ibid. p. 42.

33. Observes Harprath: "Not only the typical technique of the pen and brown acquarella, but also the accurately executed contours show this time the hand of Giulio. Especially the rendering of the eyes and of the mouths with their soft sorrowful expression reveal the autograph execution there. The little drawing was in all probability already in the collection of Vasari, who, as is known, was accustomed to integrate together fragments of leaves and join within decorative frames little drawings with others of larger dimensions in his collection" (ibid. p. 42).

34. *Lives*, trans. de Vere, vol. 6, p. 166.

35. Harprath, "Giulio Romano," p. 42.

36. *Giulio Romano: Repertorio*, vol. 1, p. 33.

37. See Rebecchini, *Private Collectors*, pp. 100–3; Giovanni Pasetti, *Giulio Romano: Il Genio e l'Invenzione* (Mantua: Tre Lune Edizioni, 2008), p. 70; *Giulio Romano: Repertorio*, vol. 1, p. 712. Not incidentally, Polissena was the mother of Isabella Boschetti, the highly influential mistress of Federico Gonzaga. For details of the relationship between their liaison and Giulio's program in the Palazzo Te, see Barbara Furlotti, "Eros and Imagery in the Court of Federico II Gonzaga," in *Art and Desire*, pp. 42–55.

38. Thematic as it evokes the cycle of a woman's life, synecdochic as that cycle is subsumed in Hermione's aging statue, with its supple "natural posture."

39. Fynes Moryson visited Mantua in 1594 and stopped at the Palazzo Te, but he says nothing of visiting San Domenico. Will Kemp traveled to Italy in 1601, and his encounter with Sir Anthony Sherley in *The Travailes of Three English Brothers* (1607) has been re-set from Rome to Venice, which is apparently the closest he came to Mantua. Thomas Coryat arrived in Mantua on June 18, 1608, staying overnight. He admired the bridge over the Mincio, the Church of Santa Barbara adjoining the Palazzo Ducale, and "three statues very curiously pourtrayed in white stone" atop the gates of the palace (*Coryat's crudities; reprinted from the edition of 1611. To which are now added, his letters from India, &c. and extracts relating to him, from various authors: being a more particular account of his travels (mostly on foot) in different parts of the globe, than any hitherto published. Together with his orations, character, death, &c. With copper-plates. In three volumes* [London: W. Cater, 1776], vol. 1, p. 146). He also records seeing his first mountebank, and concludes his account by remarking on Castiglione's tomb "about five miles from Mantua" (vol. 1, p. 150), but gives no indication that he went to see it. In 1610, William Cecil, Viscount Cranborne, the son of Sir Robert Cecil, traveled to Italy and spent four weeks in Venice, but there is no record of his having set foot in Mantua. Robert Devereux, 3rd Earl of Essex, Sir John Harington of Exton, Robert Dallington, Sir Thomas Palmer, and Thomas Coke—all with connections to Henry's court—made journeys to Italy by 1610, but did not visit Mantua as far as we know. Nor did Samuel Daniel, who met Baptista Guarini in Padua during his travels with Sir Edward Dymoke in 1590–91. He later brought forth his own version of pastoral—*The Queen's Arcadia*—at Oxford in 1605, which is likely to have come to Shakespeare's notice, though we have no written evidence that it did.

40. Although the monument occupying the far right of this composition is clearly inspired by the Strozzi tomb, its caryatids have undergone radical simplification and could not have provided the visual information Shakespeare needed to develop the scenic facts discussed above.

41. See Altman, *Improbability*, p. 319.

42. Very little is known of these earlier journeys; the evidence is virtually all inferential. See J. Alfred Gotch, *Inigo Jones* (1928) (New York: Blom, 1968), pp. 23–32; Giles Worsley, *Inigo Jones and the European Classicist Tradition* (New Haven and London: Yale University Press, 2007), pp. 5–6. What makes the lacunae especially frustrating is that handwriting analysis indicates that Jones's copy of the 1568 edition of Vasari's *Vite* had been acquired prior to 1610, perhaps on his first journey to Italy circa 1599. See A. W. Johnson, *Three Volumes Annotated by Inigo Jones* (Turku: Åbo Akademi University Press, 1997), pp. xxi–xxxi. Sometime later he annotated the chapter on Giulio, but his comments are laconic in the extreme. The same volume, as noted earlier, contains Vasari's life of Marcantonio Raimondi, who

engraved Giulio's explicitly sexual drawings for *I modi*, which, as I have suggested, probably figure in the earlier part of the play.

43. Shakespeare's indebtedness to the interchangeable "theatergrams" of Italian *commedia grave* and *commedia dell'arte* has been convincingly demonstrated by Clubb, *Italian Drama*, and in subsequent essays. It is further developed in Robert Henke, *Pastoral Transformations: Italian Tragicomedy and Shakespeare's Late Plays* (Newark: University of Delaware Press, 1997). See his "Border-Crossing in the *Commedia dell'Arte*," in *Transnational Exchange in Early Modern Theater*, ed. Robert Henke and Eric Nicholson (Burlington, VT: Ashgate, 2008), pp. 19–34, for a detailed account of the European travels of Italian actors. More recently, Henke has published a further detailed account of Shakespeare's interweaving of *commedia* material into his texts from the early 1590s through *The Tempest*. See "Shakespeare and the Commedia dell'Arte," in *Shakespeare, Italy, and Transnational Exchange: Early Modern to Present*, ed. Enza De Francisci and Chris Stamatakis (London: Routledge, 2017), pp. 53–64. Siro Ferrone provides a fascinating analysis of the changing relationship between professionalized actors and audiences in *Attori mercanti corsari: La Commedia dell'Arte in Europa tra Cinque e Seicento* (Turin: Giulio Einaudi, 1993). The standard English work on the Arte is K. M. Lea, *Italian Popular Comedy: A Study in the Commedia dell'Arte, 1560–1620 with Special Reference to the English Stage*, 2 vols. (Oxford: Clarendon Press, 1934); see esp. vol. 1, pp. 271–92.

44. For the hazards and opportunities experienced by an Italian troupe traveling between Mantua, Antwerp, Paris, London, and Lyons during the religious wars of the later sixteenth century, see Siro Ferrone, *Arlecchino: Vita e avventure di Tristano Martinelli attore* (Rome and Bari: Editori Laterza, 2006). He notes that around the time that the Martinelli troupe performed in London, a play called *The Three Sisters of Mantua*, which seems to be an English adaptation of Mantuan playwright Leone de' Sommi's *Le Tre Sorelle*, was performed at Richmond by the Earl of Warwick's Servants on December 26, 1578 (pp. 42, 265–6). I have argued elsewhere that this play may underlie *The Taming of a Shrew*, which, unlike *The Shrew*, features three sisters, albeit none of them with a trace of shrew ("Shakespeare's Talking Dumb-Shows," unpublished paper presented at the Shakespearean Theatre Conference, Stratford, Ontario, 2015).

45. See Roberta Carpani, "Il 'trionfo di Manto': festa e teatro nel età di Vincenzo I," in *Vincenzo I Gonzaga 1562–1612: Il Fasto del Potere* (Mantua: Museo diocesano Francesco Gonzaga, 2012), pp. 65–70.

46. *Almond for a Parrat*, quoted in Henke, "Border-Crossing," p. 32, from *The Works of Thomas Nashe*, ed. Ronald B. McKerrow, 4 vols. (London: Sidgwick & Jackson, 1910), vol. 3, p. 342. In *A Worlde of Wordes* (1598) John Florio defines *Francatrippa* as "a grosse, greasie,

scullionlike loggerheaded lubberlie foolish fellow" and *Parabolano* as a "parable speaker. Also a mountibanke, a pratler, a babbler, a chatter, a prater." "Harlicken" apparently refers to Arlecchino, the mask of Tristano Martinelli. "Kempino," of course, was Will Kemp, evidently considered, at least by Nashe, kin to the Italian clown.

47. *Volpone*, 2.2, in *Ben Jonson*, vol. 5. In *The Unfortunate Traveler* (1594), Jack Wilton mentions "Scoto, that dyd the juggling tricks before the queen" (Nashe, *Works*, vol. 2, p. 252).
48. Lea, *Italian Popular Comedy*, vol. 2, p. 360.
49. On Jonson's exploitation of such theatrical memories, see Altman, "Ekphrasis," in *Early Modern Theatricality*, pp. 275–7.
50. *Nichomachean Ethics*, 1094b; trans. Martin Ostwald (Indianapolis: Bobbs-Merrill, 1962). Aristotle does not refer to statistical probability here, a science that came into being in the seventeenth century AD. On this, see Ian Hacking, *The Emergence of Probability: A Philosophical Study of Early Ideas about Probability, Induction and Statistical Inference* (Cambridge: Cambridge University Press, 1975).
51. We have already noted the missing *argumentum* of *The Mousetrap*. See Chapter 1, n. 47.
52. The late Hannah Arendt makes a useful and relevant distinction between the "who-ness" and the "what-ness" of agents as they are transformed from the contingent subjects of action without determinacy to the purposeful products of art. See *The Human Condition* (Chicago: University of Chicago Press, 1958), esp. pp. 175–88.
53. The Friar foresees an ekphrastic re-creation of Hero's life taking form in Claudio's grief-infused *phantasia* as he assembles "every lovely organ of her life" unsullied by the *phantasmata* composing "every man's Hero" that Don John had implanted there as he prepared Claudio to spy at her window the night before their intended marriage.
54. Lines 165–70 appear in the Folio only.
55. For a fuller discussion of the issues broached here, see my "The Practice of Shakespeare's Text," *Style* 23.3 (1989): 466–500.
56. According to Vitruvius, caryatids represent the enslaved women of Carya, punished by the Greeks for Caryan treachery during the Persian wars (*De architectura*, 1.1.5). An indication of the unusual design of the monument may be gleaned from Giulio Ferrari, *La Tomba nell'arte italiana dal periodo preromano all'odierno* (Milan: U. Hoepli, 1916). In the more than ninety photographs shown in the section "Il Rinascimento fino ai primi del 1600," Strozzi's is the only tomb supported by caryatids.
57. The process outlined is a staple of the syncretic Aristotelian psychology that was prevalent in the period. I have discussed this process in detail in Chapter 2 above.
58. Kenneth Gross, *The Dream of the Moving Statue* (Ithaca, NY, and London: Cornell University Press, 1992), p. 16.

59. *Lives*, trans. de Vere, vol. 6, p. 165.

60. See Henry and Joannides, *Late Raphael*, pp. 162–73, on the composition of *The Transfiguration*.

61. *On the True Precepts of the Art of Painting*, ed. and trans. Edward J. Olszewski (New York: Franklin, 1977), p. 147.

62. Hence the sobriquet attending his work: *anticamente moderna e modernamente antica* (Vasari, *Le vite*, vol. 2, p. 828).

63. John Shearman argues that just such a procedure governed the drawing, now at Chatsworth, of the Sessa monument, the execution of which Giulio hoped would be awarded to his son-in-law Lorenzetto. See "Giulio Romano and the Tomb of the Duke and Duchess of Sessa," *Zeitschrift für Kunstgeschichte* 57. Bd., H. 3, Kunstgeschichte und Gegenwart: 23 (1994): 364–72.

64. As we have seen, Friar Francis's advice to Leonato in *Much Ado*, 4.1.200–54, serves as a subtext for this silent plot. In his seminal "'Living Sculptures': Ovid, Michelangelo, and *The Winter's Tale*" (*ELH* 48 [1981]: 137–67), Leonard Barkan argues that "the silence at the end of the play in which the couple can meet as statue and speechless viewer purifies the disasters of speech," both Hermione's and Leontes', that drive the action in the first half of the play. Given the aural double-entendres and misinterpretations of 1.2, this is a perceptive reading of the presentation of the statue, when Paulina says, "I like your silence; it more shows off / Your wonder" (5.3.21–2).

65. "O, thus she stood . . . when first I wooed her" (*WT* 5.3.34–6).

66. All the while remembering Dr. Johnson's confessed anxiety about editing Shakespeare's text, quoted in Chapter 1, n. 22 above. (Folio stage directions are minimal, primarily concerned to indicate entrances and exits.)

67. *Meno*, 97b–99a, trans. W. K. C. Guthrie, in *The Collected Dialogues of Plato*, ed. Edith Hamilton and Huntington Cairns (New York: Pantheon Books, 1961). Cf. *Symposium*, 202a, trans. Michael Joyce, ibid.

68. See Altman, *Improbability*, p. 143; Thomas Kyd, *The First Part of Hieronimo and The Spanish Tragedy*, ed. Andrew S. Cairncross (Lincoln: University of Nebraska Press, 1967): *ST*, 3.2.44–52; *Hamlet*, 2.2.157–9.

69. See Barbara J. Shapiro, *Probability and Certainty in Seventeenth-Century England* (Princeton: Princeton University Press, 1983), esp. pp. 163–93.

70. Sir John Hawles, *The English Man's Right* (1680), quoted in Shapiro, *Probability and Certainty*, pp. 188–90. Though it is late in the period, she argues that such writings mark the culmination of a movement in common and criminal law away from the use of quantitative proof in the civil and canon law traditions, of local juries who knew the parties and facts in the case, and of less rigorous "rhetorical circumstances"

for determining proof, although none of these actually disappeared in the seventeenth century. For Shakespeare's use of the cognitive locution associated with conscience in *Measure for Measure* and *All's Well that Ends Well*, see Chapter 5, n. 43.

"A sad tale's best for winter," but for spring a comedy is better: Time, Turn, and Genre(s) in *The Winter's Tale*

I

We are not likely ever to know why Shakespeare turned to the work of Robert Greene sometime in the year preceding 15 May 1611, when Simon Forman noted that he saw *The Winter's Tale* at the Globe.[1] But turn he did and, as we saw in Chapter 1, not just to Greene's oft-published prose tale *Pandosto*, but also to *The Second Part* and *The Third and Last Part of Conny-Catching*, and to *Mamillia* for the name of Leontes' son, as perhaps also for the name of her friend Florion, for his own Florizel.[2] The result of this bodging is a bifurcated play whose tragic and comic components stand in far stronger contrast to one another than in any of the other late plays or even the mid-career "problem plays," and is a distinctively shaped hybrid in a canon that often reflects the author's taste for serio-comic mingling. While Shakespeare's adaptation of Greene has been much commented on, studying the three elements in the subtitle of this chapter can guide us toward a deeper understanding of what he may have had in mind when he decided so drastically to transfigure Greene in his own image.

II

What might initially have caught Shakespeare's eye was the description and sales pitch printed in centered lines on the title page of the 1588 edition: "*Pandosto. / The Triumph / of Time.* // Wherein is discovered by a pleasant Historie, / that although by meanes of sinister fortune, Truth may be concea- / led, yet by Time in spight of fortune it / is most manifestly revealed. // Pleasant for age to avoyde drowsie thoughtes, / profitable for youth to eschue other wanton / pastimes, and bringing to both a / desired content. // *Temporis filia veritas.* // By Robert Greene, Maister of Artes / in Cambridge. // *Omne tulit punctum qui miscuit utile dulci.*"[3]

Following a letter to the Gentlemen Readers and a dedication to George Clifford, Earl of Cumberland, the prose narrative begins with a new title: "The Historie of / Dorastus and / Fawnia." As John Pitcher observes, the two titles reflect the overlapping plots of both *Pandosto* and *The Winter's Tale*;[4] but they also may have suggested to Shakespeare that the contiguous stories could be fashioned into two quite different plays, a tragedy and a comedy—a generic distinction that Greene seems only nominally interested in pursuing. Just as significantly, the first title and its accompanying description seems to have caused Shakespeare to consider how he could improve on Greene's misleading emphasis on time, encapsulated in the first Latin epigraph.

For while truth may be the daughter of time, in truth Time plays a quite minor role in *Pandosto*, even though the word is consistently capitalized on the title page—just as fortune is printed in lower-case letters to bolster the claim. And once the narrative begins, Time trails Fortune by a considerable length, well behind human passion and wiliness.[5] Fortune is credited with the contented marriage of Pandosto and Bellaria (157); for the birth of their young son Garinter (157); for the visit of his friend Egistus, King of Sicilia, to Bohemia (157); and for the escape of Egistus and Franion (162).[6] Bellaria declares Fortune responsible for her imprisonment (164), and Pandosto concludes that as her newborn child "came by Fortune, so he would commit it to the charge of Fortune" (166).[7] Bellaria laments that her exiled babe was "scarce born before envied by Fortune" (166), and places a little chain around her neck that, "if Fortune save thee, it may help to succor thee" (167). At her trial Bellaria declares her hope that "my patience shall make Fortune blush" (170). True to Bellaria's wishes, Fortune, "willing to show that as she hath wrinkles on her brows, so she hath dimples in her cheeks," calms the stormy sea in which the babe is being tossed, allowing it to arrive safely onshore in Sicilia (173). Following which, "It fortuned a poor mercenary shepherd that dwelt in Sicilia . . . was hard by" (173) when she came to shore, and by the time the child had reached seven years of age, "Fortune so favored him . . . that he began to purchase land, intending after his death to give it to his daughter" (175). Yet when she was sixteen, "Fortune, who all this while showed a friendly face, began now to turn her back and to show a louring countenance, intending as she had given Fawnia a slender check, so she would give her a harder mate; to bring which to pass, she laid her train in this wise" (251). And so it goes.

When Time is referred to, it is often an adjunct to a greater power, as when Bellaria fears that her reputation will be ruined, for "Report is plumed with Time's feathers" (242), and again when we are told how "Fortune is plumed with Time's feathers, and how she can minister strange causes to breed strange effects"—in this case "a meeting of all the farmers' daughters in Sicilia, whither Fawnia was also bidden as mistress of the feast" (253), and whence returning she meets Dorastus. On a few occasions Time's agency is acknowledged: Dorastus ceases his passionate complaint, "hoping that time would wear out that which Fortune had wrought," and Fawnia reasons that "Daring passions that pass measure are cut short by time or Fortune" (256). Yet in the recognition scene, when "The ambassadors rejoiced that their young prince had made such a choice, that those kingdoms which through enmity had long time been disservered should now through perpetual amity be united and reconciled" (273)—a line that clearly resonated for Shakespeare[8]— Time is merely adverbial. For *Pandosto* is Fortune's tale. After the deaths of Bellaria and Garinter, Pandosto falls into a speechless trance, to the dismay of his subjects. Declares the narrator: "This tragical discourse of Fortune so daunted them as they went like shadows, not men" (248). Such is the prevalence of Fortune, bad and good, that one is tempted to emend the subtitle to *Fortunae filia Fawnia*.

But Shakespeare took Greene's motto to heart and expanded it. Measuring and using time are important activities in *The Winter's Tale*. Polixenes' opening lines—"Nine changes of the watery star hath been / The shepherd's note since we have left our throne / Without a burden. Time as long again / Would be filled up, my brother, with our thanks, / And yet we should for perpetuity / Go hence in debt" (1.2.1–6)—not only count the months but also suggest Time's spaciousness—its capacity to be filled socially and, by implication, to be left empty. A similar emphasis is heard in the last scene, when Leontes asks, "Good Paulina, / Lead us from hence, where we may leisurely / Each one demand and answer to his part / Performed in this wide gap of time since first / We were disservered. Hastily lead away" (5.3.151–5). Leisure and haste—the human markers of temporal passage—are enjoined retroactively to fill Time's gap with the understandings that will make the restored court once again a society with a shared history.[9]

To signify its importance, Time becomes a *dramatis persona* with extraordinary agency. As the fourth act of *The Winter's Tale* opens, a winged figure bearing an hourglass appears onstage and tells the audience:

> I that please some, try all; both joy and terror
> Of good and bad, that makes and unfolds error,
> Now take upon me, in the name of Time,
> To use my wings. Impute it not a crime
> To me or my swift passage that I slide
> O'er sixteen years, and leave the growth untried
> Of that wide gap, since it is in my power
> To o'erthrow law, and in one self-born hour
> To plant and o'erwhelm custom (4.1.1–9)

He then turns his glass and assumes the role of playwright-prologue, "giv[ing] my scene such growing / As you had slept between" (16–17). Leaving Leontes to his grief, he locates himself in Bohemia, mentions Prince Florizel and Perdita, "now grown in grace / Equal with wondering" (24–5), and "what to her adheres" he calls "th'argument of Time" (27–9). As we have seen, in theatrical terms "argument" means plot (from the Latin *argumentum*), such as those that are found in classical comedies and early modern comedies and tragedies.[10] It's now Time's show.

For in turning his glass, Time does more than "slide o'er sixteen years" and assume authorship. He reverses the direction taken by the original play, in which sexual jealousy and paranoia have produced three deaths and the severing of families and friends—tragic events involving royal persons and their courtiers, mistaken judgments, recognition come too late, and apparently irreconcilable woe: "Come, and lead me / To these sorrows," says Leontes to Paulina as he goes off to view the bodies of his son and queen (3.2.240–1). In contrast, Time picks up the one promising plot line introduced in the scene just passed, when the Old Shepherd rescues the abandoned babe: "'Tis a lucky day, boy, and we'll do good deeds on't" (3.3.132–3). Like a skilled play doctor brought in by the company to avoid a theatrical disaster, Time then fashions his sequel in a new genre governed by a different mode. There is patriarchal and political power, yes, but no death and no divine oracle. This "argument" invites us to "apprehend / Nothing but jollity" (4.4.24–5), as a comic world of rural conny-catching, disguise and dance, romantic love, and intergenerational intrigue unfolds—darkened by an apparently audacious class transgression that begets royal rage—and culminates in a race across the sea in which the royal father and his conniving counselor pursue the rebel son and his betrothed, her supposed father and brother, and the witty conny-catcher, all of whom arrive seriatim at the very court where the tragic play began. There, Time yields his authority to a surrogate playwright, as the two actions are woven together in the reconciliation of surviving friends and family through a double recognition and an astonishing resurrection. Thus Time converts the genre of tragedy into the genre of comedy, then steps aside as another plotter reveals her subtler dramaturgic skills by adapting Time's comedy to the fashionable new genre of tragicomedy, or—to describe it more precisely—to a *tragedia di fin lieto* that is essentially *sui generis*, for two of the principals are irrevocably lost, even though the major tragic victims survive. Through this intricate maneuver, Shakespeare has virtually fulfilled the promise of the subtitle of Greene's *Pandosto*: "that although by meanes of sinister fortune, Truth may be concea- / led, yet by Time in spight of fortune it / is most manifestly revealed." *Virtually*, but not actually. For though Shakespeare has endowed Time with *literary* power to "plant and o'erwhelm custom" by changing the argument, he has done Greene one better by supplying Time with a sophisticated female ghost-writer who had been silently at work behind the scenes well before the winged old man had shown up onstage.[11]

To be fair, he might have found some hints in Greene. As indicated above, Greene's tale is largely a "tragical discourse of fortune." Twice he refers to comedy: at the revelation of Fawnia's identity, Egistus, "hearing this comicall event, rejoyced greatly at his sonnes good happe" (199); then Pandosto, recalling his earlier betrayal of Egistus and of Bellaria, and his recent lusting after his own daughter, "to close up the Comedy with a Tragicall stratageme, he slewe himselfe" (199). We might be tempted to consider Greene's story a "tragicomical-comitragical" tale. But these are just token gestures toward genre in a largely paratactic story of Fortune's turnings. *Pandosto* has no clearly articulated generic shape.

III

There was, however, a shapely tradition, derived from Aristotle's *Poetics*, of which Shakespeare was aware, since its avatars had reached England from Italy by the beginning of the seventeenth century. In Chapter 14 of the *Poetics*, when discussing the complex plot that arouses fear and pity and involves error, an "incurable deed," recognition, reversal of fortune, and catharsis of the two emotions, Aristotle writes that the plot in which the tragic deed is performed in ignorance and is followed by a recognition of the relationship that has been violated (as in Sophocles' *Oedipus Tyrannos*) is the *second-best* model. He reserves highest praise for Euripides' *Cresphontes* (now lost) and the extant *Iphigenia in Tauris*, in which the irredeemable deed is about to be performed in ignorance, but recognition occurs before it is enacted and there is a reversal leading to a fortunate ending.[12] This does not obviate feelings of pity and fear in the audience, for, as Stephen Halliwell writes, "the action forces us to imagine the evils, to recognize and hence to respond emotionally towards their implications; and it is this imagination, not the physical actuality of the 'incurable', which Aristotle now appears to identify as sufficient for the experience of tragedy."[13] The passage was well known to sixteenth-century Italian critics and dramatists. Francesco Robortello deemed the tragedy with the preemptive recognition and fortunate ending the "*modus omnium praestantissimus*,"[14] and Giraldi Cinzio used it to justify his own *tragedie di fin lieto* in his *Discorso intorno al comporre delle commedie e delle tragedie* of 1554. "In this species of tragedy," he writes, "the recognition or, as we prefer to call it, the identification of persons, especially has a place; through this identification those for whom we feel horror and compassion are taken from perils and from death. Among all the identifications about which Aristotle instructs us . . . that one is more praiseworthy than the others by means of which there is a change of fortune from miserable to happy."[15]

Ever alert to audience response, Giraldi recommends that

> the events in these less terrible plays ought to arise in such a way that the spectators are suspended between horror and compassion until the end, which then in turning out cheerful, leaves everyone consoled. And this holding of the spectator in suspense ought to be so managed by the poet that one does not always stand in the dark, but the action ought to go on unraveling the plot bit by bit so that the spectator sees himself guided to the end but remains doubtful of the resolution.[16]

Thus he introduces into tragedy what we might call the "tragicomic cue."[17]

It will be seen immediately that Shakespeare's entry into this subgenre of tragedy both differs from and agrees with Giraldi's *tra-*

gedia di fin lieto in important respects. Most noticeably, Giraldi's tragedies are through-written *as* tragedies. There is no excursion into comedy as there is in *The Winter's Tale*. The "holding of the spectator in suspense" about the outcome, however, is a strategy adapted by Shakespeare in several places, where he offers tragicomic cues as Giraldi recommends. After Hermione has been committed to prison in Act 2, Leontes reveals to his astonished courtiers that he has sent to the oracle of Apollo to confirm Hermione's treachery: "Come, follow us; / We are to speak in public, for this business / Will raise us all." To which Antigonus replies in an aside: "To laughter, as I take it, / If the good truth were known" (2.1.196–9). But by the end of 3.2, this prediction has proved to be a red herring, and by the end of 3.3, Antigonus is dead and not laughing one bit. There is a still earlier cue in Act 2 that the audience cannot fully appreciate until the last scene of the play. Having been accused of adultery and treason before an audience of courtiers and court ladies, Hermione exclaims to Leontes, "How will this grieve you / When you shall come in clearer knowledge, that / You have thus published me?" adding, as she departs for prison, "I never wished to see you sorry; now / I trust I shall" (2.1.96–8, 123–4). Its local meaning is that she expects to see Leontes come to his senses—just how, she doesn't say—but in retrospect it suggests that she will join the audience in witnessing Leontes' sorrow at her apparent *death*, and is actually a cue that she shall *survive to see* his repentance. There are also touches of the comic cuckold and female scold in Leontes and Paulina, leavening the incipient tragedy, as Barbara Mowat has suggested.[18] But the full barrage of tragicomic cues does not even begin until Act 5, Scene 1, with Paulina's waffling about the possibility of Leontes' remarrying—and her role in that event—which we will examine later in this chapter.

Another apparent distinction between Shakespeare's play and Giraldi's signature innovation is that some of the latter's *tragedie di fin lieto* have double endings—fortunate for the good, punitive for the evil—whereas the only negative fortunes in *The Winter's Tale* are suffered by Mamillius, an innocent casualty of his father's paranoia, and by Antigonus, a noble-minded, critical yet loyal servant of his master the king. What then is the advantage of considering *The Winter's Tale* a *tragedia di fin lieto*? Doing so calls attention to the peculiar structure of the action, which leaves us at the end of 3.2 in the position of an audience to Aristotle's "second best" kind of tragedy, where there is a misrecognition, an incurable deed is done, and the perpetrator discovers his error too late. In Shakespeare's play this is particularly horrifying, since we have come to know Hermione in all her wit and dignity, and also existentially daring, since a god has spoken in the voice of the oracle, and has been denied. The subsequent generic shift, via Antigonus's ferociously comical death—anticipated when a bear suddenly chases him off-stage and then realized in the visceral, if insouciant, description of the Clown—leaves our mouths agape and puts "case closed" to the tragic action, as we are carried off by Time's diverting argument.

This shift reinforces our impression that Shakespeare is deliberately playing with genre in his transformation of Greene's *Pandosto*. He had already been introduced to the game of mixing dramatic genres by Giraldi and Guarini when writing *Measure for Measure* and *All's Well that Ends Well* some half-dozen years earlier, but had never attempted anything so radical as to split a tragedy in two and bodge a comedy into the gap to provide connective tissue between a *tragedia di fin doloroso* and a *tragedia di fin lieto*. Greene must take some credit for this bold experiment, for his "History of Dorastus and Fawnia" supplied the raw material and was there for the taking.

But it was Giraldi who may have offered Shakespeare the *dramatic* temptation. Having praised Seneca's consistency in composing only tragedies with unhappy endings, he confesses in his *Discorso* that he himself has composed tragedies with happy endings because they are theatrically more successful: "I have written some in this manner such as *Altile*, *Selene*, *Antivalomeni*, and others simply for the benefit of the spectators, to make the plays more acceptable on the stage, and to conform myself to the practice of our time."[19] Not only that, but he has supplied some of them with a double ending: "In this sort of play, for the greater satisfaction and better instruction of the audience, those who have caused the turbulent events by which persons of ordinary goodness have been afflicted, are made to die or suffer great ills ... For it gives marvelous pleasure to the spectator when he sees the cunning taken away and those who were deceived [by them] survive at the end of the action, as the unjust and the wicked are finally overthrown."[20]

However melodramatic, this reads like a recipe whose ingredients could be adapted by an ingenious dramatist to fashion a *tragedia di fin lieto* with two endings separated by sixteen years in fictional time and some 1,800 lines in theatrical time (more than half the length of his play) in order to revisit the scene of the original unhappy ending and reveal that an invisible playwright had secretly intervened to provide a second, more satisfying ending. And that by doing so, she has not only pleased the audience but also reformed the soul of the protagonist. Due to her intervention, Leontes uniquely plays two roles in one person, that of a persecuting *cattivo*, who meets an unhappy ending in Act 3, and that of a repentant *onesto*, who knows the joy of a *fin lieto* in Act 5—each *dramatis persona* separated by a wide gap of time.

IV

Shakespeare's familiarity with Giraldi's work is well known. He drew upon the latter's collection of *novelle*, the *Ecatommiti* (1565), for both *Othello* and *Measure for Measure*. In the case of *Measure*, he seems also to have read Giraldi's *Epizia*, a *tragedia di fin lieto* that is Giraldi's dramatization of the corresponding story in his *Ecatommiti*. In the novella, Vieo (Shakespeare's Claudio), the brother of Epizia (Shakespeare's Isabella), has been condemned to death according to the laws of Innsbruck by the new governor Juriste (Shakespeare's Angelo) for having raped a young virgin. Epizia, a young virgin herself, comes to Juriste to plead for Vieo's life and, overcome by her beauty and eloquence, he promises to fulfill her request if she will go to bed with him; perhaps, he suggests, he'll even marry her afterwards. Reluctantly she agrees, but Juriste privately sends word to execute Vieo immediately, and the following morning, after she has returned home, she receives Vieo's corpse on a bier with his severed head at his feet. Suppressing her horror, grief, and rage, she seeks an audience with the Emperor. He hears her suit and summons Juriste, who, when confronted by Epizia, tremblingly confesses the truth. After marrying them in order to restore Epizia's honor, the Emperor sentences Juriste to death for having committed Vieo's crime himself and, in addition, that of promise-breach. Once more Epizia intervenes, pleading with the Emperor that if Juriste is executed she will be regarded as an avenging wife and lose whatever honor she might have regained. Complying with her wishes, the Emperor pardons Juriste and, we are told, they lived happily together thereafter. Moreover, justice and clemency, the prime virtues of a ruler, have been upheld.

Were this a tragedy rather than a novella, its *fin lieto* would seem rather tenuous, to say the least, since the happy ending is brought about by a marriage of necessity for both the seducer and his victim, who has still lost her brother—the only acknowledged *cattivo* in the plot—who makes a brief appearance and wins the sympathy of no one but his sister before he meets his just end. When Giraldi adapted it as a drama, however, he made some critical changes. In this version, Juriste has been secretly in love with Epizia for some time before she pleads for her brother's life, and her brother offers to marry his victim in order to mitigate his crime and preserve her honor. Thus the natures of both men have been softened a bit and become somewhat more sympathetic, if not to our contemporary taste. And in the third act, a messenger describes the execution of Vieo in grim detail before, in the play's final scene, the Captain of Justice (Shakespeare's Provost) announces that the decapitated body he had sent to Epizia was not her brother's after all, but that of a previously condemned prisoner who resembled him (Shakespeare's Ragozine). Whereby "Vieo is saved, Juriste is saved, Epizia's honour is saved, and so too is the honour of the woman violated by Vieo, and their pain and distress are all turned to joy."[21] *Fin lieto*, indeed—though without the kind of double ending that Giraldi had described as an instructive model in the *Discorso*, where he pointed out that the wicked schemers in his *Altile* and *Selene* get their just deserts.

If Shakespeare consulted *Epizia* as well as its prose counterpart in the *Ecatommiti* while writing *Measure for Measure*, he was surely aware of the existence of the mixed genre in Italian drama, and this connects him more firmly to the innovations of Giraldi and to those of Battista Guarini. He may not have made a hard-and-fast distinction between the *tragedia di fin lieto* and *tragicommedia*, but he certainly knew the Giraldi dramatic model and, as we shall see, Guarini's as well.

There is also some linguistic evidence that he was familiar with the controversy surrounding the *Discorso*. The treatise drew criticism for recommending the fusion of comic and tragic elements to create what some critics called "un'ibrida monstruosità."[22] The resulting mixture of high and low figures caused Giasone De Nores, follower of moral philosopher Sperone Speroni at the University of Padua, to report that he could not but feel repugnancy at this "decomposed genre," which he called a "monstrous and disproportioned composition" that mingled absurdly "a comic plot with a tragic plot, which are directly opposed to one another," thereby engendering "un ibridismo di linguaggio ora elevato ora plebeo" ("a linguistic hybridism—now high, now low").[23]

Just as suggestive for our purposes, however, is Battista Guarini's *Compendio della poesia tragicomica* of 1601, where the dramatist and polemicist defends his *Il pastor fido* against charges that it lacks unity. There are two ways in which the play may be said to be defective in unity, he argues. First, through the discordance of its two forms—tragic and comic. The other, because it has more than one plot (*soggetto*), as in many Latin comedies. In words that have a particular resonance for *The Winter's Tale*, Guarini then explains: "Concerning these allegedly 'double' forms, let us call the first by its customary name, 'mixed' (*mista*) and the second, 'cross-bred' (*innestata*)."[24] As to the first (the allegedly flawed combination of genres),

> it must be considered that tragicomedy is not made up of two integral actions, one of which is a perfect tragedy and the other a perfect comedy, joined together in such a way that they can be separated without one doing damage to the actions of the other or each damaging itself. Nor should anyone believe that it is a tragic story vitiated by the baseness of comedy or a comic action contaminated by the deaths of tragedy, because it would not then be a well-regulated form. Whoever puts together tragicomedies does not intend to compose separately either a tragedy or a comedy, but from the former and the latter a third entity that is perfect in its own kind and takes from both of them those parts that can stand together with most verisimilitude.[25]

As to its "cross-bred" or "grafted" features—of having more than one subject and action—he refers the reader to the comedies of Terence, where there are characters of the same social status but of different temperaments who follow their own lines of action. This is perhaps most familiar in the *Andria*—adapted from Menander's Greek play of the same name, with graftings from the latter's *Perinthia*—where the youths Pamphilus and Charinus are, respectively, devoted and impulsive in pursuit of their love interests, and the fathers Chremes and Simo forbearing and overbearing. This Terentian feature of *Il pastor fido*—where Mirtillo, the titular faithful shepherd who loves Amarillis, serves as counterpoint to Silvio, betrothed but indifferent to Amarillis, and who also flees the love of Dorinda—had been criticized by De Nores for defying Aristotle's preference for a single rather than double plot.[26] Moreover, argued De Nores, since Silvio is the son of the High Priest Montanus, and Mirtillo the son of a commoner, and they both come to happy endings, the playwright has violated the rule that men of high standing are tragic figures and must meet adverse fortunes, while commoners usually find happiness in the untying of the plotted knot.[27]

Guarini insists that the "mixed" form of tragicomedy must not be confused with Aristotle's "double plot," since "nothing can be 'mixed' if it is not a single entity whose parts are blended in such a way that one part cannot be recognized or separated from another."[28]

He adduces Aristotle's own *De generatione* as evidence, where in Book I the philosopher shows the difference between the *"misto"* mode of being and the *"composto."* In the former, "the parts lose their forms and constitute a third thing that is very different. In the latter, each part preserves itself in the same form as it was at first." The mixed form can be compared to the mythical Hermaphrodite and the composed form to a man and woman sexually coupling, who after their embrace revert to their individual forms. Such is not the tragicomic mode.[29] This is a sometimes bewildering argument in which the terms tend to slip their moorings, but what seems to emerge is that the tragic and comic genres, with their apparently divergent qualities of social rank, evoked emotions, and resolutions, function interdependently, and are not vitiated by the grafting of two subjects and their contrasting attitudes and lines of action within the unified new form of tragicomedy.

Which brings us to the distinctive kind of Shakespearean bodging that has not yet entered our discussion. It has often been noted that Polixenes' defense of cultivating the hybrid gillyvor—that missing flower appropriate to his age—when lecturing Perdita, who refuses "to get slips of them" because they are "nature's bastards," is suffused with peculiar ironies. For he is fully aware that his royal son is wooing this shepherd girl, and would be expected to oppose the mingling of high and low: "You see, sweet maid, we marry / A gentler scion to the wildest stock, / And make conceive a bark of baser kind / By bud of nobler race" (4.4.92–5). Were he ignorant of her putative identity as shepherd's daughter, his disquisition would be a charming bit of dramatic irony; and if she had possessed language when she was cast away as an illegitimate offspring, her repugnancy at "nature's bastards" might (with a stretch) be considered a subconscious defense mechanism. But neither situation obtains. Polixenes' words could also be regarded as an off-the-mark taunting of the "sweet maid," aimed at shaming her conscience—off-the-mark since, whatever his subtext, he is quite audibly defending cross-breeding. Or they might even be seen as a wink at the audience, inviting them to chuckle at the ignorance of both speakers, since the audience is aware of Perdita's royal identity. I propose that amid this polyvalent playfulness the exchange represents a careful Shakespearean inset that functions not only as a debate on the contested relationship between nature and art—for "the art itself is nature" (4.4.97)—which is thematically fitting given the pastoral setting,[30] but also as a metaphorical exposition of the theory of tragicomedy constructed in the Guarinian manner and set within the literary debate concerning "hybrid" genres that had roiled Italian dramatic theory since Giraldi's *Discorso* was attacked by De Nores in the 1560s.

V

To better appreciate this metadramatic exchange between Polixenes and Perdita, we should bear in mind that the work of both Giraldi and Guarini had become familiar to the London theater world by the early seventeenth century and had already influenced the plays of Shakespeare and his fellow dramatists. *Il pastor fido* was published for the first time in Venice in 1590, and in 1591 a new Italian edition was issued by John Wolfe's London printing house, sponsored and edited by the Italian language teacher Iacopo Castelvetro, and bound in the same volume with Tasso's tragicomedy *Aminta*.[31] Guarini's *Compendio* appeared in Venice in 1601, and the following year a second edition was issued, together with *Il pastor fido* and Guarini's *Annotationi*, which responded to the *querela* initiated by De Nores and subsequently joined by other Italian critics. By 1602, an English translation of the play had appeared, with a commendatory sonnet by Samuel Daniel.[32] Giraldi's *Gli Ecatommiti* had been published in 1565, and his collected plays, the 1583 *Le tragedie*, was sufficiently well known to supply material for Shakespeare, Marston, and others.[33]

As noted above, *Measure for Measure* is indebted not only to the eighth decade, fifth novella of the second part of the *Ecatommiti*, but also to Giraldi's dramatization of his own tale, *Epizia*. Shakespeare's use of English materials as well, George Whetstone's adaptation of Giraldi in his two-part *The Right Excellent and Famous History of Promos and Cassandra* (1578) and his prose *Heptameron of Civil Discourses* (1582),[34] suggests an unremitting activity of bodging that resulted in a multivalent hybrid of Giraldi and Guarini. For unlike Giraldi's *tragedia di fin lieto*, *Measure for Measure* is peppered with comic scenes and characters—"To the purpose: what was done to Elbow's wife?" (2.1.115–16); "I am as well acquainted here as I was in our house of profession: one would think it were Mistress Overdone's own house, for here be many of her old customers" (4.3.1–4)—which were probably inspired by the low-life scenes in the "two commicall discourses" of *Promos and Cassandra*. Even the psychologically complex last scene, in which Isabella, ignorant that her brother yet lives, kneels and pleads earnestly (and counter-factually) for Angelo's life, is continuously punctuated by

Lucio's impertinent interjections, until he suffers what is probably Shakespeare's response to the Giraldian tenet that the *cattivi* meet unfortunate ends: "Marrying a punk, my lord, is pressing to death, whipping, and hanging" (5.1.522–3)—mitigated by Guarini's reluctance to offer audiences a double ending.[35] The Guarinian mode of mixing high and low, comic and tragic—most evident in the controlling presence of the Duke disguised as lowly Friar Lodowick—thus intersects with the Giraldian plot. The latter, as Herrick reminds us,[36] favors the *doppio soggetto*, which here takes the form of an old betrothal between Angelo and Mariana of the moated grange, which is introduced retroactively in Act 3 to preserve Isabella's virginity, legitimize Angelo's despicable sexual bargain, and test Isabella's capacity to forgive the man who has deceived her and (she believes) has murdered her brother.[37] The final unmuffling of Claudio onstage provides the enacted recognition that both Giraldi and Guarini celebrated and yields not one, not two, but three happy endings, each with a different tonality. The result is a new dramatic entity, commonly known since the early twentieth century as a "problem play," but more accurately described as Shakespeare's first tragicomedy.[38]

His second tragicomedy, *All's Well that Ends Well* (1604–5), bears even stronger traces of Guarinian-Giraldian influence. Central to this play is the issue of joining high and low, in the persons of Bertram, Count of Rossillion, and Helena, the physician's daughter—a union that social purist Bertram resists as long as he is able. His mother the Countess takes a more enlightened view. Persuading Helena that she regards her as her natural daughter, she observes, "'Tis often seen / Adoption strives with nature, and choice breeds / A native slip to us from foreign seeds" (1.3.144–6), thereby embracing the concept of hybridization that Bertram finds so repugnant.[39]

Not surprisingly, the moral seriousness of Helena's expressed passion for Bertram is leavened almost immediately by her bawdy exchange with Parolles on the wisdom of preserving virginity, just as her decision to heal the King's disease follows instantly upon her reflection that "Our remedies oft in ourselves do lie / Which we ascribe to heaven" (1.1.216–17). The particular remedy she refers to does not, in the first instance, concern the King's illness, but her own hopeless love for Bertram, to which curing the King becomes instrumental: "The king's disease—my project may deceive me, / But my intents are fix'd, and will not leave me" (1.1.228–9).[40] She admits as much to the Countess, and with her blessing off she goes to Paris. Once there, we may recall, her cure is offered to the skeptical King in unequivocally spiritual terms: "He that of greatest works is finisher /

Oft does them by the weakest minister" (2.1.136–7). Helena is not being insincere here, but that does not mean that she is not also an intriguer, for once she has persuaded the King to accept her divinely inspired assistance, she requests her reward: "What husband in thy power I will command" (2.1.194). This is characteristic of the play's fusion of intrigue comedy and high moral purpose. As Louise Clubb has argued concerning Raffaello Borghini's *La donna costante* (1578), to which *All's Well* bears more than a family resemblance, "Love is promoted to the rank of grace and providence, and the commonplace of feigned death and burial is used as more than an example of cleverness: it is a wonder of steadfastness signifying the Unmoved Mover, who is the source of love and of the providence that controls the mutability of fortune."[41] This would stand well as a guide to Helena's behavior. She has something of the holy plotter in her—determined, self-serving, deceptive, yet virtuous, innocent, and divinely inspired—effecting the "conversion" of her callow, selfish, recalcitrant husband, who is a man that only a saint could love. Even his mother disowns him.

As evidence of Guarinian influence, to the continuously shifting moral tone of the play we must adduce the pivotal roles of prophecy and equivocal, virtually oracular speech. The first is supplied unwittingly by the hapless Bertram in his farewell letter to Helena: "When thou canst get the ring upon my finger, which never shall come off, and show me a child begotten of thy body that I am father to, then call me husband; but in such a 'then' I write a 'never'" (3.2.57–60). To which he adds a postscript: "Till I have no wife, I have nothing in France" (75). Crushed by his brutal rejection, Helena feels responsible for depriving him of his homeland, sending him to war and possible death, and decides to steal away so he may return to Rossillion. This time she makes a moral, self-abnegating decision to travel as a pilgrim to the shrine of St. Jaques le Grand (St. James of Compostella) and arrives in Florence, which, however off-route to the Spanish shrine, is also the stopping place for "four or five, to great Saint Jaques bound" (3.5.95), who are lodging at the Widow's house. Here she sees Bertram leading the Duke of Florence's army. In contrast to Painter's version of Boccaccio, in which Giletta, upon reading Beltramo's impossible conditions for acknowledging her as his wife, "purposed to finde meanes to attaine the two thinges, that thereby she might recover her husbande,"[42] Shakespeare fashions Helena's encounter as initially gratuitous—an act of unanticipated grace—out of which she then devises her bed trick, using Diana to obtain Bertram's family ring, and in the darkness of Diana's bed gives Bertram in return the ring the King had given her and conceives his child.

But not before she speaks a strangely chiasmic speech, a form of which she spoke in the second act when persuading the King to permit her to try to cure his illness, and which is reprised at the end of the play. In Act 2, Scene 1, she tells him, "I am not an imposture that proclaim / Myself against the level of mine aim, / But know I think, and think I know most sure, / My art is not past power, nor you past cure" (155–8). "Know I think" and "think I know," however rhetorically playful, signify two kinds of cognition. They are described by the Protestant divine William Perkins in this manner:

> For there be two actions of the understanding, the one is simple, which barely conceiveth or thinketh this or that: the other is a reflecting or doubting of the former, whereby a man conceives or thinks with himself what he thinks. And this action properly pertains to the conscience.[43]

So Helena is actually engaged in a truthful kind of doublespeak here. She attests her self-awareness of her thought and also her confidence that she thinks the knowledge she has is certain. It is both a modest and a presumptuous assertion, deriving from what she has previously called "inspired merit" (2.1.148).

In Florence, having seen Bertram and opportunistically schemed to fulfill the near-impossible conditions of his letter, she explains to Diana's widowed mother how to interpret what they have agreed upon: "Why then to-night / Let us assay our plot, which if it speed, / Is wicked meaning in a lawful deed, / And lawful meaning in a lawful act, / Where both not sin, and yet a sinful fact" (3.7.43–7). This time she speaks with a curiously layered equivocation that suggests oracular speech. She seems to be describing the sexual act from four perspectives: Bertram's, hers, God's, and the world's. Bertram *means* to sin, yet is performing a lawful deed; Helena *means* lawfully to gain her right as lawful wife; both, therefore, are in fact not sinning, *sub specie aeternitatis*, but to the world will seem to be engaged in sinful doing. The well-meaning Widow, having been given a purse of gold by Helena as a down payment and promised further remuneration, is not inclined to object.

The most flagrant instance of seemingly oracular equivocation, however, is heard in the climactic scene of the play. This occurs after Bertram, having arrived home to seek pardon of the King, is discovered to be wearing Helena's ring. Diana opens the ambiguous passage by putting a question to the King containing the now-loaded verb "think": "Good my lord, / Ask him upon his oath, if he does think / He had not my virginity" (5.3.184–6). When Bertram responds by deriding her as a "common gamester to the camp," she refutes him by exhibiting the ancestral ring he gave her, and Parolles is summoned as witness to the assignation. Unreliable narrator though he may be, he confirms her story in a similarly equivocating mode by telling what he'd say were he not afraid of Bertram's reprisal and then excuses himself for not saying it. "Thou has spoke all already," replies the King drily. But this is merely a preliminary to the bizarre exchange between the King and Diana that follows. The King points to the ring Bertram is wearing:

> *King*: This ring [of Helena's] you say was yours?
> *Diana*: Ay, my good lord.
> *King*: Where did you buy it? Or who gave it you?
> *Diana*: It was not given me, nor I did not buy it.
> *King*: Who lent it you?
> *Diana*: It was not lent me neither.
> *King*: Where did you find it then?
> *Diana*: I found it not.
> *King*: If it were yours by none of all these ways,
> How could you give it him?
> *Diana*: I never gave it him (5.3.270–80)

What happens between the second line of this exchange and the last is that Diana switches personae. She begins in line 271 by speaking as Helena, who had taken her place in the dark bed. She then reassumes her own person in line 273 and speaks truthfully as herself. The King is understandably puzzled:

> *King*: Wherefore hast thou accus'd him all this while?
> *Diana*: Because he's guilty, and he is not guilty.
> He knows I am no maid, and he'll swear to't.
> I'll swear I am a maid, and he knows not. (5.3.288–91)

Here is the familiar equivocation on the verb "know" that we heard in Helena's "know I think" and "think I know" in Act 2, but now there is no distancing "think" to mitigate Bertram's mistaken knowledge. The first "knows" means "thinks," but the second "knows" means "knows." He'll swear to what he thinks, while she'll swear to what he "knows not." The dialogue continues with the same play on "knows" as "thinks":

Diana: But for this lord,
Who hath abused me, as he knows himself,
Though yet he never harm'd me, here I quit him.
He knows himself my bed he hath defil'd,
And at the same time he got his wife with child.
Dead though she be, she feels her young one kick.
So here's my riddle: one that's dead is quick—
And now behold the meaning. (5.3.297–304)

Enter Helena, alive and pregnant, who asks Bertram, having fulfilled the conditions of his letter, "Will you be mine now you are doubly won?" Bertram's reply is one with which the audience, perhaps for the first time, can sympathize: "If she, my liege, can make me know this *clearly*, / I'll love her dearly, ever, ever dearly" (5.3.314–16, italics mine).

Nearly fifty years ago, G. K. Hunter examined the relationship of *Il pastor fido* and a group of plays written during the years 1603 to 1605 by Shakespeare, Marston, Middleton, and Daniel, and showed convincingly how the riddling denouements of *All's Well* and *Measure for Measure* echo those of Guarini's tragicomedy.[44] He did not emphasize, however, that the peculiar doublespeak of the last scene in *Il pastor fido* functions literally to *untie the knot* of the goddess Diana's oracle, which governs the entire action of the play. Nor that when Shakespeare picked up its tautological, self-canceling language he infused it with a quasi-divine omniscience mingled with ordinary human understanding. I quote below a sampling of the exchange between Montanus the Priest, who is about to discover that he is the father of Mirtillo, the faithful shepherd whom he is ready to sacrifice, and Mirtillo's supposed father, Carino:

Montanus: Is he thy sonne, and thou begots him not?
Carino: He is my sonne, though I begotst him not.
Montanus: Didst thou not say that he was borne of thee?
Carino: I sayd he was my sonne, not borne of mee
Montanus: How can it be sonne and not-sonne at once?
Carino: The sonne of love, and not of nature hee's.
Montanus: Why do you call him sonne?
Carino: Because I from his cradle have him nourisht still,
And ever lov'd him like my sonne.
Montanus: Bought you him? Stole you him? Where had you him?
Carino: A courteous straunger in Elidis gave me him.
Montanus: And that same straunger, where had he the child?
Carino: I gave him.
Montanus: Thou mov'st at once disdaine and laughter.

First thou him gav'st, and then thou hadst him in gift.
Carino: I gave him that which I with him had found.[45]

Clearly, Shakespeare imitates this dialogue in the final interview between the King and Diana in *All's Well*, even as he complicates it by manipulating the persona of the female speaker to further perplex her interlocutor. A similar disruption of common understanding occurs when a veiled Mariana engages in doublespeak in the final scene of *Measure for Measure*, as the Duke questions her:

> *Duke*: Is this the witness, friar?
> First, let her show [her] face, and after speak.
> *Mariana*: Pardon, my lord, I will not show my face
> Until my husband bid me.
> *Duke*: What, are you married?
> *Mariana*: No, my lord.
> *Duke*: Are you a maid?
> *Mariana*: No, my lord.
> *Duke*: A widow, then?
> *Mariana*: Neither, my lord.
> *Duke*: Why, you are nothing then: neither maid, widow, nor wife.
>   (5.1.167–77)

Lucio provides the common man's solution: "My lord, she may be a punk; for many of them are neither maid, widow, nor wife" (179–80). To this, Mariana briefly comes forth with the straightforward explanation that she has lain with Angelo, her betrothed, who doesn't know he lay with her, and offers to depose that he did so "with all th'effect of love" (5.1.184–99). But then she slides into the same kind of language that Helena and Diana were to use in *All's Well*: that Angelo "thinks he knows that he ne'er knew my body, / But knows he thinks that he knows Isabel's" (203–4). If indeed *Measure* preceded *All's Well* in order of composition, we can see Shakespeare experimenting with the "know"/"think" distinction between levels of cognition before relating it to divine grace as he does in the later play. In *Measure*, after all, there is a virtually omniscient figure, the disguised Duke who acts "like pow'r divine" (5.1.369) and knows what Isabella, Mariana, and Angelo know; more importantly, he empowers Angelo to reveal the potentiality that lies hidden in his nature, which only he has suspected:

> Lord Angelo is precise;
> Stands at a guard with envy; scarce confesses
> That his blood flows; or that his appetite

Is more to bread than stone: hence shall we see
If power change purpose: what our seemers be. (1.3.50–4)

In *All's Well* there is no comparable figure but Helena of "inspired merit," who knows what must be known in order to cure the King, marry the man she loves, and untie the knot that the recalcitrant husband then fashions when he utters his apparently impossible prophecy. But it is Guarini, drawing upon Sophocles' *Oedipus Tyrannos*, who supplies the model of a tragicomedy structured upon a prophecy whose conditions and, hence, whose true meaning cannot be discerned by any mere mortal until, with the aid of providence, they are fulfilled unintentionally by the agents of the play, and a tragic ending is averted by a recognition in which later oracles have also played a part.[46]

Interestingly, the arch-villain of Guarini's play is the nymph Corisca, confessedly a town-and-court-bred courtesan, who scorns fidelity, prides herself on having as many lovers for use as she has gowns, and has set her cap for Mirtillo. She brings about near-catastrophe when she lures Amarillis into a cave, allegedly to behold her betrothed Silvio making love to a lowly shepherd girl, and Amarillis herself is caught, along with Mirtillo, and nearly beheaded—until Mirtillo offers to sacrifice himself in her place. Hence, the original prophecy of the oracle begins to be fulfilled, and is concluded when the true identity of Mirtillo is painfully elicited from Carino under Montanus's questioning, as we have seen above.[47] Corisca herself undergoes a conversion when she sees Mirtillo and Amarillis returning from the temple where they have been married, begs pardon for her treachery, and is forgiven. Guarini explains in his *Annotationi* that this was necessary to prevent Corisca from contaminating the comic ending—punishing her would have made the play like a tragedy with a double ending and not a tragicomedy—evidently glancing at Giraldi's *tragedia di fin lieto*.[48] Prophetic structure, oracular denouement, and pardoning of the comic villain (*Measure*, 5.1.513–23; *All's Well*, 5.3.321–4) thus link *Measure for Measure* and *All's Well that Ends Well* to Guarini's tragicomedy—albeit with more than a trace of Giraldi in *Measure*.

VI

But how does this Italian influence on Shakespeare in the years 1603 to 1605 help us to understand *The Winter's Tale* of 1609–11? If *The*

Winter's Tale is a descendant of Aristotle's tragedy with a happy ending, via Giraldi and Guarini, it is a most peculiar hybrid. For as it plays out through the first four acts, it seems to be a tragedy followed by a comedy—a practice followed by neither Italian playwright. Through Act 3, Scene 2, the play follows a tragic trajectory. These acts include some tragicomic cues, as Giraldi recommends for his *tragedia di fin lieto*.[49] Despite these touches, not until 3.3 is there an extended leavening of the tragic: the seacoast setting with shepherds, associated with pastoral tragicomedy; the grotesque language of Antigonus describing his nocturnal vision of Hermione, followed by his shocking pursuit by a bear; the Old Shepherd's homespun remarks on finding the babe; and the Clown's insouciant descriptions of the foundering ship and of the helpless courtier. The Shepherd's "thou metst with things dying, I with things newborn (3.3.109–10) then authorizes Time to announce the turn to a new genre.[50]

But to fully appreciate this comic turn as *Time*'s literary property, we must consider turn in the Aristotelian sense shared by Giraldi and Guarini. In the *Poetics* the turn occurs in conjunction with the protagonist's recognition of the act he or she has performed or is about to perform in ignorance, and that act is defined by the identity of the *person* at whom it is directed. In *The Winter's Tale* there is no secret about the identity of the soon-to-be-castaway babe except to Leontes, who alone refuses to acknowledge it as his. Neither is Hermione's *person* unknown; what Leontes is willfully ignorant of is her moral nature. Though she is declared chaste by the oracle, and the "innocent babe truly begotten," he denies its truth and is about to prosecute Hermione further when Mamillius is pronounced dead. Instantly he repents, declares himself divinely punished for his injustice, and vows a future of reconciliation with wife, friend, and counselor, whom he confesses he has wronged, when Hermione, too, appears to die. The possibility of a tragedy with a happy ending, even one vitiated by Mamillius's death, is quickly transformed into the certainty of a tragedy with an unhappy ending—which is plotted out by Leontes himself in the last ten lines of the scene.

It is a false ending, of course—not present in Greene, who describes the embalming of Bellaria and her burial with Garinter—but Leontes and the audience don't know it. The subsequent turn to a new genre—initiated by the action of 3.3, appropriated narratively by Time in 4.1, and then taken up by the royals, counselor, rogue, and shepherds who play out Time's argument in 4.2–4—is thus oddly detached from the consciousness of the tragic protagonist and displaced onto the activities of others. For them,

Time authors a comedy of disguise, trickery, unmasking, and misrecognition—matters of social, familial, and moral identity that refract the tragic issues of the first part of the play and that lead all the principals to Sicilia, where the fact of the dead queen and the heirless king is still being lamented. Once there, his plot produces its first *transacted* recognition, as Perdita's identity is revealed. But this does not occur before Leontes makes an incestuous overture to his yet-unknown daughter, and is deterred by Paulina: "Sir, my liege, / Your eye hath too much youth in't. Not a month / 'Fore your queen died, she was more worth such gazes / Than what you look on now" (5.1.223–6). His recognition of Perdita, when it comes, therefore reveals that he has missed committing two "irredeemable deeds": he has not sent his only heir to her death as he had supposed and he has narrowly avoided committing incest with her.[51] But these discoveries do not on their own constitute a reversal that leads to a *fin lieto*, for his happy recognitions are experienced on still-tragic ground. As Leontes has explained to Paulina, he desires the unknown Perdita because she is a palimpsest of the lost Hermione: "I thought of her / Even in these looks I made" (5.1.226–7). Not Pandosto's broiling heat of unlawful lust is heard here, but a hopeless longing for the beauty of his lost wife, whose death he caused through moral misrecognition.

Thus Time's turn offers only a partial *fin lieto*, though it clearly bears the marks of a *doppio soggetto*. For in Act 4 Time introduces two virtually new protagonists in Perdita and Florizel. I say "virtually new" because while not new to *The Winter's Tale* as *dramatis personae*, neither of them had even a walk-on part in the Sicilian portion of the play. Florizel is talked about but not named (1.2.162–70) and Perdita exhibited but not named until Antigonus recalls his dream on the seacoast of Bohemia ("for the babe / Is counted lost for ever, Perdita / I prithee call't"; 3.3.31–3). These figures become the focus of the second action in Act 4—indeed, become "characters" in the theatrical sense discussed in Chapter 2—and their romantic courtship is attended by the residual figures of Polixenes and Camillo, now functioning respectively as conniving threatener and enabler. And one entirely new figure is introduced—Autolycus— who, like Guarini's Corisca, inadvertently helps to bring about the first recognition. In this regard, it is worth noting the thematic link between the lascivious nymph of *Il pastor fido* and Shakespeare's larcenous *Johannes fac totum*. When Corisca discovers that in spite of her malevolent plotting against Amarillis, the girl has succeeded in wedding her faithful shepherd, she undergoes—at least temporarily—a change of heart and seeks pardon. Amarillis replies generously, if skeptically:

> Howsoever now thou prov'st or friend or foe,
> I am well pleas'd the Destinies did make
> Thee the good instrument of my content.
> Happie deceits, fortunate treacheries,
> And if you please merie with us to be,
> Come then and take part of our joys with us. (5.9.77–82)

With greater nonchalance, Autolycus discovers that he has unintentionally proved the truth of his vagabond song: "But shall I go mourn for that, my dear? / The pale moon shines by night, / And when I wander here and there / I then do most go right" (4.1.15–18). After the revelation of Perdita's identity in 5.2, he reflects on the part he played in bringing it about, and is quite willing to forgo his reward in order that he may preserve his reputation:

> Now, had I not the dash of my former life in me, would preferment drop on my head. I brought the old man and his son aboard the prince; told him I heard them talk of a fardel, and I know not what; but he at that time over-fond of the shepherd's daughter—so he then took her to be—who began to be much seasick and himself little better, extremity of weather continuing, this mystery remained undiscovered. But 'tis all one to me, for had I been the finder-out of this secret it would not have relished among my other discredits. (5.2.111–21)

Giraldi had praised the play with a double ending precisely because it provided more than one recognition and peripety, the most exciting elements of a good plot.[52] Shakespeare seems to have embraced that principle even as he kept his audiences largely in the dark about the second ending to come. For in accordance with Giraldi's caution that the "spectator should be held in suspense but not always in the dark," in Act 5, Scene 1 he reintroduces the tragicomic cue. The scene opens with Leontes expressing a grief still fresh after sixteen years of mourning the wife whose death he had caused, and with Paulina just as resolutely resuming her sixteen-year-old recrimination for his apparently irredeemable folly. When Cleomenes chides her for her lingering bitterness and Dion reminds her "What dangers, by his highness' fail of issue, / May drop upon his kingdom," she insists on the impossibility of replacing Hermione—"There's none worthy, / Respecting her that's gone (5.1.34–5)—and reminds them of the gods' will that "King Leontes shall not have an heir / Till his lost child be found" (39–40). While her remarks will stir audience awareness that Perdita is even now making her way to Sicilia, they do nothing to suggest that Hermione, too, has survived. Moreover, what next falls from her lips raises serious doubts about the reliability of Paulina's judgment: "Which that it shall [his lost child be found] / Is all as monstrous to our human reason / As my Antigonus to break his grave / And come again to me, / Who, on my life, did perish with the infant" (40–4). Her oath notwithstanding, what she says is both true and not true—Antigonus *is* dead, but Perdita is alive. Her remark, though, may subtly suggest to an attentive listener that what is "monstrous to our human reason" can simply indicate the limitations of our human reason and thus (irrationally) raise hope for succor. There are more things in heaven and earth, Horatio. . .

Giraldian waffling indeed. As the scene proceeds, the dialogue becomes increasingly cryptic, as Paulina concentrates on the question of remarriage, and virtually goads Leontes to recall the perfections of his dead wife and the impossibility of his ever finding another like her. "No more such wife, therefore no wife," he concedes (56); "Fear thou no wife; / I'll have no wife, Paulina" (68–9). Then suddenly, a volte-face on her part: "Will you swear / Never to marry but by my free leave?" she asks (69–70). When Cleomenes objects, "You tempt him overmuch," she modifies the proposed oath: "Unless another / As like Hermione as is her picture / Affront his eye" (73–5). Upon which a further concession is offered, an unexpected prediction, and a request: "Yet if my lord will marry—If you will, sir, / No remedy but you will—give me the office / To choose you a queen" (76–8). To which Leontes readily accedes—"My true Paulina, / We shall not marry till thou bidd'st us"—and Paulina apparently reneges again: "That / Shall be when your first queen's again in breath. / Never till then" (81–4). This existential cat-and-mouse game—now you'll marry, now you won't—in which we can imagine auditors sharply turning their heads left to right and back again as at a tense tennis match, is then cut short by the entrance of a Gentleman who announces the arrival of "One who gives out himself Prince Florizel, son of Polixenes, with his fair princess" (85–6).

VII

Such are the varied ways in which tragedy and comedy have interpenetrated in *The Winter's Tale*. Nearly three acts of tragic development, lightly seasoned with tragicomic cues; one scene of tragicomic transition on the coast of Bohemia; a deliberate takeover by comic playwright Time at the beginning of Act 4, who fills the remaining scenes of the act with performers playing out his argument. And a fifth act that begins in tones of tragic lamentation but incrementally introduces irrational comic alternatives that leave an audience truly puzzled about the possibility of recuperation, since nothing has been said to indicate that Hermione's "picture" (a term that includes "statue") even exists as an instrument with which to measure the virtues of a second wife, or that after sixteen years it is actually possible to discover that "your first queen's again in breath." In this respect, Shakespeare has shifted the sort of cryptic dialogue he had used in the final recognition scenes of *Measure for Measure* and *All's Well that Ends Well* to a position in this play well before either of the two recognitions and peripeties take place—the first conveyed via ekphrasis in 5.2, the second through enactment in 5.3. As a result, he teasingly draws out the intermingling of tragic and comic by more than 450 lines until the action has reached its astonishing conclusion, bringing forth a woman "as like Hermione as is her picture" to "affront his eye" *and* revealing that his "first queen's again in breath."

If comedy and tragedy intermingle through language, mood, event, and spectacle, so, too, do they intermingle with "the times," as Shakespeare attaches genre change to seasonal change. From Polixenes' early concern that "No sneaping [biting] winds at home" injure his pastoral kingdom in his absence (1.2.13) and Mamillius's declaration that "A sad tale's best for winter" (2.1.25), to Autolycus's raffish spring lyric "When daffodils begin to peer" (4.2.1) and Perdita's entrance as "Flora, peering through April's front" (4.4.2–3), thence to her melancholy invocation of Ovid's Proserpina, whose gathered spring flowers—now past their season in Bohemia—remind us of the loss of Perdita to Sicily (4.4.116–29), to Leontes' greeting to the young visitors who enter his barren palace, "Welcome hither, / As is the spring to th'earth" (5.1.150–1), Shakespeare harmonizes the transition from tragedy to comedy to something in between the two with the complex feelings inspired by seasonal passage in a fallen world ruled by Time.

But Time's scope has boundaries. After all, "A shepherd's daughter, / And what to her adheres, which follows after, / Is th'argument of Time" (4.1.27–9). When Time's plot draws to its promised end, the Tale is taken up by another authorial usurper who gives it a final turn so that Leontes, who is outside Time's remit, can perform his second recognition. Leontes had not recognized the true identity of his victim in Act 3 before perpetrating the incurable deed, as in Aristotle's example of Oedipus; in truth, we now learn, he did not perform the deed at all, but only seemed to—for Hermione's death was a fiction secretly authored by Paulina for everyone in the theater to see. Her ferocious baiting of him in 3.2 after that apparent death, resumed relentlessly in 5.1, is suddenly illuminated when we discover that she has done so in order to bring him gradually through repentance to the state of grace in which a true recognition is possible. For now his recognition of Hermione (and through her, of himself) is more than factual. It is insightful and amending, renovating both their beings. When Giulio Romano's alleged statue is revealed and Leontes is stirred by "her natural posture," he also acknowledges her nature—"as tender / As infancy and grace"—and his own obduracy, "Being more stone than it" (5.3.23, 26–7, 38). Shocked by the marks of time on her face—"Hermione was not so much wrinkled, nothing / So aged as this seems" (28–9)—he is led by Paulina to long for her in the form that Giulio, Time's supposed apprentice, carved her: "As she lived now" (32).[53] When impossible signs of life are seen in the statue, he heeds Paulina's injunction—"It is required / You do awake your faith" (94–5)—and surrenders rational agency. It is at this moment that the former self-appointed author is publicly invoked by his surrogate playwright: "'Tis time; descend; be stone no more," Paulina tells the statue, which comes alive in response to Leontes' recognition. *Temporis filia veritas.* But Tempus must defer to a literary midwife who has secretly fashioned a *tragedia di fin lieto* in order that truth may be born.[54]

Notes

1. Pitcher offers a circumspect review of the likely dates of composition in his introduction to Arden 3, pp. 84–93.
2. The name has been traced to *Amadis de Grecia*, "one of Feliciano de Silva's continuations of *Amadis de Gaulle*" (see *The Winter's Tale*, ed. G. H. P. Pafford [London: Methuen, 1963], p. 164). But why—*pace* Jason Lawrence—look further than Greene?
3. Words and lineation are from the 1588 edition printed by Thomas Orwin for Thomas Cadman. It is not certain that the 1588 edition was Shakespeare's source, but he seems to have used one of the first three editions (1588, 1592, 1599), since the oracle's prediction in the 1607 and 1609 editions differs slightly (substituting "die" for "live") from the earlier editions and from the corresponding lines in the play (3.2.130–3). On the other hand, if the publication of the fifth edition

of *Pandosto* inspired him to revisit Greene, he could just as easily have made his mark by substituting "live" for the more recent "die."

4. *The Winter's Tale*, ed. Pitcher, p. 95.

5. Subsequent page references are to Bullough, *Narrative and Dramatic Sources*, vol. 8, which follows the 1588 edition and supplies its missing pages from the 1592 edition.

6. I assume readers are familiar with the names of characters in *Pandosto*, but as a refresher: Pandosto = Leontes; Egistus = Polixenes; Bellaria = Hermione; Franion = Camillo; Garinter = Mamillius; Porrus = Old Shepherd; Fawnia = Perdita; Dorastus = Florizel.

7. Cf. *WT* 2.3.177–81.

8. *WT* 5.3.154–5.

9. For a sensitive account of Time's purview in the play, see Inga-Stina Ewbank, "The Triumph of Time in *The Winter's Tale*," *REL* 5 (1964): 83–99. More recently B. J. Sokol has pointed out that "There are over a hundred mentions of time or its measurement in the play, and many of these provide metaphors or images for states of mind, perception or judgment, as when Hermione says she loves Leontes 'not a jar o' th' clock behind / What lady she her lord' (I.ii.43–4)" (*Art and Illusion*, p. 197, n. 14).

10. Cf. the prologues of *Tamburlaine I and II*, Jonson's *Volpone* and *The Alchemist*, *Romeo and Juliet*, and Claudius's anxious remark while hearing Hamlet's *Mousetrap*, which we discussed earlier: "Have you heard the argument? is there no offence in't?" (*Hamlet*, 3.2.232–3).

11. In describing Time's transformation of the tragic trajectory of the first three acts of *The Winter's Tale* into a play written in a new genre (comedy) governed by a different mode (pastoral), I am invoking the distinction argued by Paul Alpers in *What Is Pastoral?* (Chicago: University of Chicago Press, 1996). Alpers presses us to recognize pastoral's emphasis on the relationship of the individual's power to that of his world and, more formally, the playfulness accorded by pastoral to its inhabitants—both evident in Act 4. See esp. pp. 44–78, 204–22.

12. See *Poetics*, trans. Janko, 1454a1–10.

13. *Aristotle's Poetics* (Chicago: University of Chicago Press, 1998), p. 182.

14. *In librum Aristotelis de arte poetica explicationes* (Florence, 1548), p. 163.

15. "E in questa specie di tragedie ha specialmente luogo la cognizione, od agnizione che la vogliam noi dire, delle persone, per la qual agnizione sono tolti dai pericoli e dalla morte coloro dai quali veniva l'orrore e la compassione. E tra tutte le agnizione che c'insegna Aristotile ... quella è lodovole sovra le altre per la quale nasce la mutazion della fortuna da misera a felice." *Discorso intorno al comporre delle commedie e delle tragedie* (1554), in G. Giraldi Cinzio, *Scritti Critici*, ed. Guglielmo Guerrieri Crocetti (Milan: Marzorati, 1973), pp. 183–4.

The translation is that of Allan H. Gilbert, *Literary Criticism: Plato to Dryden* (Detroit: Wayne State University Press, 1962), p. 255, slightly modified by me. I am using Crocetti's text rather than Susanna Villari's *Discorso intorno al comporre della tragedia e comedia* (Messina, 2002) because, while her scrupulous edition includes marginal additions by both the author and his nineteenth-century editor Salamone Camarini, many of these are now conjectural due to the mutilation of the exemplar by its book-binder. In a few cases they have rendered the text illogical or self-contradictory.

16. "Si debbono nondimeno far nascere gli avvenimenti di questi men fiere tragedie in guise che gli spettatori tra l'horrore e la compassione stiano sospesi insino al fine, il qual poscia riuscendo allegro gli lasci tutti consolati. E questo far stare sospeso l'auditore, dee però essere condotto talmente dal poeta che egli non stia sempre nelle tenebre, ma dee l'azione di parte in parte andare sciogliendo la favola di modo che lo spettatore si veda menare al fine, ma stia dubbioso a che egli debba riuscire" (Crocetti, p. 184; trans. Gilbert, pp. 256–7, slightly modified by me).

17. This term will be elaborated below.

18. *The Dramaturgy of Shakespeare's Romances* (Athens: University of Georgia Press, 1976), pp. 15–20. Mowat further argues that the "tragic" portion of the play is not really tragic, since Shakespeare refrains from revealing qualities in Leontes with which an audience might sympathize, unlike his treatment of Othello or Macbeth. Without recourse to Giraldi, she detects a genre ambivalence running through the entire play, including Act 4.

19. "Nondimeno noi, n'abbiam composta alcuna a questa imagine, come l'Altile, La Selene, gli Antivalomeni e le altre, solo per servire agli spettatori e farle riuscire piú grate in iscena, e conformarmi piú con l'uso dei nostri tempi" (Crocetti, p. 184, translation mine).

20. "Ed [il far morire] in questa sorte di favola [I malvagi, o patir gravi mali, è introdotto] per piú contentezza, e per maggior ammaestramento di quelli che ascoltano, [veggendo puniti] coloro che erano stati cagione degli avvenimenti turbolenti, onde le mezzane persone erano state travagliate nella favola" (Crocetti, p. 184; trans. Gilbert, p. 257, modified by me).

21. See G. Giraldi Cinzio, *Epizia: An Italian Renaissance Tragedy*, ed. Philip Horne (Lewiston: Mellen Press, 1996): "Salvo è Vieo, è salve Iuriste, e salvo / È d'Epizia l'onor e l'onor anche / De la violate donna da Vieo; / E le angosciose doglie in gioia tutte / Rivolte sono" (V.vii.2824–8). The Claudio figure is also preserved in Whetstone's *Promos and Cassandra*, published five years before *Epizia*, but it lacks the explanation for his substitution by a reprobate who is "so alike in features to Vieo as to appear the very image of Vieo himself" (*Epizia*, ll. 2720–1, trans. Horne, p. xxx). This suggests that if Shakespeare did read Whetstone,

he also read Giraldi's play. Horne argues that "the correspondence between *Measure for Measure* and *Epizia* in this respect supports the theory that Shakespeare knew the dramatic version of the story as well as the *novella*. Some verbal reminiscences point in the same direction." Cf. Lawrence, *"Who the devil"*, pp. 140–1.

22. Crocetti, p. 23.

23. Crocetti, p. 24.

24. "Delle quali favole ... chiameremo la prima col nome solito 'mista,' e la seconda 'innestata.'" *Il Compendio della poesia tragicomica* [*De la Poésie Tragi-Comique*], trans. and annotated by Laurence Giavarini (Paris: Honoré Champion, 2008), p. 196; cf. Gilbert, p. 506.

25. "Quanto alla prima, bassi a considerare, che la tragicommedia non è composta di due favole intere, l'una della quali sia perfetta tragedia, e perfetta commedia l'altra, congiunte insieme di modo che ambedue si possano disunire senza che l'una guasti i fatti dell'altra o ciascuna i suoi propri. Ne dessi altresi credere ch'ella sia una storia tragica viziata con le bassezze della commedia, o favola comica contaminata con le morti della tragedia, perciocché ne cotesto sarebbe retto componimento, conciosiacosaché chiunque fa tragicommedie non intenda di comporre separata o tragedia o commedia, ma di questa e di quella un terzo, che sia perfetto in suo genere, e abbia di ambedue loro quelle più parti che verisimilmente possano stare insieme" (Giavarini, pp. 196, 198, translation mine; cf. Gilbert, p. 507).

26. "Double plot" is not to be confused with a double ending, of which Aristotle also disapproved. See *Poetics*, 1453a31–6.

27. See Giavarini's quotations from De Nores on p. 340, nn. 32–3. Aside from his perverse denial of good fortune to men of high birth, De Nores seems not to have read very carefully, since Mirtillo and Silvio turn out to be brothers, descended from the same noble father.

28. In this, he may have been reflecting on Giraldi, whose *tragedie di fin lieto* included the double ending disparaged by Aristotle (see n. 19 above). Giraldi used the term *mista* for Aristotle's "double," which is contrary to Guarini's meaning, and Guarini probably wanted to make that clear. See Marvin T. Herrick, *Tragicomedy* (Urbana: University of Illinois Press, 1962), pp. 67–73.

29. *Compendio*, pp. 198–200. Indeed, he adds that the overheard spasms experienced by lovers are caused by the failure of their bodies to fully mingle, as do their souls, despite their desires.

30. On the ubiquity of the topos in Italian pastoral, see Clubb, *Italian Drama*, pp. 125–71, esp. 168–71.

31. For details of Castelvetro's activities as editor in the period 1584–91, see Lawrence, *"Who the devil"*, pp. 190–6. For Wolfe's career in publishing Italian texts, see John Lievsay, *The Englishman's Italian Books 1550–1700* (Philadelphia: University of Pennsylvania Press, 1969).

32. Attesting to its familiarity, Lady Politic Would-be torments Volpone

with her erudition: "Here's *Pastor Fido* . . . All our English writers, /
I mean such, as are happy in th' Italian, / Will deign to steale out of this
author, mainly" (*Volpone*, 3.4.86–9).

33. For an informative discussion of Italian books on the London literary
market, see G. K. Hunter, "Italian Tragicomedy on the English Stage,"
Renaissance Drama 6 (1973): 123–48, esp. 125–9.

34. See *Measure for Measure*, ed. J. W. Lever (Methuen: London, 1965),
pp. xxxv–xlv.

35. For an analysis of Isabella's counter-factual arguments, see Altman,
Improbability, pp. 355–63. Guarini's refusal to contaminate tragicomedy with a double ending is discussed below.

36. *Tragicomedy*, p. 64.

37. In Giraldi's dramatic version of his novella, the fact that Epizia's
brother Vieo has been spared is announced before she pleads for
Juriste's life, thus motivating her new desire for clemency. Isabella's
plea is therefore utterly selfless—a direct response to Mariana's plight.
The *doppio soggetto* of Mariana's betrothal, however, is not without
problems of its own. "Here comes a man of comfort, whose advice /
Hath often still'd my brawling discontent," she says as the Friar enters
at 4.1.9–10. Suddenly a long-time back-story joins the continuous
short-time action of the representation, suggesting that the Duke had
been making a habit of disguising himself as Friar Lodowick, a practice
barely hinted at during his interview with Friar Thomas at the beginning of 1.3.

38. Whether *Measure for Measure* preceded or followed *All's Well that
Ends Well* has long been uncertain. I follow the dating of Stanley Wells
and Gary Taylor, *William Shakespeare*.

39. The Countess is Shakespeare's invention. She doesn't exist in Boccaccio's
Decameron III, 9, or in William Painter's English translation in *The
Palace of Pleasure*, his most likely sources. Her speech suggests
Shakespeare's alertness to the theme of hybridization that informs the
mixed Italian genre into which he has ventured. In Painter, Beltramo's
sneering response to the proposed marriage touches lightly on the
subject, but emphasizes its literal, not metaphorical significance: "The
Counte knew her wel, and had already seen her, although she was
faire, yet knowing her not to be of a stocke convenable to his nobility,
skornefully said unto the king, 'Will you then (sir) give me a Phisition
to wife?'" (Bullough, *Narrative and Dramatic Sources*, vol. 2, p. 391).

40. The seriousness of her reflection is emphasized by means of a fourteen-
line sonnet in heroic couplets.

41. *Italian Drama*, p. 73. Again, Helena's feigned death is Shakespeare's
addition. Thus her appearance in the final scene—"one that's dead
is quick"—is presented to the onstage audience as a miraculous resurrection. Clubb's third chapter, "Woman as Wonder" (pp. 65–89),
offers a detailed analysis of the providential *commedia grave* tradition

from which Shakespeare adapted both *All's Well* and *Measure for Measure*.

42. Bullough, *Narrative and Dramatic Sources*, vol. 2, p. 392.

43. *William Perkins, 1555–1602: English Puritanist*, ed. and intro. Thomas F. Merrill (Nieuwkoop: B. De Graaf, 1966), pp. 7–8. Note how this concept of "thinking and knowing" relates to Sir John Hawles's observation about jurors' decisions quoted in Chapter 4, n. 70: "They don't swear the Bill is True, but that they in their Consciences believe that it is so."

44. "Italian Tragicomedy on the English Stage," pp. 140–8.

45. *Il pastor fido*, 5.3.30–3, 38–9, 58–66, in *Three Renaissance Pastorals: Tasso, Guarini, Daniel*, ed. Elizabeth Story Donno (Binghamton: MRDS, 1993), pp. 155–6. The translation is that of the 1602 edition, which Hunter uses, noting the close imitation of Guarini's Italian in several parts of *All's Well*.

46. Mirtillo, who had first seen Amarillis in Elide, his adoptive homeland, returned to the house of Carino, his supposed father, at news of the latter's illness, but became ill himself through longing for Amarillis. Carino, once recovered, consulted an oracle that told him Mirtillo would not regain health until he went to Arcadia, and so dispatched him, but there Mirtillo had to endure a life of unrequited love because he found Amarillis betrothed to Silvio, son of Montanus the High Priest. In 5.1 Carino turns up in Arcadia himself and tells his friend Uranio that yet another oracle ordered him to return to his native land, Arcadia, where he would again enjoy life with Mirtillo. These oracles are all instruments of divine providence.

47. A brief refresher: in the Golden Age, the shepherd Amintas had sacrificed himself at Diana's altar rather than kill his beloved, the unfaithful Lucrina, who then slew herself in remorse. Arcadia was condemned by the angry goddess to an annual virgin sacrifice, to which was added a law that any woman found unfaithful in love would die unless another was willing to die in her stead. Diana's oracle then proclaimed to the Arcadians: "*No end there is to that which you offends, / Till two of heavens issue love unite; / And for the auncient fault of that false wight* / A faithful Shepheards *pittie make amends*" (*The Faithful Shepherd*, 1.2.193–6, in Donno, *Three Renaissance Pastorals*). Amarillis is descended from Pan's seed, Silvio, the younger brother of Mirtillo, from that of Hercules. Mirtillo, who has offered to die in Amarillis's stead, and is believed lost by Montanus, is not identified as Montanus's elder son until 5.5, at which time the original prophecy is unexpectedly fulfilled.

48. See Battista Guarini, *Opere*, ed. Marziano Guglielminetti (Turin: Unione Tipografico-Editrice Torinese, 1971), p. 712, n. *a*.

49. There are further "tempering" cues. As Robert Henke has shown, the arboreal metaphors used in 1.1 to describe Leontes' and Polixenes'

boyhood, and Polixenes' extended simile of "twinned lambs" in 1.2, are genre signifiers of pastoral tragicomedy (*Pastoral Transformations*, pp. 92, 101–3).

50. For a detailed account of the ambiguous nature of the stage bear see Clubb, *Italian Drama*, pp. 140–52.

51. In keeping with his plan for a happy ending, Shakespeare has played down in Leontes the passion of Greene's Pandosto who, "broyling at the heat of unlawfull lust," first courts Fawnia, then tries to bribe her, then threatens her, and, at her persistent denial, "flong away from her in a rage: swearing if in shorte time she would not be wonne with reason: he would forget al courtesie, and compel her to grant by rigour" her body to his lust (Bullough, *Narrative and Dramatic Sources*, vol. 8, pp. 194–6). Pandosto "(calling to mind how first he betraied his friend Egistus, how his jealousie was the cause of Bellarias death, that contrarie to the law of nature hee had lusted after his own Daughter) moved with these desperate thoughts, he fell into a melancholie fit, and to close up the Comedie with a Tragicall strategeme, he slew himself" (ibid. p. 199).

52. Though he had not anticipated that there might be a sixteen-year interval between the ending for the *cattivo* and the ending for the *onesto*, or that he would be the same person.

53. Ewbank remarks on the unexpected qualification of time's power as Leontes expresses longing for the statue: "Hermione . . . is a living proof that 'Love's not Time's fool, though rosy lips and cheeks / Within his bending sickle's compass come' (Sonnet cxvi). These sonnet lines could perhaps also paraphrase the truth that time has finally revealed to Leontes: paradoxically, time has at last in its triumph brought about its own defeat" ("The Triumph of Time," p. 99).

54. Authorship and performance are recurrent themes in *The Winter's Tale*. In 1.2.186–9, Leontes puns on "Go play, boy" as playing shades from child's game to Hermione's sexual play to his playing the part of a cuckold, a theatrical metaphor that resumes with Perdita and Camillo in Act 4, talking of playing parts. But it is Paulina who gradually emerges as the hidden playwright and actor from late 3.2 to 5.1 to 5.3. Hence the temptation to cast the same actor in the roles of Paulina and Time, as was done with Judi Dench in Kenneth Branagh's production of *The Winter's Tale* at the Garrick Theatre in London in 2016.

Bodging Theatrical Faith

I

Bodging a theatrical script is the practice of stitching verbal and visual patches into one's text in unexpected ways to produce a dramatic hybrid for the stage. In "verbal," I include words, phrases, sentences, and patterns of speech that can be traced to written or spoken language outside the play. These would encompass such locutions as those that passed from *Il pastor fido* into *All's Well that Ends Well* and *Measure for Measure*. By "visual," I refer specifically to those vivid patches of dialogue that "lead objects before our eyes"— whether natural or artificial—by means of ekphrases, though visible actions—what we now call "stage business" or "theatergrams"—are also among the materials available for recycling. Bodging involves insight into the rightness of often improbable conjunctions of materials that function so well together that their union commands assent, despite—or perhaps because of—its unpredictability. It is born of ingenuity, which, we are told by the humanist Juan Luis Vives, is a God-given power to enable unaccommodated man to construct his world through "the lively keenness of an *ingenium* full of spontaneous play."[1] Its success lies in the eyes and ears of the bodger and his or her perceivers, who discover a "breakthrough into a new reality," according to philosopher Ernesto Grassi, where "the metamorphosis of man takes place."[2] We have seen that Shakespeare was an inveterate bodger, using many kinds of materials to stitch together his plays—as, truth to tell, were most of his contemporaries, all trained in the arts of literary imitation, ekphrasis, ethical representation, topical dialectic, and the myriad other devices taught by classical and contemporary rhetoricians. The question that the foregoing account of *The Winter's Tale* inevitably raises, however, is whether one can bodge up faith.

II

The peculiarity of Paulina's injunction to Leontes, "It is required / You do awake your faith," is that it seems to demand he arouse a dormant religious faith in the possibility of Hermione's resurrection *and* to direct the theater audience to do so as well, although they are involved only vicariously in the crisis confronting Hermione's family and friends onstage. Of them, as, by extension, of us today (who may or may not be believers), what does Paulina demand? To answer this, we must recall that she is not only Paulina the *dramatis persona* of court lady who once served the apparently dead queen and, currently, Paulina the *character* of priestess-magician presenting us with a stone image of that queen. She is also, as we soon discover, Paulina the behind-the-scenes *dramatist* who has usurped the role of play-doctor from Time—indeed, preceded him in usurpation—having collaborated for sixteen years with her diegetic client to supply a quite different dramatic ending from the one Shakespeare has led Leontes and the audience to anticipate. In that role she is the instrument of a more subtle kind of bodging: Shakespeare's silent embrace of one of the recently denizened forms of Italian tragicomedy. As Hermione soon explains to Perdita, "thou shalt hear that I, / Knowing by Paulina that the oracle / Gave hope thou wast in being, have preserved / Myself to see the issue" (5.3.125–8). Tricky Will, without drawing attention to what he was doing, has slipped in an inaudible, invisible bodge to dupe us into believing that Hermione is dead and concealed it for nearly two more acts, only to pull it out from behind a curtain in the form of a Giulian "statue" that reveals she was alive all the while. By doing so, he offers us the unique pleasure of participating in a *tragedia di fin lieto*.

Much has been written in recent years about the question of faith in the final scene of *The Winter's Tale*. Michael O'Connell has addressed the interpenetration of sacred and theatrical ritual in the context of idolatry, as the audience unexpectedly find themselves evoked as potential respondents to Paulina's injunction. "What becomes most significant theatrically is the way the scene comes to insist on faith in what is seen," he writes, having reviewed the antitheatrical animus rooted in the reformers' distrust of images. And this extends beyond the stage. "Leontes' response to her is a command both to the court and the audience: 'Proceed; / No foot shall stir.' As theatrical performance testifies, the faith and complicity of the audience are also at stake; if anyone indeed made a move to leave, one senses, the scene itself could not proceed."[3] Marion O'Connor has shown in even more detail how the action self-consciously plays to the still-sensitive post-Reformation issues of *maleficium*, conjuration, and image-making, arguing that by the time the statue is revealed the stage has virtually been set for the adoration of a St. Hermione.[4] For Leontes tells the statue, "There's magic in thy majesty, which has / My evils conjured to remembrance"; Perdita asks, apotropaically, "And give me leave, / And do not say 'tis superstition, that / I kneel and then implore her blessing"; while Paulina reminds them, in the language of an image-making witch, that "the stone is mine," threatens "I could afflict you farther," yet denies that she is "assisted / By wicked powers" (5.3.39–40, 42–4, 58, 75, 90–1).

Focusing on the mixed emotions attending Hermione's "coming to life" sixteen years after her apparent (and Mamillius's real) death, Elizabeth Williamson has traced the event to the resurrection scenes of medieval Catholic drama—especially to what she calls its "affective technology," through which feelings of both joy and loss experienced by the apostles at Jesus's tomb are transmitted to audiences. "Many early modern dramas," she writes, "can be construed as having an interest in the sacred insofar as they work to access the emotional charge associated with the original religious narrative. The force of that narrative comes not just from the theology behind the event, but also from the entertainment value of suspense, which was a factor in both the Catholic drama and in the commercial theater." Such plays as Thomas Heywood's *How a Man May Choose a Good Wife from a Bad*, John Day's *Law Tricks*, Thomas Middleton's *A Chaste Made in Cheapside*, and John Mason's *The Turk*, she points out, perform generic variations on the resurrection theme. She further reminds us that Shakespeare himself had experimented in different ways with such scenes in *Romeo and Juliet*, *Much Ado About Nothing*, *Othello*, and *Pericles*, so that audiences attending *The Winter's Tale* may have been ready to pick up the mixed signals of resurrection provided in 5.1.[5]

These critical approaches to the question of faith in the context of contemporary religious controversy are surely correct.[6] Still, they do not take into sufficient account the active piecing-together of the scenic narrative of the fifth act, which Shakespeare seems deliberately to have crafted in accordance with the tragical-comical aesthetic of

Giraldi Cinzio that we observed in the previous chapter. For the caution that "spectators should be held in suspense but not always stand in the dark" is so hotly pursued in the first eighty-four lines of 5.1 that audience members must be aware by the time Florizel's arrival is announced that their emotional and intellectual expectations are being actively manipulated by Paulina (and, behind her, by Shakespeare). This means that they will certainly have acquired by then an increased interest in the crafting of the play—affording them a certain critical distance—which may have been aroused, as we shall see, even before Time's takeover in 4.1, then augmented by the steward's surprising revelation that there exists a statue of the queen "in the keeping of Paulina" (5.2.93), followed by the Second Gentleman's startling remark: "I had thought she had some great matter there in hand, for she hath privately twice or thrice a day, *ever since the death of Hermione*, visited that removed house" (5.2.102–6, italics mine). One can imagine the curiosity that then arose in the minds of first-time auditors at early performances— "What is *that* about?" they must have wondered—especially those who were familiar with *Pandosto*, where no resurrection—religious or humanly plotted—is ever a possibility.

But plotting is at the heart of the matter—in this case unseen, unheard plotting. Only in retrospect is one led to scan Paulina's line in 3.2, "Look down / And see what death is doing" (dismissed by Leontes), and, when she returns after Hermione has been carried from the court, to question her frantic cry, "The queen, the queen, / The sweetest, dearest creature's dead . . . I say she's dead—I'll swear it [although no swearing is heard]. If word nor oath / Prevail not, go and see." She is offering ocular proof that a now-humbled Leontes readily accepts—"Prithee bring me / To the dead bodies of my queen and son"—and then concludes, definitively, "Come, and lead me / To these sorrows" (3.2.145–6, 197–8, 200–1, 231–2, 239–40). In the dramatic moment, the intensity of Paulina's passionately acted grief and the finality of Leontes' actual remorse leave no room for skepticism.[7]

From there on, however, Shakespeare's bodging becomes more evident. New to the language of the play is the grotesque imagery Antigonus uses in the next scene to describe his vision of Hermione (3.3.15–36), followed by his "superstitiously" Catholic decision that she was a revenant spirit, and then by his astonishing "Exit, pursued by a bear" (57 S.D.). I have discussed the first two passages in Chapters 3 and 5 in the context of ekphrasis and genre development, respectively, but here I want to call attention to how all three are likely to have registered with Shakespeare's early audiences. For a sophistic oscillation of affect and cognition is induced in 3.3. Antigonus is a good and upright man, not without a sense of humor, trapped in a cruel mission he had sworn to undertake toward the end of the most physically violent scene in the play (2.3.129–91). When he next appears, auditors are likely to regard him sympathetically as he confides in them, yet will also note the slightly risible hyperbole of the head-wagging, the triple bowing, and the "two spouts" that Hermione's weeping eyes have become in his memory. Their identification with Antigonus thus loosened, they might then greet more critically his belief that "This was no slumber," that the image which had appeared and spoken to him was indeed a spirit of the dead, "and that / Apollo would—this being indeed the issue / Of King Polixenes—it should here be laid, / Either for life or death, upon the earth / Of its right father" (3.3.41–5). Their knowledge that the oracle had pronounced the "innocent babe truly begotten" (3.2.132) would confirm their sense that Antigonus is not a reliable interpreter of his oneiric experience—yet the vision's reported words, "For this ungentle business / Put on thee by my lord, thou ne'er shalt see / Thy wife Paulina more" (33–5), might raise concern for him. His tender settling the child on the ground would solicit further sympathy. The final indignity of Antigonus being chased off the stage by a bear clashes so violently with the gentler feelings they have just been experiencing that they would realize only after it had happened—as they looked at one another in astonishment—that the playwright's primary interest was to provide them with a horrendous, mouth-gaping entertainment for which they were entirely unprepared.[8]

The homiletic grumbling of the unwitting Shepherd who then enters will in itself function as a kind of emotional let-down, literally as a low "comic relief" from the auditors' close encounter with a bloodthirsty farce that must have left many of them gasping or—less charitably—roaring with laughter. We should probably allow for several beats before the Shepherd even enters, so that the audience can turn their attention to him in order that he be heard at all. Thus recovered to enjoy the Shepherd's homely satire of youthful sex, they are bestirred to yet another mode of response by Clown's attempts to outdo his father by describing in russet yeas and honest kersey noes the sea action and land action he's witnessed—"now the ship boring the moon with its mainmast, and anon swallowed with yeast and froth, as you'd thrust a cork into a hogshead. And then for the land-service, to see how the bear tore out his shoulder-bone, how he cried to me for help, and said his name was Antigonus a nobleman!"

(3.3.89–95). Clown's final gesture of courtesy to the honest courtier marks the base uses to which he has come: "I'll go see if the bear be gone from the gentleman, and how much he hath eaten. They are never curst but when they are hungry. If there be any of him left, I'll bury it" (3.3.125–9). Agreeing to assist him, the Shepherd tells his son, "'Tis a lucky day, boy, and we'll do good deeds on't" (135–6). Thus the very dark event, mingled with good-natured humor, offers practical comedy that evokes yet again a new level of mental apprehension and emotional pleasure.

Enter a winged figure with an hourglass who tells the audience, "I . . . / Now take upon me, in the name of Time, / To use my wings" (4.1.1–4). The sudden appearance of a pageant personification is yet another arrant intrusion (if we count the bear-chase) upon the more naturalistic mode of representation that governs the play.[9] Yet this Shakespearean bodge has both a dramaturgic and a rhetorical function. Importuning the audience to "Impute it not a crime / To me or my swift passage that I slide / O'er sixteen years, and leave the growth untried / Of that wide gap" (4–7), Time can self-righteously elide Greene's account of Fawnia's nurture by shepherd and wife—slipping around Sir Philip Sidney's old charge, still maintained by Ben Jonson, that the English stage was "faulty both in place and time, the two necessary companions of all corporal actions."[10] And Time can authorially set the next scene, using language similar to that of the Chorus in *Henry V*, as he invites the audience to "imagine me, / Gentle spectators, that I may now be / In fair Bohemia"—and lists its chief *dramatis personae*: "a son o'th'king's, which Florizel / I now name to you; and with speed so pace / To speak of Perdita" (19–21, 22–4). The rhythmic function of his entry is equally important. Time restores dignity to the proceedings in sixteen rhymed couplets. Thus flattered and elevated—even soothed by the regularity of the pentameter rhyme—after being stirred to compassion, doubt, and shocked horror (or mirth) by the mingled modes of comedy, serious drama, and ferocious farce in the previous scene, auditors may now relax in the confidence that they are in friendly and experienced hands.

III

I am taking the liberty of offering this precis of material that readers are already familiar with in order to introduce my concluding thesis: virtually all of Time's "argument" (Act 4, Scenes 2–4) is a bodged-up variety show that offers a succession of entertaining diversions designed to woo an audience who will grow increasingly enamored of the maker's ingenuity in giving them pleasure, so that when they are asked to awake their faith at the end of the play they cannot but reciprocate.

Intrigue and disguise take over as the action resumes and prompts a different kind of attentiveness in those standing in the yard and seated in the stalls. We find Polixenes, presumably looking somewhat older, trying to convince his now-bosom counselor Camillo, anxious to return to Sicilia and "the penitent king, my master," to help him check out the unprincely pastime of his son, the aforementioned Florizel (4.1.22), "seldom from the house of a most homely shepherd," who "hath," Camillo supplies, "a daughter of most rare note." Polixenes has heard as much and fears she is "the angle that plucks our son hither." Whereupon he declares, "Thou shalt accompany us to the place, where we will, not appearing what we are, have some question with the shepherd, from whose simplicity I think it not uneasy to get the cause of my son's resort thither" (4.2.37–50). The plan thus set in motion . . .

. . . It's time for a little musical conny-catching comedy. I mean, of course, the first entrance of Autolycus, singing "When daffodils begin to peer," interspersed with some candid autobiographical snatches of prose before Clown enters—the first time we have seen him since his memorable description of Antigonus being gnawed by a bear. Which gives Autolycus the chance to exhibit the skill he's just told us about—by playing a half-dead victim who has been beaten and robbed by one Autolycus who was "once a servant of the prince" (twice told), then picking gullible Clown's pocket (4.3.1, 13, 86–7) and, when alone onstage, promising us more of the same at the sheep-shearing feast.[11]

Rhapsodic love-talk follows. "These your unusual weeds to each part of you / Does give a life; no shepherdess, but Flora / Peering in April's front. This your sheep-shearing / Is as a meeting of the petty gods, / And you the queen on't" (4.4.1–5). Thus Florizel to Perdita, dressed as Queen of the Feast. It is our first glimpse of grown-up Perdita. She is as pretty, sweet, and modest as we would have her—and worried that Florizel's father might pass this way and find his princely son "vilely bound up" as the shepherd Doricles, with herself in "borrowed flaunts." Florizel-cum-Doricles urges her to "Apprehend / Nothing but jollity" (24–5), and justifies his masquerade by reference to the gods who disguised themselves for love (Jupiter as a bull, Neptune as a ram, Apollo as a shepherd).

His allusions to rape, which might raise some eyebrows among his offstage listeners, prove to be strategic, for he immediately backs off the threat, declaring the superiority of his love, for "my desires / Run not before mine honour, nor my lusts / Burn hotter than my faith" (33–5)—and we are reassured. Still, Perdita is apprehensive that their intended marriage will prove an impossibility. Florizel's further assurances that "I cannot be / Mine own, nor anything to any, if / I be not thine" (44–6) are interrupted by the arrival of the Shepherd, Polixenes, and Camillo, and the notes then turn decidedly academic.

After some paternal scolding for not behaving like a proper hostess, Perdita shifts to her lecture mode, offering a lesson in botanical lore: "Give me those flowers there, Dorcas. Reverend sirs, / For you there's rosemary and rue; these keep / Seeming and savour all the winter long. / Grace and remembrance be to you both" (73–6). To Polixenes' wry retort, "Well you fit our ages / With flowers of winter," Perdita grows apologetically lyrical: "Sir, the year growing ancient, / Not yet on summer's death, nor on the birth / Of trembling winter, the fairest flowers o'th' season / Are our carnations and streaked gillyvors, / Which some call nature's bastards; of that kind / Our rustic garden's barren" (78–84). Lyric then segues into an increasingly heated nineteen-line debate on the relationship of horticultural and natural growth (85–103).[12] Following which, Perdita waxes lyrical again, offering Polixenes and Camillo "flowers / Of middle summer, and I think they are given / To men of middle age" (106–8)—then suddenly grows elegiac as she realizes she has nothing for young Doricles, Mopsa, and Dorcas: "O Proserpina, / For the flowers now that, frighted, thou let'st fall / From Dis's wagon! . . ." (116 ff). Her plangent catalogue of the spring blooms that had disappeared from the earth when Ceres' daughter was abducted in Sicily by the god of the underworld will be recognized by many listening as a sobering reminder of the dead Hermione's loss of her own daughter and Leontes' role in that abduction. So again we find in these mingling modes of speech and their accompanying tonalities the continuous exercising of affect and understanding—inducing a psychological athleticism not all of which will be perceived by any single auditor, but which is likely to be experienced in the aggregate by all of them.

More lyrical love-talk ensues, then a tragicomic cue offered by an unknowing Polixenes, struck by Perdita's beauty: "Nothing she does or seems / But smacks of something greater than herself" (157–8). It raises a momentary hope that he possesses a saving intuition when, just as suddenly, Clown cries "Come on, strike up!" (167), and—God save the mark!—we are distracted by "a dance of Shepherds and Shepherdesses" (S.D. 167). During this interlude, the Shepherd and Polixenes move downstage and we hear the newly rich rustic boast to the undercover king, "If young Doricles / Do light upon her, she shall bring him that / Which he dreams not of" (180–2). It is another tragicomic cue to be savored by the audience, if not by the speaker or his interlocutor.

At this point, the mode changes once again to low comic, as a servant announces the arrival of a pedlar who "has the prettiest love songs for maids, so without bawdry . . . with such delicate burdens of dildos and fadings, 'jump her and thump her'"; "He hath ribbons of all the colours i'th'rainbow; points more than all the lawyers in Bohemia can learnedly handle, though they come to him by th'gross" (194–7, 206–8). Enter Autolycus disguised, singing a pedlar's pitch, followed by some snitty backchat between the jealous Mopsa and Dorcas, whom Clown tries to appease with gifts of ballads, including one that "goes to the tune of 'Two Maids Wooing a Man,'" sung by the girls challenging a two-timing male, whose response is sung (appropriately) by Autolycus. And just when we think we'll get back to Florizel and Perdita, the servant enters again to announce the arrival of "three carters, three shepherds, three neatherds, three swineheards that have made themselves all men of hair," who offer to dance. "One three of them, by their own report, sir, hath danced before the king" (4.4.329–31, 342–3). Ah! A topical allusion! This variety show goes on—and on.

Matters grow serious following the dance—indeed, rise gradually to sound a tragic note, as Florizel attempts to enlist his disguised father as witness to his betrothal, and Polixenes, tearing off his disguise, declares in contempt, "Thou art too base / To be acknowledged. Thou a sceptre's heir / That thus affects a sheephook?" (422–4). Any inclination to find amusement in his synecdoche is tempered immediately by his threats to the lives of both the Shepherd and his daughter, especially by his parting words to Perdita: "if ever henceforth thou / These rural latches to his entrance open, / Or hoop his body more with thy embraces / I will devise a death as cruel for thee / As thou art tender to't" (442–6). He sounds as ferocious here as Leontes did when he threatened to burn her alive as a baby. Auditors may want to—and perhaps did at the Globe—shout out Perdita's true identity, but at this moment in the performance, with neither Rogue nor Clown onstage, the fourth wall is impermeable, so their knowledge is of no use in resolving the crisis playing out before them.

Instead, they are led to find relief in the more piquant pleasures of multiple onstage intrigues. After Polixenes stalks out, Perdita falls into despondency, and the Shepherd berates Florizel and his daughter for bringing ruin upon him, Florizel insists that he will not even now break his faith to Perdita, and tells Camillo that the two of them will run away to sea together. Camillo, finding an opportunity to fulfill his own desire to return to Sicily, persuades Florizel to sail to Leontes as emissary of his father and marry Perdita there. He will provide a script, "The which shall point you forth at every sitting / What you must say, that he shall not perceive / But that you have your father's bosom there / And speak his very heart" (566–9). Thus arises the first intrigue—among Florizel, Perdita, and Camillo—bringing theatrical plotting audibly to the observers' consciousness. The notion of crafting a play is developed further with the reappearance of Autolycus. After he jovially tells us of his success in stealing purses from the entranced rustics listening to Clown's ballad-singing, Camillo spots him, insists he exchange clothes with Florizel, and orders Perdita to take Florizel's hat, muffle her face, and "disliken / The truth of your own seeming" (654–7), thereby furnishing the plot with costumes. Perdita picks up her cue: "I see the play so lies / That I must bear a part" (659–60).

My point is that the audience is getting a behind-the-scenes look at what they have been enjoying all along: theatrical craft. A second plot then ensues. Camillo, solus: "What I do next shall be to tell the king / Of this escape, and whither they are bound . . . / To force him after, in whose company / I shall re-view Sicilia, for whose sight / I have a woman's longing" (666–71). Overhearing the plot, Autolycus resolves to keep their secret: "I hold it the more knavery to conceal it, and therein am I constant to my profession" (684–6). Enter Shepherd and Clown—and a third intrigue. Through a last, salutary act of conny-catching, Autolycus culls more gold from the frightened pair by promising to bring them aboard the king's ship where they can prove the girl is none of their flesh and blood, and then turns to his admirers in the audience with a satisfied grin: "If I had a mind to be honest, I see Fortune would not suffer me—she drops booties in my mouth" (835–6). Conspirators all, we happily wait to see what happens next.

IV

It's not what we expect, for Time's argument is overtaken by Paulina's argument. It is in this scene, Act 5, Scene 1, that the manipulation of expectation begins—regarding the possibility of Leontes' remarriage to "another / As like Hermione as is her picture" (5.1.73–4)—which we examined in the previous chapter. But with the arrival of Prince and Perdita, the plot reverts to that of Act 4 and the dress rehearsal the audience had been allowed to witness through the medium of Camillo's ekphrasis: "Methinks I see / Leontes opening his free arms and weeping / His welcomes forth; asks thee there, 'Son, forgiveness!' / As 'twere i'th' father's person; kisses the hands / Of your fresh princess; o'er and o'er divides him / 'Twixt his unkindness and his kindness" (4.4.552–7). Now Leontes performs the actual staged version of Camillo's scene *in propria persona*: "Most dearly welcome, / And your fair princess—goddess—O, alas, / I lost a couple that 'twixt heaven and earth / Might thus have stood, begetting wonder, as / You, gracious couple, do" (5.1.129–33). The audience's memory of having been present at the drafting of this scene cannot but strike them with the sense that they are privileged patrons and endear them further to the invisible artificer.

With this in mind, we can reposition the extensive ekphrases of the reunions in 5.2 within a deeper perspective. There are three locations involved in viewing the events that these ekphrases concern: (1) that of the *unseen dramatis personae* who are said to have experienced at first hand the discovery of the shepherd girl's identity, her reunion with her real father, and the meeting of the two kings; (2) that of the *visible* courtiers who describe these events—and of their onstage listeners, who turn the words they hear into images in their own fantasies, to which they then respond in speech and action; and (3) that of the *theater audience* who watch the courtiers and hear their ekphrases and the responses of their listeners—whom they simultaneously imitate by bodging for themselves, with imaginative variations, the otherwise unseen events going on in Leontes' receiving chamber. It is a tour de force of multiple scripting, which, by supplying lines for only one set of speakers, represents the interiorities of two sets, and manipulates the interiorities of three sets.

Thus with all enabled pen our bending author pursues his story, and thus his audience make love to their employment. Although we cannot construct a graph that precisely traces their oscillating emotions and understandings from moment to moment, *The Winter's*

Tale is a psychagogic casebook illustrating how Shakespeare led his audience through the many kinds of enjoyment available in his theater—by varying dramatic genres and literary modes, locus and platea entertainments, naturalistic, conventional, and allegorical representations, visible plots and invisible intrigues, and by thematizing and enacting playwriting and performing. Their affective and cognitive capacities so fully and so pleasurably exercised, what else can a grateful audience do but comply when Paulina invokes her dramaturgic authority to "make the statue move indeed" if they awake their faith? Leontes has already answered for them: "No settled senses of the world can match / The pleasures of that madness," he says; "What you can make her do / I am content to look on; what to speak / I am content to hear" (5.3.72–3, 91–3). *Ecstasis*, not ekphrasis, awaits.

But the play isn't over. The settled senses return, as Leontes asks Paulina to help fill in the circumstances that have brought them to this *fin lieto*: "Lead us from hence, where we may leisurely / Each one demand and answer to his part / Performed in this wide gap of time since first / We were dissevered. Hastily lead away" (5.3.152–5). Shakespeare has written the last word. We the audience will never hear the performers' additions to his script, as they question each other and re-enact the scenes of their lives during the past sixteen years. We'll just have to fantasize their responses and bodge them together in our imaginations.

Notes

1. See Chapter 1, n. 35.
2. See Chapter 1, n. 40. It is the "metamorphosis of man," Grassi suggests, because we are transactional creatures. When we discover new relationships among the disparate elements of our given environment we ourselves are inevitably modified by our own insights and creations. The idea of participatory invention goes back at least as far as Aristotle, who believed that we become virtuous by performing virtuous actions, whose content will vary according to the perceived circumstances in which they are taken (*Nichomachean Ethics*, 1103b, 1104a, 1106a).
3. Michael O'Connell, *The Idolatrous Eye: Iconoclasm and Theater in Early Modern England* (Oxford: Oxford University Press, 2000), pp. 138–42.
4. Marion O'Connor, "'Imagine Me, Gentle Spectators': Iconomachy and *The Winter's Tale*," in *A Companion to Shakespeare's Works*, ed. Richard Dutton and Jean Howard, 4 vols. (Oxford: Blackwell, 2003), vol. 4, pp. 365–88, esp. 375–82.

5. Elizabeth Williamson, "Things Newly Performed: The Resurrection Tradition in Shakespeare's Plays," in *Shakespeare and Religious Change*, ed. Kenneth J. E. Graham and Philip D. Collington (New York: Palgrave Macmillan, 2009), pp. 110–32.

6. For more secular psychological and literary approaches, see T. G. Bishop's fascinating study, *Shakespeare and the Theatre of Wonder* (Cambridge: Cambridge University Press, 1996), esp. pp. 161–75, and Peter Platt's excellent *Reason Diminished: Shakespeare and the Marvelous* (Lincoln and London: University of Nebraska Press, 1997), pp. 153–68.

7. Our acceptance of the reality of Hermione's death is mediated by Leontes' belief in Paulina's truthfulness, which we, too, have no reason to doubt. What we don't know at this moment is not only that Hermione's death is Paulina's fiction, but that the lady-in-waiting is a skilled stage director, as attested at the end of the play by Leontes himself, who wants to know *how* Hermione could have survived, "for I saw her, / As I thought, dead, and have in vain said many / A prayer upon her grave" (5.3.139–41). Shakespeare has imagined Paulina staging a death and burial so convincing that Leontes' conviction remains the audience's reference point until the last moments of the play.

8. Unprepared, that is, for it to occur in *this* play. Many in the audience may have seen something like it before. The republication of the popular *Mucedorus* in 1610, when the comedy was performed by the King's Men before King James, may suggest a further example of Shakespeare's bodging, for the third scene opens with the stage direction "Enter Segasto running and Amadine after him, being pursued with a bear." *Drama of the English Renaissance*, ed. Fraser and Rabkin, vol. 1, p. 466. In this play, the bear is slain by the eponymous hero and thence becomes a symbol of his heroism. If the bear episode in *The Winter's Tale* is a Shakespearean patch, it does not work to the advantage of the unfortunate Antigonus, who has taken the place of the cowardly Segasto, a courtier who leaves the heroine Amadine to fend for herself before Mucedorus comes to her rescue with the bear's head on a pike.

9. Cf. "Enter Rumor, painted full of tongues" in *Henry IV, Part 2*, which, though a personification like Time, opens the play as Prologue, and does not constitute a sudden change to the allegorical mode from the naturalistic.

10. *An Apology for Poetry*, p. 134.

11. Some in the audience may even recognize his riff on Greene's "plaine Country farmer, a man of good wealth, who had a well lined purse, onely barely thrust up in a round slop," to whom the Foist in St. Paul's "cried alas honest man helpe me, I am not well, & with that sunck down suddenly in a sown," as "the pore Farmer seeing a proper yong

Gentleman (as hee thought) fall dead afore him, stept to him, helde him in his armes, rubd him & chaft him . . . whilest the Foist drewe the farmers purse and away" (*The Second Part of Conny-Catching*, p. 40).

12. Its ironies were discussed in Chapter 5.

Bibliography

Akrigg, G. P. V. *Shakespeare and the Earl of Southampton* (London: Hamish Hamilton, 1968).

Alpers, Paul. *What Is Pastoral?* (Chicago: University of Chicago Press, 1996).

Altman, Joel B. "Ekphrasis," in *Early Modern Theatricality*, ed. Henry S. Turner (Oxford: Oxford University Press, 2013), pp. 270–90.

———. *The Improbability of Othello: Rhetorical Anthropology and Shakespearean Selfhood* (Chicago: University of Chicago Press, 2010).

———. "The Practice of Shakespeare's Text," *Style* 23.3 (1989): 466–500.

———. *The Tudor Play of Mind: Rhetorical Inquiry and the Development of Elizabethan Drama* (Berkeley: University of California Press, 1978; rpt. 2020).

———. "Vile Participation: The Amplification of Violence in the Theater of *Henry V*," *Shakespeare Quarterly* 42.1 (1991): 1–32.

———. "Virtual Presence and Vicarious Identity in the First Tetralogy," in *Shakespeare Up Close: Reading Early Modern Texts*, ed. Russ McDonald, Nicholas D. Nace, and Travis D. Williams (London: Arden Shakespeare, 2012), pp. 234–44.

Arendt, Hannah. *The Human Condition* (Chicago: University of Chicago Press, 1958).

Aristotle. *De somniis*, in *The Basic Works of Aristotle*, ed. and intro. Richard McKeon (New York: Random House, 1941).

———. *Nichomachean Ethics*, trans. Martin Ostwald (Indianapolis: Bobbs-Merrill, 1962).

———. *Poetics*, trans. Richard Janko (Indianapolis and Cambridge: Hackett, 1987).

Armenini, Giovanni Battista. *On the True Precepts of the Art of Painting*, ed. and trans. Edward J. Olszewski (New York: Franklin, 1977).

Ascham, Roger. *The Schoolmaster* (1570), ed. Lawrence V. Ryan (Ithaca, NY: Cornell University Press, 1967).

Aste, Richard. "Giulio Romano as Designer of Erotica: *I modi*, 1524–25," in *Giulio Romano, Master Designer*, ed. Janet Cox-Rearick (New York: Hunter College of the City University of New York, 1999), pp. 44–53.

Baldwin, Thomas W. *On the Literary Genetics of Shakespeare's Plays, 1592–1594* (Urbana: University of Illinois Press, 1959).

——. *William Shakspere's Small Latine and Lesse Greeke*, 2 vols. (Urbana: University of Illinois Press, 1944).

Barkan, Leonard. "'Living Sculptures': Ovid, Michelangelo, and *The Winter's Tale*," *ELH* 48 (1981): 137–67.

Barron, Kathryn. "The Collecting and Patronage of John, Lord Lumley (c. 1535–1609)," in *The Evolution of English Collecting: Receptions of Italian Art in the Tudor and Stuart Periods*, ed. Edward Chaney (New Haven and London: Yale University Press, 2003), pp. 125–58.

Bate, Jonathan. *How the Classics Made Shakespeare* (Princeton and Oxford: Princeton University Press, 2019).

——. *Shakespeare and Ovid* (Oxford: Clarendon Press, 1993).

Belsey, Catherine. *Shakespeare and the Loss of Eden* (New Brunswick, NJ: Rutgers University Press, 1999).

Berry, Francis. *The Shakespearean Inset: Word and Picture* (London: Routledge, 1965).

Bevington, David, et al., eds. *English Renaissance Drama* (New York: Norton, 2002).

Bishop, T. G. *Shakespeare and the Theatre of Wonder* (Cambridge: Cambridge University Press, 1996).

Blanch, William Harnett. *Dulwich College and Edward Alleyn: A Short History of the Foundation of God's Gift College at Dulwich, Together with a Memoir of the Founder* (London: E. W. Allen, 1877).

Bolgar, R. R. *The Classical Heritage and its Beneficiaries from the Carolingian Age to the End of the Renaissance* (London and New York: Cambridge University Press, 1954).

Bonner, S. F. *Roman Declamation in the Late Republic and Early Empire* (Berkeley: University of California Press, 1949).

Bracken, Susan. "Copies of Old Master Paintings in Charles I's Collection: The Role of Michael Cross (*fl.* 1632–60)," *British Art Journal* 3.2 (Spring 2002): 28–31.

——. "The Early Cecils and Italianate Taste," in *The Evolution of English Collecting: Receptions of Italian Art in the Tudor and Stuart Periods*, ed. Edward Chaney (New Haven and London: Yale University Press, 2003), pp. 201–19.

Bruster, Douglas. *Quoting Shakespeare: Form and Culture in Early Modern Drama* (Lincoln and London: University of Nebraska Press, 2000).

Bullough, Geoffrey. "'The Murder of Gonzago': A Probable Source for *Hamlet*," *MLR* 30.4 (October 1935): 433–44.

——. *Narrative and Dramatic Sources of Shakespeare*, 8 vols. (New York: Columbia University Press, 1957–75).

Carpani, Roberta. "Il 'trionfo di Manto': festa e teatro nel età di Vincenzo I," in *Vincenzo I Gonzaga 1562–1612: Il Fasto del Potere* (Mantua: Museo diocesano Francesco Gonzaga, 2012).

Chamberlain, John. *The Letters of John Chamberlain*, ed. N. E. McClure, 2 vols. (Philadelphia, 1939).

Chambers, E. K. *The Elizabethan Stage*, 4 vols. (Oxford: Clarendon Press, 1923).

———. *William Shakespeare*, 2 vols. (Oxford: Clarendon Press, 1930).

Chaney, Edward, ed. *The Evolution of English Collecting: Receptions of Italian Art in the Tudor and Stuart Periods* (New Haven and London: Yale University Press, 2003).

Cheney, Patrick. *Shakespeare, National Poet-Playwright* (Cambridge: Cambridge University Press, 2004).

Chettle, Henry. *Kind-Hearts Dream. Conteining Five Apparitions with their Invectives agains abuses raigning. Delivered by severall Ghosts unto him to be publisht, after Piers Penilesse Post had refused the carriage* (London: William Wright, 1592).

Cinzio, G. Giraldi. *Epizia: An Italian Renaissance Tragedy*, ed. Philip Horne (Lewiston: Mellen Press, 1996).

———. *Scritti Critici*, ed. Guglielmo Guerrieri Crocetti (Milan: Marzorati, 1973).

Clare, Janet. *Shakespeare's Stage Traffic: Imitation, Borrowing and Competition in Renaissance Theatre* (Cambridge: Cambridge University Press, 2014).

Clubb, Louise George. *Italian Drama in Shakespeare's Time* (New York and London: Yale University Press, 1989).

———. *Pollastra and the Origins of "Twelfth Night"* (Burlington, VT: Ashgate, 2010).

Coleridge, Samuel T. *Shakespearean Criticism*, ed. T. M. Raysor, 2nd edn, 2 vols. (London: Dent, 1960).

Coryat, Thomas. *Coryat's crudities; reprinted from the edition of 1611. To which are now added, his letters from India, &c. and extracts relating to him, from various authors: being a more particular account of his travels (mostly on foot) in different parts of the globe, than any hitherto published. Together with his orations, character, death, &c. With copper-plates. In three volumes* (London: W. Cater, 1776).

Cox-Rearick, Janet, ed. *Giulio Romano, Master Designer* (New York: Hunter College of the City University of New York, 1999).

Crane, Mary Thomas. *Framing Authority: Sayings, Self, and Society in Sixteenth-Century England* (Princeton: Princeton University Press, 1993).

Cust, Lionel. "The Lumley Inventories," *Walpole Society* 6 (1918): 15–35.

Daileader, Celia R. "Back Door Sex: Renaissance Gynosodomy, Aretino, and the Exotic," *ELH* 69.2 (2002): 303–34.

D'Arco, Carlo. *Monumenti di pittura e scultura trascelti in Mantova e nel suo territorio* (Mantua, 1827).

Di Majo, Ippolita. *Raffaello e la sua scuola* (Florence: Il Sole 24 ORE, E-ducation.It, 2007).

Donno, Elizabeth Story, ed. *Three Renaissance Pastorals: Tasso, Guarini, Daniel* (Binghamton: MRDS, 1993).

Duncan-Jones, Katherine. *Ungentle Shakespeare: Scenes from his Life* (London: Arden, 2001).

Dundas, Judith. *Pencils Rhetorique: Renaissance Poets and the Art of Painting* (Newark and London: University of Delaware Press, 1993).

Eden, Kathy. "Literary Property and the Question of Style," in *Borrowed Feathers: Plagiarism and the Limits of Imitation in Early Modern Europe*, ed. Hall Bjornstad (Oslo: Unipub, 2008), pp. 21–38.

Elam, Keir. "'At the cubiculo': Shakespeare's Problems with Italian Language and Culture," in *Italian Culture in the Drama of Shakespeare and his Contemporaries*, ed. M. Marrapodi (Burlington, VT: Ashgate, 2007), pp. 99–110.

——. *Shakespeare's Pictures: Visual Objects in the Drama* (London: Bloomsbury, 2017).

Elze, Karl. *Essays on Shakespeare*, trans. L. Dora Schmitz (London: Macmillan, 1874).

Enterline, Lynn. *Shakespeare's Schoolroom: Rhetoric, Discipline, Emotion* (Philadelphia: University of Pennsylvania Press, 2012).

Erasmus, Desiderius. *Desiderius Erasmus of Rotterdam, On Copia of Words and Ideas*, ed. and trans. Donald B. King and H. David Rix (Milwaukee: Marquette University Press, 1963).

Esdaile, Katherine. *English Church Monuments 1510–1840* (London: Batsford, 1946).

Evans, G. Blakemore, et al., eds. *The Riverside Shakespeare*, 2nd edn (Boston and New York: Houghton Mifflin, 1997).

Ewbank, Inga-Stina. "The Triumph of Time in *The Winter's Tale*," *REL* 5 (1964): 83–99.

Farinella, Vincenzo, and Giovanni Agosti. "Su Roberto Longhi, la scultura e il Classicismo," *Quaderni di Palazzo Te* 2.3 (1985).

Ferrari, Daniela, ed. *Giulio Romano: Repertorio di fonti documentarie*, intro. Amedeo Belluzi, 2 vols. (Mantua: Ministerio per I Beni Culturale e Ambientali Ufficio Centrale per I Beni Archivisitici, 1992).

Ferrari, Giulio. *La Tomba nell'arte italiana dal periodo preromano all'odierno* (Milan: U. Hoepli, 1916).

Ferrone, Siro. *Arlecchino: Vita e avventure di Tristano Martinelli attore* (Rome and Bari: Editori Laterza, 2006).

——. *Attori mercanti corsari: La Commedia dell'Arte in Europa tra Cinque e Seicento* (Turin: Giulio Einaudi, 1993).

Florio, John. *A Worlde of Wordes* (1598) (Hildesheim and New York: Georg Olms Verlag, 1972).

Fowler, Alastair. *Renaissance Realism: Narrative Images in Literature and Art* (Oxford: Oxford University Press, 2003).

Fraser, Russell A., and Norman Rabkin, eds. *Drama of the English Renaissance*, 2 vols. (New York and London: Macmillan, 1976).

Frede, Dorothea. "The Cognitive Role of *Phantasia*," in *Essays on Aristotle's De Anima*, ed. Martha C. Nussbaum and Amelie Oksenberg Rorty (Oxford: Clarendon Press, 1992), pp. 279–95.

Gent, Lucy, ed. *Albion's Classicism: The Visual Arts in Britain, 1550–1660* (New Haven and London: Yale University Press, 1995).

Gilbert, Allan H. *Literary Criticism: Plato to Dryden* (Detroit: Wayne State University Press, 1962).

Gotch, J. Alfred. *Inigo Jones* (1928) (New York: Blom, 1968).

Grassi, Ernesto. *Renaissance Humanism: Studies in Philosophy and Poetics* (Binghamton: Medieval and Renaissance Text Society, 1988).

Greenblatt, Stephen, and Peter G. Platt, eds. *Shakespeare's Montaigne: The Florio Translation of the Essays: A Selection* (New York: NYRB, 2014).

Greene, Robert. *Greene's Groatsworth of Wit; Bought with a Million of Repentance* (1592). Attributed to Henry Chettle and Robert Greene, ed. D. Allen Carroll (Binghamton: Medieval and Renaissance Texts and Studies, 1994).

———. *A Notable Discovery of Coosnage, 1591; The Second Part of Conny-Catching, 1592*, ed. G. B. Harrison (Edinburgh: Edinburgh University Press, 1966).

Greene, Thomas M. *The Light in Troy: Imitation and Discovery in Renaissance Poetry* (New Haven and London: Yale University Press, 1982).

Grosart, A. B., ed. *The Life and Complete Works in Prose and Verse of Robert Greene, M.A.*, 15 vols. (New York: Russell & Russell, 1964).

Gross, Kenneth. *The Dream of the Moving Statue* (Ithaca, NY, and London: Cornell University Press, 1992).

Guarini, Battista. *Il Compendio della poesia tragicomica* [*De la Poésie Tragi-Comique*], trans. and annotated by Laurence Giavarini (Paris: Honoré Champion, 2008).

———. *Opere*, ed. Marziano Guglielminetti (Turin: Unione Tipografico-Editrice Torinese, 1971).

Gurr, Andrew. "The Many-Headed Audience," *Essays in Theatre* 1.1 (1982): 52–62.

Hacking, Ian. *The Emergence of Probability: A Philosophical Study of Early Ideas about Probability, Induction and Statistical Inference* (Cambridge: Cambridge University Press, 1975).

Hagstrum, Jean. *The Sister Arts: The Tradition of Literary Pictorialism and English Poetry from Dryden to Gray* (Chicago: University of Chicago Press, 1958).

Halliwell, Stephen. *Aristotle's Poetics* (Chicago: University of Chicago Press, 1998).

Hamill, John. "The Ten Restless Ghosts of Mantua: Shakespeare's Specter Lingers over the Italian City," *Shakespeare Oxford Newsletter* 39.3 (2003): 1, 12–16.

Hardy, Barbara. *Shakespeare's Storytellers: Dramatic Narration* (London: Peter Owen, 1997).

Harprath, Richard. "Giulio Romano e la conoscenza della Loggia delle Cariatidi dell'Eretteo," *Quaderni di Palazzo Te* 2.3 (1985).

Hartt, Frederick. *Giulio Romano*, 2 vols. (New Haven: Yale University Press, 1958; rpt. 1981).

Hearn, Karen, ed. *Dynasties: Painting in Tudor and Jacobean England 1530–1630* (Peterborough: Tate Gallery, 1995).

Heffernan, James A. W. *Museum of Words: The Poetics of Ekphrasis from Homer to Ashbury* (Chicago: University of Chicago Press, 1993).

Henke, Robert. "Border-Crossing in the *Commedia dell'Arte*," in *Transnational Exchange in Early Modern Theater*, ed. Robert Henke and Eric Nicholson (Burlington, VT: Ashgate, 2008), pp. 19–34.

———. *Pastoral Transformations: Italian Tragicomedy and Shakespeare's Late Plays* (Newark: University of Delaware Press, 1997).

———. "Shakespeare and the Commedia dell'Arte," in *Shakespeare, Italy, and Transnational Exchange: Early Modern to Present*, ed. Enza De Francisci and Chris Stamatakis (London: Routledge, 2017), pp. 53–64.

Henry, Tom, and Paul Joannides, eds. *Late Raphael* (New York: Thames & Hudson, 2013).

Herrick, Marvin T. *Tragicomedy* (Urbana: University of Illinois Press, 1962).

Hervey, Mary F. S. "A Lumley Inventory of 1609," *Walpole Society* 6 (1918): 36–46.

Hollander, John. *The Gazer's Spirit: Poems Speaking to Silent Works of Art* (Chicago and London: University of Chicago Press, 1995).

Honigmann, E. A. J. *Shakespeare: The Lost Years* (Manchester and New York: Manchester University Press, 1998).

———. *Shakespeare's Impact on his Contemporaries* (London: Macmillan, 1982).

Hooker, Richard. *Of the Laws of Ecclesiastical Polity*, ed. A. S. McGrade and Brian Vickers (New York: St. Martin's Press, 1975).

Horace. *Satires, Epistles and Ars Poetica*, trans. H. Rushton Fairclough (London: Heinemann Ltd, 1966).

Hotson, Leslie. *The First Night of Twelfth Night* (New York: Macmillan, 1954).

Huloet, R. *Abcedarium Anglico Latinum* (London, 1552).

Hunter, G. K. "Italian Tragicomedy on the English Stage," *Renaissance Drama* 6 (1973): 123–48.

Hutson, Lorna. *Circumstantial Shakespeare* (Oxford: Oxford University Press, 2015).

Johnson, A. W. *Three Volumes Annotated by Inigo Jones* (Turku: Åbo Akademi University Press, 1997).

Johnson, Samuel. *Johnson on Shakespeare*, ed. Arthur Sherbo, in *The Yale*

Edition of the Works of Samuel Johnson, 9 vols. (New Haven: Yale University Press, 1968).

Jones, Ernest. *Hamlet and Oedipus* (Garden City, NY: Doubleday, 1955).

Jonson, Ben. *Ben Jonson*, ed. C. H. Herford and Percy Simpson, 11 vols. (Oxford: Clarendon Press, 1925–63).

Kerrigan, John. *Shakespeare's Originality* (Oxford: Oxford University Press, 2018).

Kleinbub, Christian K. *Vision and the Visionary in Raphael* (University Park: Pennsylvania State University Press, 2011).

Knight, Jeffrey Todd. *Bound to Read: Compilations, Collections, and the Making of Renaissance Literature* (Philadelphia: University of Pennsylvania Press, 2013).

Krieger, Murray. *Ekphrasis: The Illusion of the Natural Sign* (Baltimore: Johns Hopkins University Press, 1992).

Küster, Bärbel. "Copies on the Market in Eighteenth-Century Britain," in *Marketing Art in the British Isles, 1700 to the Present: A Cultural History*, ed. Charlotte Gould and Sophie Mesplède (Burlington, VT: Ashgate, 2012), pp. 179–94.

Kyd, Thomas. *The First Part of Hieronimo and The Spanish Tragedy*, ed. Andrew S. Cairncross (Lincoln: University of Nebraska Press, 1967).

Laertius, Diogenes. "Zeno," in *Lives of Eminent Philosophers*, trans. R. D. Hicks (London: Harvard University Press, 1970), vol. 2, pp. 111–262.

Land, Norman E. *The Viewer as Poet* (University Park: Pennsylvania State University Press, 1994).

Lawrence, Jason. *"Who the devil taught thee so much Italian?" Italian Language Learning and Literary Imitation in Early Modern England* (Manchester: Manchester University Press, 2005).

Lea, K. M. *Italian Popular Comedy: A Study in the Commedia dell'Arte, 1560–1620 with Special Reference to the English Stage*, 2 vols. (Oxford: Clarendon Press, 1934).

Lear, Jonathan. *Aristotle: The Desire to Understand* (Cambridge: Cambridge University Press, 1988).

Levi, Alda Spinazzola. "Monumenti inediti di Mantova in rapporto con l'arte di Giulio Romano," *Atti della Pontificia Accademia Romana di Archeologia* 21 (1944–45): 213–39.

Lievsay, John. *The Englishman's Italian Books 1550–1700* (Philadelphia: University of Pennsylvania Press, 1969).

Longhi, Roberto. "Le Cariatidi della sepultura Strozzi in S. Andrea di Mantova sono imitate dall'antico," *Quaderni di Palazzo Te* 2.3 (1985): 31–2.

Lucian, trans. A. M. Harmon, vol. 1 (London: Heinemann, and New York: Macmillan, 1913).

Lyne, Raphael. *Memory and Intertextuality in Renaissance Literature* (Cambridge: Cambridge University Press, 2016).

McGill, Scott. *Plagiarism in Latin Literature* (Cambridge: Cambridge University Press, 2012).

Mack, Peter. *Elizabethan Rhetoric: Theory and Practice* (Cambridge: Cambridge University Press, 2002).

Marrapodi, Michele, ed. *Shakespeare, Italy, and Intertextuality* (Manchester: Manchester University Press, 2004).

Marston, John. *Antonio and Mellida*, ed. G. K. Hunter (Lincoln: University of Nebraska Press, 1965).

Matteuchi, Vittorio. *Le chiese artistiche del Mantovano* (Mantua, 1902).

Meek, Richard. *Narrating the Visual in Shakespeare* (Burlington, VT: Ashgate, 2009).

Melzi, Robert. "From Lelia to Viola," *RenD* 9 (1966): 67–81.

Millar, Oliver, ed. *Abraham van der Doort's Catalogue of the Collections of Charles I* (Glasgow: Walpole Society, 1960).

———, ed. *The Inventories and Valuations of the King's Goods, 1649–1651* (Glasgow: Walpole Society, 1972).

Miola, Robert S. "Seven Types of Intertextuality," in *Shakespeare, Italy, and Intertextuality*, ed. Michele Marrapodi (Manchester: Manchester University Press, 2004), pp. 13–25.

———. *Shakespeare's Reading* (Oxford and New York: Oxford University Press, 2000).

Miyamoto, Bénédicte. "'Making Pictures Marketable': Expertise and the Georgian Art Market," in *Marketing Art in the British Isles, 1700 to the Present: A Cultural History*, ed. Charlotte Gould and Sophie Mesplède (Burlington, VT: Ashgate, 2012), pp. 119–34.

Montefusco, Lucia Calboli. "Ενάργεια et ενέργεια: l'évidence d'une demonstration qui signifie les choses en acte (*Rhet. Her.* 4, 68)," in *Demonstrare: Voir et faire-voir: forme de la demonstration à Rome*. Proceedings of the International Colloquium in Toulouse, 18–20 November 2004, compiled by Mireille Armisen-Marchetti (Toulouse: Presses universitaires du Mirail/Centre national du livre, 2005), pp. 43–58.

Moss, Ann. *Printed Commonplace-Books and the Structuring of Renaissance Thought* (Oxford: Clarendon Press, 1996).

Moulton, Ian Frederick. *Before Pornography: Erotic Writing in Early Modern England* (Oxford: Oxford University Press, 2000).

Mowat, Barbara. *The Dramaturgy of Shakespeare's Romances* (Athens: University of Georgia Press, 1976).

Muir, Kenneth. *Shakespeare's Sources* (London: Methuen, 1957).

Nashe, Thomas. *The Works of Thomas Nashe*, ed. Ronald B. McKerrow, 4 vols. (London: Sidgwick & Jackson, 1910).

Nuttall, W. L. F. "King Charles I's Pictures and the Commonwealth Sale," *Apollo* (October 1965): 302–9.

O'Connell, Michael. *The Idolatrous Eye: Iconoclasm and Theater in Early Modern England* (Oxford: Oxford University Press, 2000).

O'Connor, Marion. "'Imagine Me, Gentle Spectators': Iconomachy and

The Winter's Tale," in *A Companion to Shakespeare's Works*, ed. Richard Dutton and Jean Howard, 4 vols. (Oxford: Blackwell, 2003), vol. 4, pp. 365–88.

Ovid. *Metamorphoses*, trans. Frank Justus Miller, Loeb Classical Library (London: Heinemann, 1921–22).

Palfrey, Simon, and Tiffany Stern. *Shakespeare in Parts* (Oxford: Oxford University Press, 2007).

Panzanelli, Roberta, ed. *The Color of Life: Polychromy in Sculpture from Antiquity to the Present* (Los Angeles: J. Paul Getty Museum, 2008).

Pasetti, Giovanni. *Giulio Romano: Il Genio e l'Invenzione* (Mantua: Tre Lune Edizioni, 2008).

Pasquin, Antoine Claude [Valery]. *Voyages historiques et litteraires en Italie pendant les années 1826, 1827, et 1828, II* (Paris, 1831).

Perkins, William. *William Perkins, 1555–1602: English Puritanist*, ed. and intro. Thomas F. Merrill (Nieuwkoop: B. De Graaf, 1966).

Petrarch. *Petrarch: Sonnets and Songs*, trans. Anna Maria Armi (New York: Grosset & Dunlap, 1968).

Pigman, G. W. "Versions of Imitation in the Renaissance," *Renaissance Quarterly* 33 (1980): 1–32.

Plato. *The Collected Dialogues of Plato*, ed. Edith Hamilton and Huntington Cairns (New York: Pantheon Books, 1961).

Platt, Peter G. *Reason Diminished: Shakespeare and the Marvelous* (Lincoln and London: University of Nebraska Press, 1997.

———. *Shakespeare and the Culture of Paradox* (Burlington, VT: Ashgate, 2009).

———. *Shakespeare's Essays: Sampling Montaigne from Hamlet to The Tempest* (Edinburgh: Edinburgh University Press, 2020).

Polansky, Ronald. *Aristotle's "De anima"* (Cambridge: Cambridge University Press, 2007).

Praz, Mario. "Shakespeare's Italy," in *The Flaming Heart: Essays on Crashaw, Machiavelli, and Other Studies of the Relations between Italian and English Literature from Chaucer to T. S. Eliot* (New York: Norton Library, 1973; rpt. of 1958 original), pp. 146–67.

Puttenham, George. *The Arte of English Poesie* (1589), ed. Baxter Hathaway (Kent: Kent State University Press, 1970).

Quintilian. *Institutio oratoria*, trans. H. E. Butler, 4 vols. (Cambridge, MA: Harvard University Press, 1961).

Rebecchini, Guido. *Private Collectors in Mantua, 1500–1630* (Rome: Edizioni di Storia e Letteratura, 2002).

Redford, George. *Art Sales: A History of the Sales of Pictures and Other Works of Art*, 2 vols. (London: Whitefriars, 1888).

Robertson, Martin. *A History of Greek Art*, 2 vols. (Cambridge: Cambridge University Press, 1975).

Robortello, Francesco. *In librum Aristotelis de arte poetica explicationes* (Florence, 1548).

Rymer, Thomas. *The Critical Works of Thomas Rymer*, ed. Curt A. Zimansky (New Haven: Yale University Press, 1956).

Schoenbaum, S. *William Shakespeare: A Compact Documentary Life* (New York: Oxford University Press, 1977).

Schofield, Malcolm. "Aristotle on the Imagination," in *Essays on Aristotle's De Anima*, ed. Martha C. Nussbaum and Amelie Oksenberg Rorty (Oxford: Clarendon Press, 1992), pp. 249–77.

Scholz, Bernard F. "*Ekphrasis* and *Enargeia* in Quintilian's *Institutionis Oratoriae Libri XII*," in *Rhetorica Movet: Studies in Historical and Modern Rhetoric in Honour of Heinrich F. Plett*, ed. Peter L. Oesterreich and Thomas O. Sloane (Leiden: Brill, 1999), pp. 3–24.

Seneca. *Ad Lucilium Epistulae Morales in Three Volumes*, trans. Richard M. Gummere (Cambridge, MA: Harvard University Press, 1962).

Severi, Rita. *Shakespeare's Mantua: A Cultural Itinerary/La Mantova di Shakespeare: Itinerario Culturale* (Mantua: Sonetti, 2016).

Shackford, Mary Hale. "Shakespeare and Greene's *Orlando Furioso*," *MLN* 39 (1924): 54–6.

Shakespeare, William. *The First Folio of Shakespeare*, prepared by Charlton Hinman (New York: W. W. Norton & Company, Inc., 1968).

———. *Hamlet*, ed. Harold Jenkins (London and New York: Methuen, 1982).

———. *Love's Labour's Lost*, ed. G. R. Hibbard (Oxford and New York: Oxford University Press, 1990).

———. *Measure for Measure*, ed. J. W. Lever (Methuen: London, 1965).

———. *The Riverside Shakespeare*, 2nd edn, ed. G. Blakemore Evans et al. (Boston and New York: Houghton Mifflin, 1997).

———. *The Taming of the Shrew*, ed. Brian Morris (London and New York: Methuen, 1981).

———. *Twelfth Night*, ed. Keir Elam (London: Arden Shakespeare, 2008).

———. *The Winter's Tale*, ed. Stephen Orgel (Oxford: Oxford University Press, 1996).

———. *The Winter's Tale*, ed. G. H. P. Pafford (London: Methuen, 1963).

———. *The Winter's Tale*, ed. John Pitcher (London: Arden Shakespeare, 2010).

Shapiro, Barbara J. *Probability and Certainty in Seventeenth-Century England* (Princeton: Princeton University Press, 1983).

Shapiro, James. *1606: William Shakespeare and the Year of Lear* (London: Faber and Faber, 2015).

Shearman, John. "Giulio Romano and the Tomb of the Duke and Duchess of Sessa," *Zeitschrift für Kunstgeschichte* 57. Bd., H. 3, Kunstgeschichte und Gegenwart: 23 (1994): 364–72.

Sidney, Sir Philip. *An Apology for Poetry or The Defence of Poesy*, ed. Geoffrey Shepherd (London: Nelson, 1965).

Skinner, Quentin. *Forensic Shakespeare* (Oxford: Oxford University Press, 2014).

Smith, G. Gregory, ed. *Elizabethan Critical Essays*, 2 vols. (Oxford: Oxford University Press, 1904).

Sokol, B. J. *Art and Illusion in The Winter's Tale* (Manchester: Manchester University Press, 1994).

———. *Shakespeare's Artists* (London: Bloomsbury, 2018).

Stern, Tiffany. "The Dumb Show in *Hamlet*," in *Shakespeare Up Close: Reading Early Modern Texts*, ed. Russ McDonald, Nicholas D. Nace, and Travis D. Williams (London: Arden Shakespeare, 2012), pp. 273–81.

Stevens, Andrea. *Inventions of the Skin: The Painted Body in Early English Drama, 1400–1642* (Edinburgh: Edinburgh University Press, 2013).

Stopes, Charlotte Carmichael. *The Life of Henry, Third Earl of Southampton, Shakespeare's Patron* (Cambridge: Cambridge University Press, 1922).

Strong, Roy. *Henry, Prince of Wales, and England's Lost Renaissance* (London: Thames & Hudson, 1986).

Struever, Nancy. *The Language of History in the Renaissance: Rhetoric and Historical Consciousness in Florentine Humanism* (Princeton: Princeton University Press, 1970).

Tafuri, Manfredo. "Giulio Romano: linguaggio, mentalita, committenti," in *Giulio Romano: Saggi di Ernst H. Gombrich, Manfredo Tafuri, Sylvia Ferino Pagden, Christoph L. Frommel, Konrad Oberhuber, Amedeo Belluzzi e Kurt W. Forster, Howard Burns* (Milan: Electa, 1989), pp. 15–63.

Talvacchia, Bette. *Taking Positions: On the Erotic in Renaissance Culture* (Princeton: Princeton University Press, 1999).

———. "That Rare Italian Master and the Posture of Hermione in *The Winter's Tale*," *Literature, Interpretation, Theory* 3 (1992): 163–74.

Taylor, Gary. "Collaboration," in *Shakespeare in our Time*, ed. Dympna Callaghan and Suzanne Gossett (London and New York: Bloomsbury Arden, 2016), pp. 141–9.

———, and John Lavagnino, eds. *Thomas Middleton: The Collected Works* (Oxford: Clarendon Press, 2007).

Thorne, Alison. *Vision and Rhetoric in Shakespeare: Looking through Language* (New York: St. Martin's Press, 2000).

Tumelson II, Ronald A. "Robert Greene, 'Author of Playes,'" in *Writing Robert Greene*, ed. Kirk Melnikoff and Edward Gieskes (Burlington, VT, and Aldershot: Ashgate, 2008), pp. 95–114.

Turner, James G. *Eros Visible: Art, Sexuality and Antiquity in Renaissance Italy* (New Haven and London: Yale University Press, 2017).

Vasari, Giorgio. *Lives of the Most Eminent Painters, Sculptors, and Architects by Giorgio Vasari*, trans. Gaston du C. de Vere, 10 vols. (London: Medici Society, 1912–14).

———. *Le vite de' piú eccellenti architetti, pittori, et scultori italiani, da Cimabue, insino a' tempi nostri*, edition by Lorenzo Torrentino, Florence, 1550, ed. Luciano Bellosi and Aldo Rossi, 2 vols. (Turin: Einaudi, 1991).

Viani, Elisa. *L'Avvelenamento di Francesco Maria I della Rovere Duca d'Urbino* (Mantua, 1902).

Vives, Juan Luis. *De causis corruptarum artium*, in *Joannis Ludovico Vivis Valentini Opera omnia* . . . (1782–90), 8 vols. (London: Gregg, 1964).

Waddington, Raymond B. *Aretino's Satyr: Sexuality, Satire, and Self-Projection in Sixteenth-Century Literature and Art* (Toronto: University of Toronto Press, 2004).

Watson, Gerard. *The Stoic Theory of Knowledge* (Belfast: Queen's University Press, 1966).

Webb, Ruth. *Ekphrasis: Imagination and Persuasion in Ancient Rhetorical Theory and Practice* (Burlington, VT: Ashgate, 2009).

Wells, Stanley, and Gary Taylor. *William Shakespeare: A Textual Companion* (New York: Norton, 1997).

Whalley, J. Irene. "Italian Art and English Taste: An Early Seventeenth Century Letter," *Apollo* (September 1971): 184–91.

Whinney, Margaret. *Sculpture in Britain, 1530 to 1830* (Harmondsworth: Penguin, 1964).

Wilks, Timothy. "Art Collecting at the English Court from the Death of Henry, Prince of Wales to the Death of Anne of Denmark (November 1612–March 1619)," in *Journal of the History of Collections* 9.1 (1997): 3–48.

———. "'Paying Special Attention to the Adornment of a Most Beautiful Gallery': The Pictures in St. James's Palace, 1609–49," *The Court Historian* 10.2 (2005): 149–72.

Williams, Richard L. "Collecting and Religion in Late Sixteenth-Century England," in *The Evolution of English Collecting: Receptions of Italian Art in the Tudor and Stuart Periods*, ed. Edward Chaney (New Haven and London: Yale University Press, 2003), pp. 159–200.

Williamson, Elizabeth. "Things Newly Performed: The Resurrection Tradition in Shakespeare's Plays," in *Shakespeare and Religious Change*, ed. Kenneth J. E. Graham and Philip D. Collington (New York: Palgrave Macmillan, 2009), pp. 110–32.

Wilson, J. D. *What Happens in Hamlet* (Cambridge: Cambridge University Press, 1967).

Wilson, Rawdon. *Shakespearean Narrative* (Newark: University of Delaware Press, 1995).

Wilson, Thomas. *The Rule of Reason*, ed. Richard S. Sprague (Northridge, CA: San Fernando State College Renaissance Editions, 1972).

Wolk-Simon, Linda. "Raphael, Giulio Romano, and the Business of Love," in *Giulio Romano: Art and Desire*, ed. Barbara Furlotti, Guido Rebecchini, and Linda Wolk-Simon (Milan: Electa, 2019), pp. 28–43.

Wood, Jeremy. "Taste and Connoisseurship at the Court of Charles I: Inigo Jones and the Work of Giulio Romano," in *The Stuart Courts*, ed. Eveline Cruickshanks (Stroud: Sutton Publishing, 2000), pp. 118–40.

Worsley, Giles. *Inigo Jones and the European Classicist Tradition* (New Haven and London: Yale University Press, 2007).

Yates, Frances A. *John Florio: The Life of an Italian in Shakespeare's England* (Cambridge: Cambridge University Press, 1934).

Index

References to images are in *italics*; references to notes are indicated by n.

EU representative:
Easy Access System Europe
Mustamäe tee 50, 10621 Tallinn, Estonia
Gpsr.requests@easproject.com

www.ingramcontent.com/pod-product-compliance
Lightning Source LLC
Chambersburg PA
CBHW071712170526
45165CB00005B/1990